BRIDGES 2

S.D. Robinson
Series Editor

BRIDGES 2

S. D. Robinson · S. D. Bailey · H. D. Cruchley · B. L. Wood

Prentice-Hall Canada Inc., Scarborough, Ontario

Canadian Cataloguing in Publication Data

Robinson, Sam, 1937–
    Bridges 2

For use in schools.
Includes index.
ISBN 0-13-081951-4

1. Communication — Juvenile literature. I. Title.

P91.2.R63 1985   001.51   C84-099667-5

Accompanying Material

Bridges 1, 2, 3, 4 student texts and Teacher's Guides

Prentice-Hall, Inc., Englewood Cliffs, New Jersey
Prentice-Hall International, Inc., London
Prentice-Hall of Australia, Pty., Ltd., Sydney
Prentice-Hall of India Pvt., Ltd., New Delhi
Prentice-Hall of Japan, Inc., Tokyo
Prentice-Hall of Southeast Asia (PTE) Ltd.,
    Singapore
Editora Prentice-Hall do Brasil Ltda., Rio de
    Janeiro
Prentice-Hall Hispanoamericana, S.A., Mexico

Credits

Project Editor: Iris Skeoch
Production Editor: Jane Springer
Coordinating Editor: Miriam London
Production: Monika Heike
Design: Michael van Elsen
Illustrators: Victoria Birta, Pat Cupples
    Karen Reczuch
Composition: Compeer Typographic Services Ltd.

ISBN 0-13-081951-4

2   3   4   5   89   88   87   86

Printed and bound in Canada by T.H. Best Printing
    Company Ltd.

Policy Statement

Prentice-Hall Canada Inc., Educational Book
Division, and the authors of *Bridges* are
committed to the publication of instructional
materials that are as bias-free as possible.
The student text was evaluated for bias prior
to publication.

The authors and publishers also recognize
the importance of appropriate reading levels
and have therefore made every effort to ensure
the highest degree of readability in the student
text. The content has been selected, organized,
and written at a level suitable to the intended
audience. Standard readability tests have been
applied at several stages in the text's
preparation to ensure an appropriate reading
level.

Research indicates, however, that readability
is affected by much more than word or
sentence length; factors such as presentation,
format and design, none of which are
considered in the usual readability tests, also
greatly influence the ease with which students
read a book. These and many additional
features have been carefully prepared to ensure
maximum student comprehension.

TABLE OF CONTENTS

ACKNOWLEDGEMENTS

The *Bridges Series* grew over a period of four years. It is not the product of any one person or of a group of people. Rather, it is the result of the work of many people, each of whom has left a special mark on the series.

As a result, we the authors of *Bridges* have many people to thank for their help and encouragement and downright hard work. We sincerely acknowledge these contributions.

Several teachers field-tested early drafts of chapters for *Bridges 1* and *Bridges 2*, pointing out the good and clearly telling us what would and would not work in classrooms. Our appreciation, then, to these teachers: Laurie Ball, John Barton, Brendan Bitz, Gordon Bland, Shelley Bryan, Irene Danaher, Lillian Fowler, Del Fraser, Shirley Gange, Wilma Gautier, Ellen Hagan, Donna-lou Holbrow, Eileen Leverington, Irene Loewen, Linda March, Phil McAmmond, Michelle Meugot, Lale Merdsoy, Al Mitchell, Dave Mumford, Donna Noonan, Cheryl Olischefski, Diane Page, Irene Sawchuk, Christine Vernon, Gerri Walker, and Marion Widlake. We have an extra thank you for Betty Thorpe and Mark Silverstein who pilot-tested an earlier version of *Bridges 1*. And we acknowledge, too, the help of Julie Ashcroft, Sheila Brooks, Don Cassidy, Bill Chin, Dan Clarke, Micki Clemens, Joan Lawrence, Harry MacNeil, Bill Talbot, and especially Karen Holm, and Neville Hosking, all of whom cleared the administrative way to make this classroom work possible. And a grateful thank you to Christtine Fondse, Saskatoon Public School Board, and William Ewart, Regina Public School Board, for their help in writing and revising material for *Bridges 1* and 2.

We also owe a special thank you to those at Prentice-Hall who guided this series from its first stumbling steps to this finished product. Joe Chin and Monika Heike are to be commended for their untiring efforts in coordinating art and manufacturing. To project editor, Iris Skeoch and production editors Mia London and Jane Springer — thank you for the care and attention, and even love, that you have given to *Bridges*. Your cooperation and helpfulness got us over many a rough spot, and your professionalism has made *Bridges* a better series.

To Dorothy Greenaway, who worked with *Bridges* from its first stages, thank you for being a first-rate editor. Without your cheerfulness, your optimism, and your drive, we would still be mired in the jungle of first drafts.

The authors,
S.R., S.B., D.C., B.W.

Credits

Every reasonable effort has been made to find copyright holders of the following material. The publishers would be pleased to have any errors or omissions brought to their attention. For permission to use the following material in this textbook, we thank:

Sources

p. 25 Excerpt from journal in "North of Reindeer: The 1940 Trip of Prentice G. Downes" by Robert H. Cockburn in *The Beaver*, Spring, 1983;

p. 43 Excerpt from "Fog" by Ethel Wilson in *Mrs. Golightly and Other Stories*, (Toronto: Macmillan, 1961, p. 97);

p. 45 "Imprecise Orders Linked To Near-Crash", November 5, 1984, *Saskatoon Star Phoenix*;

p. 61 Excerpt from "Be It Ever So Humble, . . ." by Eric Nicol in *A Herd of Yaks*, (Toronto: Ryerson Press, 1962);

p. 61 Excerpt from "History of Punctuation" by John Farrell in *The Creative Teacher of Language*, McGraw-Hill, 1965;

p. 62 "Racoon" from *Outdoors Canada* © 1977 The Reader's Digest Association (Canada) Ltd., Montreal;

p. 75 Excerpt from *Ten Lost Years* by Barry Broadfoot. © 1973 by Barry Broadfoot. Reprinted by permission of Doubleday and Company, Inc.;

p. 81 Excerpt from *Never Sleep Three in a Bed* by Max Braithwaite. Used by permission of the Canadian Publishers, McClelland and Stewart Limited, Toronto;

p. 120 "Motto" from *Panther and the Lash: Poems of Our Times* by Langston Hughes, (New York: Alfred A. Knopf, Inc. 1967);

p. 121 Excerpt from *The Root Cellar* by Janet Lunn, (Toronto: Lester and Orpen, 1981). Also available in paperback from Penguin Canada;

p. 122 Excerpt from *Cape Breton Harbour* by Edna Staebler, used by permission of The Canadian Publishers, McClelland and Stewart Limited, Toronto;

p. 150 Material adapted from *The Biological*

Timebomb, by G.R. Taylor, (New York: New American Library, 1968);

p. 151 Excerpts from *North by 2000* by H.A. Hargreaves © 1975 by Peter Martin Associates. Used by permission of Clarke Irwin (1983) Inc.;

p. 166 "Pen Pal in a Bottle" reprinted from *Owl* magazine with permission from the Young Naturalist Foundation, publisher of *Owl* and *Chickadee* magazines for children.

p. 157 "Medical Breakthrough . . . Life Expectancy" by Phyllis Watts, (written as part of a class newspaper exercise at Burnaby South Senior School);

p. 169 "Tongue Twisters" from *An Almanac of Words at Play* by Willard Espy (New York: Potter, 1975;

p. 178 Excerpt from "The Explosion Window" by Betty Sanders Garner, *Canadian Children's Annual* © 1978 Pottach Publications, 1977;

p. 182 "Thanadelthur" by Sylvia Van Kirk in *The Beaver*, Spring, 1974;

p. 191 "Migraine 'vocabulary' studied", February 17, 1982, *Saskatoon Star Phoenix*;

p. 192 "Word Association" game and "Simile Making Activity" from *Dreams and Challenges* by M. Ramsden, (Toronto: Macmillan);

p. 196 "The Saws were Shrieking" by W.W.E. Ross in *Shapes and Sounds: Poems by W.W.E. Ross*, Ed. Raymond Souster and John Robert Columbo. (Don Mills, Ontario: Longmans Canada, 1968);

p. 202 "Alphabet Poem" by Stephen Scobie in *When Is a Poem* by Florence McNeil (Toronto: League of Canadian Poets, 1980);

p. 203 "Red Ferrari", *ibid*;

p. 207 "The White Pony" by Morley Callaghan from *Morley Callaghan's Stories*, (Toronto: Macmillan, 1967);

p. 210 "A Pine Tree" and "Time Running Out"; p. 217 "A Painting" from *Prints In the Sand*, published by the Ministry of Education B.C.;

p. 212 "Dylan Thomas Portrait Poems" and "Eza Pound Couplets" adapted from *Dreams and Challenges* by M. Ramsden, Toronto: Macmillan;

p. 215 "I Am A Play" from *Their Own Spe-*

cial Shape by Brian Powell, reprinted by permission of Collier Macmillan Canada, Inc; The idea for a "poem portrait" also came from Their Own Special Shape;

p. 216 "This Is Just To Say" William Carlos Williams, Collected Earlier Poems of William Carlos Williams. Copyright 1983 by new Directions Publishing Corporation. Reprinted by permission of New Directions;

p. 217 "The World's Greatest Baton-Twirler" by Susan M. Foster. (Written in class at Burnaby South Senior School);

p. 218 "Highway 6, Ten A.M." page 61 of Zodiac, Canadian Council of Teachers of English;

p. 223 Reprinted from Fly Away Paul by Paul Davies. Copyright © 1974 by Paul Davies. Used by permission of Crown Publishers, Inc.;

p. 245 "Platform Notes" by Tim Bryson in Fran A. Tanner's Creative Communication Projects, 1973;

p. 246 "A Space For Me To Solve" by Geraldine Rubia in Easterly: 60 Atlantic Writers, 1978;

p. 247 "Instructor" by E.F. Dyck in Number One Northern: Poetry from Saskatchewan, ed. Robert Currie et al, (Moose Jaw: Coteau, 1977);

p. 248 "Grade Five Geography Lesson" by Barry Stevens in Number One Northern: Poetry from Saskatchewan, ed. Robert Currie et al, (Moose Jaw: Coteau, 1977);

p. 296 From A Queen In Thebes by Margaret Laurence. Used by permission of The Canadian Publishers, McClelland and Stewart Limited.

p. 318 "Ogopogo" by Mary Moon printed by permission of Douglas and McIntyre Publishers.

Photos

Cover Ramp 1, Chris Temple. Courtesy of Bau-Xi Gallery and Imperial Oil Limited. Photographed in Toronto by Robert and Brenda Skeoch.

p.1 Government of the North West Territories and the National Film Board of Canada; p.3 top: John Ruge; bottom: Clarence Brown; p.4 top: Cary Grossman; bottom: Bill Hoest; p.5 Vahan Shirvanian; p.11 A September Gale, Georgian Bay, Arthur Lismer, The National Gallery of Canada (NGC), Ottawa; p.21 A Buffalo Pound, Paul Kane. Courtesy of the Royal Ontario Museum (ROM), Toronto, Canada; p.25 Photo: Mrs. E.G. Downes; p.28 Blunden Harbour, Emily Carr, NGC; p.32 © 1982 United Feature Syndicate; p.42 Illustration by Roland Dingman, Campus Life Magazine; p.46 The Ferry, Quebec, James Wilson Morrice, NGC; p.54 top: reprinted with permission— the Toronto Star Syndicate; bottom: © Universal Press Syndicate; p.58 Martha Campbell; p.59 Bill Levine; p.64 Three Frigates in a Storm; John O'Brien; NGC; p.67 John Ruge; p.68 Nurit Karlin; p.74 © Universal Press Syndicate; p.78 © 1960 United Feature Syndicate; p.79 Association of Universities and Colleges of Canada; p.84 A Circle of Gladness, ROM; p.98 Val Valentine; p.104 April Fool, Reprinted from The Saturday Evening Post © 1943 The Curtis Publishing Company; p.111 Tribute Co. Syndicated Corporation; p.112 © 1984, Archie Comic Publications Inc.; p.113 © 1966 United Feature Syndicate; p.117 Petro-Canada; p.119 Madeleine de Vercheres, Philippe Hébert, Le Musée du Québec; p.125 top: Randy Hall; bottom: Clarence Brown; p.130 Canada Post Corporation; p.142 © 1974 United Feature Syndicate; p.143 © 1967 United Feature Syndicate; p.144 left: Martha Campbell; right: © King Feature Syndicate, Inc.; p.170 St. Paul's Church, Halifax, William Eager, ROM; p.179 Betty Sanders Garner; p.180 National Geographic World, 1981, p.19; p.183 Public Archives Canada, #C-62630; p.188 © 1984 United Feature Syndicate; p.189 Cathy, Universal Press Syndicate; p.195 Hans Hubman, Black Star; p.198 Dizlo Studios; p.199 Library of Congress, Washington, D.C.; p.200 Dick Hemingway; p.203 Hart Leavitt; p.213 Atlantic Storm, Alfred Eisenstadt, Life Magazine, c. 1943; p.214 Hart Leavitt; p.221 Winnipeg Free Press; p.222 top: By permission of Johnny Hart and News Group Chicago Inc.; bottom: © King Feature Syndicate, Inc.; p.223 Ron Davis; p.226 RILEY, Bridget. Current. 1964. Synthetic polymer paint on composition board, 58⅜ × 58⅞" (148.1 × 149.3 cm). Collection, The Museum of Modern Art, New York. Philip Johnson Fund; p.230, 231 and 232 Seymour Simon, The Optical Illusion Book. New York: Four Winds Press, 1976; p.233 Dick Hemingway; p.234, 235 and 236,

BRIDGES 2

BEGINNINGS

The photograph on the opposite page shows the construction of a railway in the Northwest Territories. It is a major achievement because it stands for people working together to accomplish a difficult task. But the railway also allows people to connect with each other more easily. It is a **bridge** that allows them to communicate.

In a way this photograph is a symbol for *Bridges 2*. It symbolizes the ideas that are a part of this book. Just as the railway helped the people of the Northwest Territories gain control over a difficult terrain, so *Bridges 2* will guide you through a study of communication. Just as the main purpose of this railway is to help people communicate with each other, so the main purpose of *Bridges 2* is to help you grow as you learn to communicate with others.

The **thought web** below illustrates the various skills in communication: **listening, speaking, writing, reading**, and **viewing**. It also shows you some other topics that are also part of communication: **language, media** and **visual literacy**. *Bridges 2* will connect you with these topics and skills.

Chapters and Links

The main parts of this textbook are its **chapters**, which are printed on white paper. The chapters give you information about the skills of communication or about a topic in communication. For example, a chapter may focus upon the skill of speaking. It will also contain exercises that encourage you to practise learning and writing. Other chapters will provide you with information about what language is, and require you to practise some of the skills of communication at the same time.

The sections between each chapter, on tinted paper, are called **links**. Links provide extra practice with the skills of communication, particularly speaking, listening, and viewing. Your teacher may use these link activities in various ways. Some will be used to help you learn the skills discussed in each chapter. Others will be used on their own, when your class has a few minutes left over from some other lesson. Your teacher may omit some of the link activities that don't fit the particular needs of your class.

Thinking About Communication

Throughout this textbook, you will find signs like this: *Activity*. Activities give you some definite tasks to do, tasks that will help you grow in your ability as a communicator. These first activities ask you to do some thinking about what communication is, and what you might want to learn about communication.

Activity 1   About Communication

Use the questions beneath each cartoon to hold a class discussion about the meaning of *communication*. These questions will get you started. You will be able to add many more ideas.

1. Cartoon 1
   a. What does the following statement mean? *This cartoon has a simple message, but a complex meaning*.
   b. How do you think the writer in this cartoon feels about his task? How do you know?
   c. How do you feel when you are given a writing task to do? Why do you feel this way?
   d. Talk about some of the writing assignments you have done in other years. Which ones did you enjoy doing? Which ones did you not enjoy? Why?

"Chapter one, page one . . ."

    e. How do you go about doing your writing assignments?
    f. Do you know anyone who makes his or her living as a writer? Have you ever thought of becoming a writer?

2. Cartoon 2
    a. What does this cartoon say about writing?
    b. What concerns do you have about making errors in your writing?
    c. How do you handle your problems with spelling, punctuation, capitalization, and other concerns?
    d. How do you learn what is correct in writing?

"We now come to the influence of ~~Hegel~~ ~~Hobbes~~ ~~Herder~~ Kant on modern thought."

"That's a window, honey. There are no commercials."

3. Cartoon 3
   a. What does this cartoon say about communication?
   b. How important is television as a means of communication?
   c. What do you know about television and its role in our society?
   d. How accurate is the cartoon in describing the role of television in your life?

"I see that our next speaker needs no introduction."

4. Cartoon 4
   a. Why is everyone leaving the room?
   b. What is the message about communication in this cartoon?
   c. How important are the skills of speaking and listening in your life? Why?
   d. What are some of the things you need to learn about listening and speaking? Why?

"The King is in his counting house."

5. Cartoon 5
   a. What is the message about communication in this cartoon?
   b. What changes do you think will occur as a result of computers and other new forms of communication?
   c. What do you think communication will be like fifty years from now? Why?
   d. What experiences have you had with some of the newer methods of communication?

Activity 2 *Pulling Your Ideas Together*

This activity will help you think about and organize your discussion about the cartoons in Activity 1. Use the following questions to start a class discussion:

1. Which skill or skills of communication are considered in each cartoon?

2. Which is the best cartoon? Why?

3. What does the skill of *viewing* involve? How important is it in your life?

4. Develop a class list of the objectives of things to be learned about each of the communication skills: writing, speaking, listening, viewing.

5. Collect cartoons about communication to make a class display. Use these cartoons and pictures to begin a class discussion about communication and its place in the modern world.

LINK 1 A

Follow the directions to build a **thought web** that outlines some ideas and facts about you:

1. Draw an oval shape in the centre of your page and put the word *me* inside it.

2. Think of something special about you. Place this idea inside another oval, and connect it with a line to the *me* oval.

3. If there is something about this second idea that you want to record, create another oval, write your idea inside it, and attach it with a line to the second oval. Keep this up until you have exhausted all of your thoughts connected with this second idea.

4. Think of something else about you. Attach this third idea to the *me* oval. Add other ovals to this third idea until you have recorded all of your thoughts.

5. Return to the *me* oval and add a fourth thought, and a fifth thought. Keep this up until you have several ideas about this *special me* recorded in your thought web.

Note: A thought web is a process of organizing your thoughts and can be used any time you want to explore your ideas and thoughts on a subject. It can be used in any school subject or in any area of your life, for example, when you are trying to make a decision.

Use your work in Link 1 B to introduce each other.
1. Divide into pairs. Each member of the pair explains his or her *Me* thought web to the other member.

2. Take notes while your partner is explaining his or her thought web to you.

3. Form small groups, with three or four pairs in each group. Each member of the pairs will introduce his or her partner to the small group.

4. Next, introduce your partner to the whole class.
   Here is an example of such an introduction:
   > I would like you to meet Lydia. She loves horses, travel, and swimming. Lydia spent her summer holiday on her grandpa's farm. She hopes to make the school volleyball team this fall.

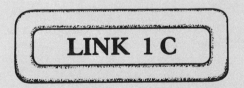

As a whole class, follow these directions to construct a thought web that will outline some information about the students in your class.

1. Draw an oval in the middle of a chalkboard or a large piece of paper and put the word *us* in it. (Or, you may use the name of your class, such as 8C, as the word for the oval.)

2. Each member of your class, in turn, will contribute one idea to this class thought web from the web that he or she created for Link 1 A.

3. As each class member adds to the class thought web, he or she might give a short talk about this personal web. This talk could be a minute or less in length.

4. Keep this up until all students have added something of themselves to the class thought web.

Note: If you run out of ideas, keep doodling on your thought web by running your pencil over and over one of your ovals. Do this until you get your next idea. Keep your pencil moving. This will help you generate or think up ideas.

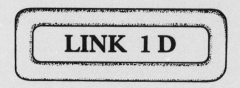

LINK 1 D

This activity gives you some practice in using a thought web to spark ideas for writing.

1. Look again at the photograph of the railway in the Northwest Territories. Consider it for at least a minute and a half.

2. In your notebook, construct a thought web to record your response to this photograph:
   a. In the centre oval, write the one main word that came to you as you were looking at the photograph.
   b. Keep adding ideas to your thought web. Some of the words may have occurred to you while you are viewing the photograph. Others may come into your mind while you are actually building the thought web.

3. Choose two or three parts of your thought web — the branches of the web that you like best.
   a. Change the words in each branch into complete sentences and write them in your notebook.
   b. Use one of the words from your thought web as a title for these sentences.
   When you put all of these sentences together, you have a **paragraph** that presents your response to the photograph.

Note: A response to this photograph is not the same as a description of the photograph. A **description** would involve a group of sentences that explain what you see in the photograph. Your **response** to the photograph examines the words and ideas that you associate with this picture, and perhaps expresses your feelings about it. There is quite a bit of *you* involved in your response. There is only a little bit of *you* involved in a description.

What has happened in September?

September 1, 1557 — Jacques Cartier, a famous Canadian explorer, died.

September 1, 1914 — The last passenger pigeon died in a Cincinnati zoo.

September 5, 1755 — Six thousand Acadians were deported from Nova Scotia. This event set the theme for Longfellow's poem "Evangeline."

September 7, 1533 — Queen Elizabeth I of England was born.

September 12, 1959 — Russia's Lunik II landed on the moon.

September 14, 1759 — General Montcalm died. Montcalm fought in the Battle of the Plains of Abraham, defending Quebec City from the British.

September 20, 1917 — The Quebec Bridge was completed.

September 22, 1959 — A baby gorilla was born in a zoo, at Basel, Switzerland.

September 27, 1066 — William the Conqueror set sail from France to conquer England.

CHAPTER 1

SEPTEMBER —
A CHALLENGE

A September Gale, Georgian Bay, Arthur Lismer

A challenge is a kind of demand that is placed on you. You prepare yourself to cope with it and then you confront it head-on. Sometimes you are successful, and sometimes not.

The way you go about meeting a challenge is important. In one sense, your knowledge of how to meet challenges may be more important than your success in meeting them.

You can learn how to cope with challenges. Consider the task of learning to write as one of the challenges you have to meet. This chapter will help you meet that challenge.

When you learn to write you accomplish two things. First, writing is of value to you personally. Most people have something inside that needs to be said. Writing can do this for you. It's a way to get your inner thoughts on a page so that you know what they are and what you think about them.

Second, you learn to write so that you can communicate with others. To do this, you have to find a way to present your ideas to other people. You connect with others.

Something else happens, too. When you write for others, the people you are writing for react to you. They are influenced by your writing, both by what you say and how you say it. And they make decisions not only about what to write but about you yourself.

Much of the writing practice that takes place in this textbook focuses on writing as a way to connect with others. To do this, you will learn about **the writing process**. Your knowledge of this writing process will help you to meet the challenge of writing.

Activity 1A Testing Your Courage

People react to challenges in different ways. A situation that frightens one person may not bother another person at all. The following activity gives you the task of considering different kinds of challenges.

1. Read the list of challenges carefully.

2. Rewrite the list in your notebook, putting it in a new order. Start with the situation you believe presents the greatest challenge and end with the one that presents the least challenge.

Challenging Situations

a. You have to give a speech in front of three hundred people.
b. You have been asked to go hang-gliding or mountain-climbing.
c. You see someone beating up on another person who is crying for help.

d. You are supposed to stay alone in a deserted house.

e. You wake up and realize that your house is on fire.

f. You have wandered into a yard guarded by a hostile, unchained watchdog.

g. You have been receiving threatening letters and phone calls.

3. As a class, discuss your lists. Try to reach class agreement on the most challenging and least challenging situations.

4. In your notebook, write a few sentences describing how you would handle each of these challenges.

THE CHALLENGE OF THE WRITING PROCESS

This section presents you with the writing task for this chapter. This task, then, becomes your personal challenge. What you have to learn is *how* to meet this challenge.

Your Writing Task

The first page of this chapter tells you about some of the significant events of September. Your writing task is to express your ideas and feelings about *September*.

This piece of writing will be your own personal statement about *September*, something creative and unique. It is a piece of writing that you write for yourself, but you may share it with others.

Don't despair. You will not be left on your own to do this writing.

The rest of this chapter will take you through the stages in the writing process.

The Writing Process

This diagram outlines the **stages in the writing process**. The next section outlines exactly what is involved at each stage and explains how to go about using the techniques for each stage of your writing.

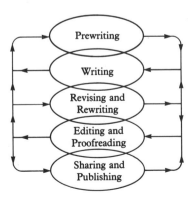

Prewriting

Writing

Revising and Rewriting

Editing and Proofreading

Sharing and Publishing

From the diagram, it looks as if the writing process is a series of steps that follow sequentially, one after the other. To some extent this is true. Yet the writing process is not so clearly defined. You may find that you flip back and forth from one stage to the other. While you are involved with prewriting, for example, you may find that you are also doing some revising and editing of your work. Moving from one stage to another is a very normal way to use the process.

In this text, however, you will be taken through each stage one at a time, as you go about your writing tasks. This will allow you to master the process of writing.

If you think back to the introduction of this chapter, you will remember *that the experience of knowing how to solve a problem may be as important as the solution itself.* So, on to the writing process!

THE STAGES IN THE WRITING PROCESS

Challenge 1: Prewriting

The first step in the writing process is the **prewriting stage**. When you get set to write, you make several decisions: why you want to write; who you want to read what you write; how you want them to think or feel; what you want to say; what facts or details you should include; what form of writing you want to use.

One challenge of the prewriting stage is to gather your ideas and facts. Here are some ideas you can use:

a. talking to another person or a group
b. listening to discussions or radio programs
c. reading
d. observing carefully
e. watching films
f. looking at pictures, maps, or diagrams
g. using the library
h. conducting surveys
i. asking questions
j. keeping a journal
k. brainstorming ideas with a partner or group
l. using a thought web
m. developing a word cache
n. sitting and thinking by yourself

Activity 1B   Prewriting for September

To begin your writing task, you will have to do some prewriting for the topic *September*.

1. Construct a thought web, with the word *September* in the middle oval. Let your mind wander to create as many connections with *September* as you can.

2. Share thought webs with a fellow student. If you see any word association in your partner's web that means something to you, add it to your own thought web.

3. Use any other prewriting technique from the list above that will help you think about *September*.

Often you will be given the **form** for your writing task with your assignment. It will say such things as these: write a paragraph, write an essay, write a letter, write a report. These are examples of the forms you can use in writing.

You are free to choose your own form for your *September* assignment.

Activity 1C   Choosing a Form for September

This activity will help you choose a form for your writing task.

1. Read the following list of writing situations and rewrite it in your notebook. Place the *most difficult* writing situation first on your list. Then add the others to your list in descending order of difficulty. End the list with the *easiest* writing situation for you.

Challenging Writing Situations

a. Your teacher asks you to write a twelve-line rhymed poem.

b. You write a letter to your pen pal in Denmark to tell him or her about a holiday you are going to have.

c. You are assigned a ten-page report for your science class.

d. You write to yourself in your secret diary (it has a secure lock on it).

e. You have to write a business letter for your class to order a new program for your microcomputer.

f. You have to write a four-line, unrhymed poem for a school contest.   →

g. You are assigned a descriptive paragraph to write for English class.

h. You have to write a script with a group of friends for a play that your class will perform before the school assembly.

i. You have to create a newspaper ad for your school play.

j. You have to write a classified ad to run in your community newspaper to find your lost dog.

2. Discuss your lists as a whole class.

3. As a class, add to the list of writing forms given in the *Challenging Writing Situations*.

4. Copy the whole list into your notebook.

5. Now that you have a list of possible writing forms, choose the form you want to use for your writing assignment on the topic *September*.

Challenge 2: Writing

The next step in the writing process is **writing the first draft**.

At this stage, let your writing carry you along. Try to get everything down on paper, without worrying about whether or not it is completely correct. You can make major changes to your writing during the next stage in the writing process.

Activity 1D   Writing September

This activity will give you an easy way to get the first draft of *September* down on your page.

1. Look at the thought web you constructed in Activity 1B and choose the one part of it that interests you most.

2. Write one word from this part of the thought web at the top of a fresh sheet of paper.

3. Use this word as a starting point and write continuously about this topic for three minutes. This technique is called *fast writing*.

Note: Keep your pen working during the entire three minutes. If you can't think of anything new to say, just keep writing your main word on your page until some new ideas come.

4. Repeat these first three steps with a second topic from your thought web in Activity 1B.

Challenge 3: Revising and Rewriting

The third step in the writing process is **revising and rewriting**.

At this stage, there are some basic things you can do to make improvements in your writing:

1. **Add** new ideas, examples, facts, and information.

2. **Remove** ideas, examples, facts, and information.

3. **Replace** some details with others that seem more appropriate.

4. **Rearrange** details and ideas in the most effective order.

Activity 1E *Revising* September

This activity will help you do some thinking about your writing on *September.*

1. Reread both of the fast writings you did for Activity 1D and choose the piece of writing you like better.

2. To this piece of writing, add *two* new facts or ideas. You can do this by adding words to your existing sentences, or by adding new sentences to your piece of writing.

3. Find *four* words in your writing that could be scratched out without changing the meaning too much. Decide whether to delete them or leave them as they are.

4. Look for *two* ideas or words in your writing that could be improved by using different words. Make this change.

5. Find *one* sentence that could go better in a different place in your writing. Draw an arrow from the first word in this sentence to the spot where it could go.

6. Think of *four* different titles you could use for your piece of writing and write them on the back of your page.

7. Make up *two* first or *topic sentences* for your piece of writing and write them on the back of your page.

8. Make up *two* last or concluding sentences that could do for this piece of writing and write them on the back of your page.

9. Read your piece of writing to a partner and ask for comments. Make notes on what your partner says.

Activity 1F Rewriting September

Now that you have done some revising of your piece of writing, it is time to rewrite it and compose a second draft.

1. Study the changes you made to your writing by *adding*, *removing*, *replacing*, or *rearranging* words or sentences.

2. Decide which changes improve your writing and which ones do not.

3. Make the changes that you want. Don't be afraid to keep what you wrote originally. Your revisions were done just to give you some choices. Now is the time to make your choice.

4. Choose which of your *topic sentences* you prefer. Your topic sentence should be an interesting opening for your writing.

5. Do the same with your *concluding sentences*.

6. Finally, decide upon the best title for your writing.

7. When you have considered all of these choices, write your second draft of *September*.

Challenge 4: Editing and Proofreading

When you reread your second draft, you may want to make some final changes to the words, sentences, or descriptive details. These changes tend to be smaller than those you make at the revising stage. This process is called **editing**. Writers edit their work in order to make it more pleasant to read or easier to understand.

You may also want to make changes in order to correct mistakes in the mechanics of your writing: spelling, punctuation, or capitalization. This process is called **proofreading**. Writers proofread their work to be sure that they have followed the rules of writing and that others will easily understand what they mean in their writing. These rules are called **conventions**, or normal ways of doing things.

Activity 1G Editing and Proofreading September

1. Edit your writing by looking for any small changes that you can make.

2. Next, use this checklist to help you proofread your writing to be

certain that you are following the conventions of writing:

a. Start at the end of your piece of writing and read it backwards, one sentence at a time. If any of your sentences don't make sense when you read them in isolation, change them. Each sentence should be clear to the reader and to you.

b. Make sure that you have capitalized all important words in your title. (Prepositions are not usually capitalized.) Check, too, to make certain that your title is centred on your page and that you have left a line between the title and the first line of the body of your writing.

c. Check to make certain that each paragraph is indented at least two centimetres.

d. Be sure to use the following homophones correctly:

too	She went *too*.	(also)
two	*two* horses	(number)
to	*to* the game	(direction)
there	*t + here*	(direction)
their	*their* house	(ownership or possession)
they're	*They're* going with me.	(contraction: they are)
it's	*It's* the beginning of a new year.	(contraction: it is)
its	The dog hurt *its* paw.	(ownership or possession)

3. Read your writing to your partner and ask him or her for a final comment on it. Work together to make your writing say exactly what you want it to say. Do the same thing for your partner.

Activity 1H   Writing a Final Draft of September

Now that you have finished editing and proofreading your writing, you can write the final draft.

1. Choose a fresh page. (Check with your teacher to see what size page is preferred.)

2. Plan to do a quality job in presenting your writing:
   a. Centre your title on the page.
   b. Leave at least one line between the title and the beginning of your writing.
   c. Leave margins around both sides of your work and at the top and bottom of your page.
   d. Use ink for your final draft and try for a good clear handwriting.

3. Sign your name to your work.

Challenge 5: Publishing and Sharing

The final stage in the writing process is **publishing and sharing** your work. You wrote your reaction to *September* just to please yourself. You were, in other words, your own **audience**. You may want to share this writing with someone else. Sharing or publishing your writing could mean many things:

   a. mailing a letter you wrote to a friend
   b. sending your writing to the editor of your community newspaper
   c. sending a story to the editor of a magazine
   d. sharing your work with a small group of classmates or reading it aloud in class
   e. displaying the writing on a bulletin board or making up a writing book
   f. putting your writing in a helium-filled balloon, sending it off in the wind, and waiting to hear from the person who finds it
   g. handing in a homework assignment to your teacher
   h. keeping your writing in your own folder and continuing to use it only to communicate with yourself

Activity 11 Sharing or Publishing September

1. **Form small groups of three to five students.**

2. **Decide upon one way your class could share or publish the *September* writings. You may use some of the suggestions in the list or, better still, make up your own possibilities.**

3. **Then, each group will report its suggestion to the whole class.**

4. **The suggestions should be listed on the board. Then the class can decide how to go about sharing or publishing the *September* writings.**

Challenge Accomplished

This chapter has given you two challenges: to produce an interesting and creative piece of writing about *September*, and to work with and understand the writing process.

The first of these challenges is over. You should be proud of your accomplishment. The second challenge is still with you — to learn to use the writing process whenever you write, whether it is in English, history, science, or math.

LINK 2 A

A Buffalo Pound Paul Kane

In 1846, Paul Kane journeyed westward across Canada to study and sketch life in Western Canada. Eventually he travelled from Fort Garry in Manitoba, past Fort Edmonton, up the Athabasca River to Jasper, across the Rocky Mountains, and all the way to Vancouver Island. When he returned home in 1848, he had over five hundred sketches of the Canadian West. One hundred of these paintings are now in the Royal Ontario Museum in Toronto.

1. Study Kane's *A Buffalo Pound* for a minute and then write your response to these questions in your notebook:
   a. What contrast can you find between the lines on the left side of the painting and those on the right side? What is the effect of this difference?
   b. What ideas about the Canadian West is Kane presenting in this painting? How might they have been received by the people back in Eastern and Atlantic Canada?

2. In your notebook, write a description of the scene that appears in Kane's painting.

3. In your notebook, write your personal response to this painting. *Remember:* A description provides an account of what you can see in the painting. Your personal response includes your feelings and ideas about the painting.

LINK 2 B

Paul Kane did not make his trip on his own. In the same way, you do not need to venture forth on your writing journeys alone. You need companions to help you and to give advice.

It is very likely that you will work with one or more students at the several stages of the writing process. Sometimes you may work with only one student: your **writing partner**. At other times, you may work with a group of two or more students: your **writing team**.

Here are some of the ways you can work with others to improve your writing:

Prewriting: Talking to your partner or team may help you get ideas, ask questions, discover facts, choose examples or details, decide on a topic, or pick out an audience for your work.

Writing: You do most of the work at this stage, but your partner can help out if you're looking for the right word, a good example, or an interesting detail.

Revising and Rewriting: Your partner gets the chance to look over the first draft of your writing and to offer advice. At this point, your partner, or writing group, may suggest how to improve your writing by adding, removing, replacing, or rearranging details and ideas.

Editing and Proofreading: A partner with a keen eye, a dictionary or thesaurus, and a sharp pencil may help you at this stage. He or she can point out such problems as these: spelling mistakes, capitalization and punctuation mistakes, incomplete or run-together sentences, unclear or incorrect word choice.

Sharing and Publishing: When you write or type your finished copy, your partner or writing team may be your first official audience and may suggest who else would enjoy reading your work.

1. Think about what you would like your writing partner or writing team to do for you. In your notebook, write a list of these things.

2. Next, make a list of things you have to offer a writing partner to enable him or her to grow in the skill of writing.

3. Use your two lists to write a *Help Wanted* advertisement for a writing partner.
   Remember: Help Wanted ads are very brief. They are usually only a few sentences in length, but they must contain the essential information. Your ad will include ideas about what you want in a writing partner and what you can give in return.

4. Place the ad on your classroom notice board and wait to see who answers it.

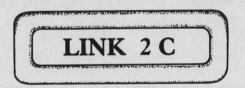

LINK 2 C

You may want to organize your writing according to whether it is **private writing** or **public writing**. The best place for your private writing is probably a diary or journal. Link 2 D describes the journals of Prentice Downes, who explored Canada's northland, and tells you how you can set up a journal.

Your public writing — the writing you do to share with an audience — presents you with a different problem from your private writings. There are countless ways to publish writing: reading aloud, mailing letters to the newspaper, putting up bulletin board displays, printing stories in a class booklet.

Like every writer, you will have to choose a method of storing your public writing. During the school year, you may go back and reread some of the writing you did earlier. This is an excellent way to find out how you are growing in your writing skills.

Activity

One suggestion is that you save your writing in a folder. The folder could be a plain file folder, a ring binder, or even a box. Make a table of contents for your folder, and record the date of each piece as you add it to your collection. You will want to be able to find things easily when you need to look at something you wrote earlier. Keeping a writing folder will help you to measure your progress and build on what you have learned.

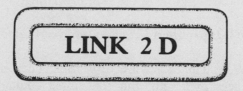

LINK 2 D

Some people write for themselves. They keep a journal in which they record things that they see and things that they think about. These are private writings. Writers often use their journal writings as a source of ideas for their public writings.

Prentice G. Downes, a school teacher, went on several long trips across Canada's northland. He kept a journal account of his ventures. These private journals are being edited and someday will appear in print as a book.

On July 30, 1940, Downes and his partner camped in their sleeping rolls, as a herd of deer migrated nearby. The click of deer hooves within five feet of their beds kept them awake most of the night. In the morning, Downes hid in some bushes to photograph the deer migration. The following page shows part of his journal entry for the day.

Activity

You might want to start writing a journal. Find a book for yourself and start. Set aside a definite time each day to write, even if you can find only four or five minutes. And keep it up.

Use your journal as a place to record your ideas. It can be a valuable source of ideas for you as you do your writing assignments. It is also an excellent place to practise and experiment with writing.

One very ludicrous habit the deer have occurs when they are puzzled. They stand still and face one but often throw one hind leg out in the most ridiculous fashion thus

Prentice Downes, July, 1940

In fact, one big buck entirely obscured the view-finder. It has been a thrilling thing — first to hear them coming at a distance and then having them swim across directly to one and get out of the water; they stop, shake themselves, the cows grunt, the calves give a bleat or two, then they clamber up the steep slope beside me so close I could jump and grab a fawn. There is great individual difference in their appearance. Some of the bucks are still almost white with winter hair. Some of the younger ones are dark chocolate and in full summer coat. Some are very mottled. The little fawns are a tawny buckskin hue. As they swim, the head is well above water and tilted upward, the horns lying back; the tail, just a tuft, also rides above the water. They swim powerfully and without noise — (two are coming now). Having 'snapped' them, I go on. They are almost semi-aquatic in habit — swimming from point to point, island to island, in long strings. When a large band crosses, it seems usually that one takes the lead considerably in advance of the others.

R. H. Cockburn, *North of Reindeer: The 1940 Trip Journal of Prentice G. Downes.*

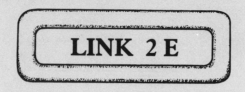

LINK 2 E

Read Downes's journal once more and use your own journal to write some of your thoughts about it. These questions will start your thinking:

1. What is your overall reaction to Downes's journal entry? Do you like it? Why or why not?

2. Would you like to go on a trip with him? Why?

3. What does this journal entry tell you about Downes as a person?

4. Do you think he enjoyed his adventure? Why?

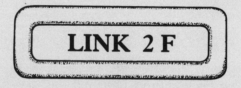

LINK 2 F

1. Use your journal to record some observations you have made.

2. Add a sketch in your journal, like the one Downes drew. Sketches are helpful in describing things, and they are especially useful if you decide later to use your journal notes to write a report or make a presentation on the topic you have been writing about in your journal.

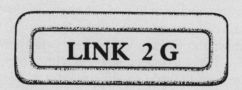

LINK 2 G

A title is a kind of ad for your writing. This link activity gives you practice creating titles.

1. Write the answers to each of these situations in your notebook.

2. Brainstorm your suggestions in small groups of four or five students.

   - For each situation, choose the best title from the suggestions in your group.

   - Write your titles on a large piece of paper and display them for your class.

What Would Be a Good Title for . . .

a) a novel in which a fourteen-year-old boy from Winnipeg and a fifteen-year-old Inuit boy are lost on the tundra in the Arctic?
b) a short story in which two teenaged girls are lost in a spaceship that is travelling to Venus?
c) a poem about the wonders of each of the provinces of Canada?
d) an editorial in a newspaper that is commenting on the relationship between the Prime Minister and the Leader of the Opposition?
e) a movie about a teenager who is in conflict with his or her parents?
f) a television situation comedy about a classroom in a school that overlooks the Bay of Fundy?

Discussion: As a class, discuss this question: What makes a good title?

Blunden Harbour Emily Carr

Blunden Harbour, which was completed in about 1929, shows totem poles in Blunden Harbour. Blunden Harbour is a village of the Kwakiutl Indians in British Columbia. The Kwakiutl are known for their gift-giving ceremonies or potlatches. At a potlatch, the host or hostess gives many gifts to the guests. This next chapter is about a special kind of gift: the gift of writing. For this reason, the chapter is called *A Writing Potlatch*.

A WRITING POTLATCH

Giving a gift can mean many things — buying something special, making a one-of-a-kind present, or even promising several hours of your time to help someone. People enjoy giving and getting different and imaginative gifts.

Writing is another way for you to give gifts to people. You can give them information and ideas. You can amuse and entertain them. You can express your feelings and emotions. This is your own writing potlatch.

In this chapter, you will have the opportunity to put your gift-giving imagination to work. You will be able to choose from several writing projects about different kinds of gifts. You will also be asked to try several different things in your writing:

- following the writing process from start to finish
- working with a writing partner
- using your writing folder to store your work

THE WRITING PROCESS

Later in this chapter you will be asked to write about the steps you would take to choose a suitable gift for someone. Remember that there are also steps for you to take as you go through the writing process.

prewriting   Get set to write by choosing your topic, your reader, and your ideas.

writing	Put what you have to say down on paper in your first draft.
revising and rewriting	Make improvements to your first draft in one or more ways: • add new ideas and information • remove weak or unnecessary material • replace some ideas with better ones • rearrange the order of your ideas.
editing and proofreading	Improve your writing by making changes so that it is correct as well as easy and pleasant to read.
sharing and publishing	Give your finished writing to the readers you planned to read it. Decide whether they reacted the way you wanted them to and whether you should make any changes the next time you go through the writing process.

YOUR WRITING PARTNER

Many of the activities in this chapter set you up to work with a writing partner. You and your partner can help each other in several ways:

• Discuss ideas before you start to write.
• Help with problems as you write.
• Make suggestions to improve your first draft as you revise and rewrite.
• Point out corrections as you edit and proofread.
• Be the first official audience for your finished writing.

Note: If you did Link 2 B, does this list look anything like the *Help Wanted* ad you wrote?

Activity 2A   Gifts and Giving

If you spend some time thinking about gifts and gift-giving, you will get yourself set for the writing projects in this chapter.

1. Make up a gift list of the perfect present you might give to each of these people. You can spend not more than $5.00 on any one gift. Write your ideas in your notebook.
   a. a preschool child
   b. another student (someone you don't know very well), whose name you drew in a class gift exchange

   c. a pen pal in another country
   d. the parents of a friend who invited you to visit over the summer holidays
   e. an adult who has been helpful to you, such as a sports coach or music teacher
   f) someone you admire greatly but don't know personally, such as a singer or great athlete

2. As a whole class, discuss your lists of *perfect* gifts. Give some thought to this question: what makes the perfect gift?

Activity 2B   What Should I Give to . . .

1. What gift would you give to each of these people? Write your answers in your notebook.
   a. your member of parliament
   b. a movie star who visits your community
   c. a football hero who talks with your class
   d. a blind person who addresses your school assembly
   e. a dog who saves a baby from a burning building

2. Share your ideas as a whole class. When you give your idea, be prepared to state why you would give this particular gift.

Activity 2C   Saying Thanks

1. Work with your writing partner to discuss the proper ways to express thanks for a gift — whether your really like it or not.

2. In your notebook, make a list of the appropriate ways to say thank you for a gift.

3. In your notebook, write down your solutions to each of these problems:
   a. Your grandmother has given you a toque and you hate toques. Besides, it's knitted in the school colours of your school's biggest rival. Your grandmother will undoubtedly want to see you wearing this toque.
      How do you say thanks?
   b. An old school friend of your parents has sent you a birthday gift. This person does not live near you. Unfortunately, this person thinks you are ten years younger than you really are and sent you an expensive toy suitable for a preschool child.
      How do you say thanks?

c. Someone you don't really like much wants to become your close friend. This person has given you a fancy gift, spending more money than he or she really should have.
How do you say thanks?

4. Work with your writing partner. Choose one of the situations in 3 and work out the conversation that would take place between the person who gave the gift and the person who received the gift.
Be prepared to act out your conversation for your class.

Incredible Presents

Over the centuries, people have given each other some incredible presents. Imagine what it would be like to get one of these gifts.

- In 1888, an artist named **Vincent Van Gogh** cut off the lobe of his left ear and presented it to a girl named Rachel, saying, "Keep this object like a treasure."

- About 1340, an English knight named **Sir Godfrey Luttrell** left home to fight in the Crusades. He told his wife before he left her that his heart would always be with her. When he died, his heart was sent back to her in a casket.

- In 1152, **Eleanor of Aquitaine** married Henry Plantagenet, Count of Anjou. As a wedding present, she gave him the entire Duchy of Aquitaine, about one-third of modern-day France.

- In 1301, for his son's sixteenth birthday, **King Edward I** gave young Prince Edward a whole country, the Principality of Wales.

- The people of France gave the **Statue of Liberty** to the United States as a token of friendship. With its pedestal, the statue stands over one hundred metres high. Its observation platform is eighty metres up in the air.

- The Cullinan diamond, the largest gem diamond ever discovered, was given to **King Edward VII** by the Transvaal Government for his sixty-sixth birthday. It is 3106 carats and weighs about 600 grams.

- The oldest of all great diamonds is the Koh-i-nor, discovered in 1304. Now part of the British Crown Jewels, it was a gift to **Queen Victoria** from the East India Company.

Activity 2D   Talking about Gifts

You can learn interesting information by asking several different people the same question. For this activity, you will conduct a survey of at least five people. Choose people or informants who are not in your class.

1. Ask each person the following questions and record the answers in your notebook:
    a. What is the most unusual or imaginative gift you have ever been given?
    b. What special occasion is the most important time for a person to receive a gift? Why?

2. The class may hold a vote to decide on the most unusual or imaginative gift anyone reported from the surveys.

3. The class may also draw up a list of occasions that are celebrated with gift-giving.

Activity 2E   Fantastic Gifts

Work by yourself on the following questions to come up with a list of ideas about gifts that are completely "out of this world." Write your ideas in your notebook so that you can use them for an activity later in this chapter.

1. What do you think might happen if you were given a gift:
    a. that only you could see and that was invisible to everyone else?
    b. that made up its own games when you tried to play with it?
    c. that could change its size and shape?
    d. that was jealous of your other possessions?

2. Pick out your best idea and be prepared to share it with the class.

WRITING ABOUT GIFTS

This section offers you the chance to write about two types of gifts — gifts from the Magic Shop or gifts that nobody wants. Read on. You will find a description of each situation.

Choice 1: Magic Shop Gifts

You want to buy a very special gift for someone. None of the stores you visit has anything you like. Finally you come to a dark little shop on a quiet street. In the window is a sign that says *Buy someone a gift from the magic shop*. As you enter, you see a mysterious man standing behind the counter. The shelves are loaded with strange, exciting-looking objects.

"Welcome," says the man. "Pick any gift you like. Just remember that this is a magic shop. One of these gifts has a *curse* on it. Another one comes alive sometimes. A third one will change the life of the person who gets it. Now make your choice."

If you choose *Magic Shop Gifts* your writing task will be to write the story of what happens when you choose a gift from the Magic Shop.

Choice 2: Unwanted Gifts

You have been asked to write an advice column for the local newspaper. You want to keep your identity completely secret, so you use the name *Kim Kolumn* for your contribution to the newspaper.

This letter has just arrived in your mail. Read it carefully and think about your answer.

Dear Kim Kolumn:

I need help desperately! Every time I pick out a gift for someone, everything goes wrong. People never like what I choose for them. Sometimes they return the presents to the store. Sometimes they give them away to other people. At other times, they just hide the presents in the basement.

Last week, I picked out a surprise present for my dog Duffy. Duffy took it right out and buried it in the back yard, like this . . .

I need your advice. Please tell me what I need to know to pick out good gifts for other people. Can you explain some simple rules for me to follow? I need to know how to choose presents that other people will appreciate and enjoy.

Yours truly,

Confused

If you choose *Unwanted Gifts*, your writing task will be to write your reply to Confused. Your reply should give a clear report of your opinions on how to pick out gifts that people will appreciate and enjoy.

Activity 2F   Questions to Think About

In this activity you will work with a small group of students to talk about the two choices: *Magic Shop Gifts* and *Unwanted Gifts*. After you have talked about the following questions, decide which topic you will write about.

1. *Magic Shop Gifts* offers you a choice of three gifts: one that has a curse on it, one that comes alive sometimes, or one that will change the life of the person who gets it. Each member of the group should give at least one answer or suggest one idea for these questions:
   a. Which kind of gift would you prefer to get: the one with the curse on it, the one that comes to life or the one that can change a person's life? Why?
   b. What would be the worst thing that could happen?
   c. What would be the best thing that could happen?
   d. How would you know which gift you had received?

2. *Unwanted Gifts* asks for advice about choosing appropriate gifts. If you could give only one piece of advice, what would it be?

3. Look back at your ideas from the previous activities in this chapter. Pick out the ideas you could use for *Magic Shop Gifts*. Pick out the ideas you could use for *Unwanted Gifts*. Make notes about these ideas in your notebook.

4. Think carefully about what you have discussed in your group and written in your notebook.
   a. Choose the topic you want to write about.
   b. Find a writing partner who has chosen the same topic as you.

If you chose to write about *Magic Shop Gifts*, do Activity 2G. If you chose to write about *Unwanted Gifts*, do Activity 2H.

Prewriting

Activity 2G   Magic Shop Gifts

1. Work by yourself to find some ideas for your story. Write short answers to these questions in your notebook:
   a. Make up interesting names for three people who might be in your story.
   b. Make up two details to describe each of them.

c. List one place besides the Magic Shop where some of the action might take place.

d. List two details to describe this place.

e. Make a list of three objects that you might buy in the Magic Shop.

f. What is the funniest thing that could happen? the most mysterious? the most surprising?

2. Work with your writing partner to gather ideas. Share your lists and help each other think some more about this story:

a. Suggest one more person who might be in the story.

b. Suggest one statement that each of the people in the story might say.

c. Decide why your group of characters might go to the place you picked out, and what they might do there together.

d. Decide which object is the gift

  • that comes alive sometimes

  • that has a curse on it

  • that will change the receiver's life

3. Working alone, look over the list of ideas you discussed with your writing partner. Reexamine the ideas you recorded in Activity 2F and choose three ideas that you might use in your story about the Magic Shop gift.

Activity 2H Unwanted Gifts

1. Working by yourself, write short responses to these problems in your notebook.

a. Make a list of three people who seemed to enjoy the gifts you gave them, and list the gifts as well.

b. Make a list of three gifts you have received that you liked. Why did you like each of them?

c. Make a list of three gifts you have received that you disliked. Why did you dislike them?

d. If you had $10.00 to spend, what would you pick to give

  • your parents?

  • your brother or sister?

  • your best friend?

  • your grandparents?

  • someone who has done you a favour?

2. Which of these gifts would you like to receive? Write this list in your notebook in order from the most enjoyable to the least enjoyable:

a. a surprise gift
b. a useful gift
c. something beautiful
d. a gift of money

e. something helpful for school
f. a gift to start a hobby
g. a gift of clothes
h. friendship

3. Work with your writing partner to gather ideas. Share your lists and ask your partner to help you with these statements:

   a. Ask for your partner's opinion about the three gifts you gave to other people. Also, ask your partner's opinion about the gifts you would give if you had $10.00 to spend. Do you both agree that these gifts would be appreciated and enjoyed?

   b. Compare what your partner thinks about the kinds of gifts that would be the most enjoyable and least enjoyable to receive. Do you both agree on one list?

   c. Work with your partner to decide why people would or would not enjoy the kinds of gifts on the list you have just made.

4. Working alone, think about the discussion you had with your partner and go back over your notes from Activity 2F. Decide upon at least three details that you can use to help answer Confused's letter.

It is important at this point in your writing to think about the person who will read it: your audience. For this writing task, you will be writing for someone you know quite well, such as one of your classmates.

Activity 2I   An Audience

Work with a writing partner or a writing group to consider the audience for *Magic Shop Gifts* or *Unwanted Gifts*:

1. What kind of story do the students in your class like to read? What kind of advice column would be interesting for them?

2. Would an older friend of yours like to read the same story or advice column?

3. What things can you do with your story or letter to interest your classmates? an older friend?

4. On your own, make notes, giving yourself some advice about things that you should do with your writing in order to interest your audience.

Writing

Write your story about *Magic Shop Gifts* or *Unwanted Gifts*. Use most of the ideas you have gathered. Do not worry about whether everything is completely correct. You can go back later and make corrections. Get your ideas on paper as quickly as you can.

Revising and Rewriting

Activity 2J   Revising Magic Shop Gifts

1. Exchange papers with your writing partner, who will help you by answering these questions:
   a. Would the story be more interesting if it were told from the point of view of another character?
   b. Is there one place where you should tell *why* something happened?
   c. What are three more descriptive words to refer to objects, actions, or places?
   d. Where is one place in which some more action might take place?
   e. Is there another ending for your story?

Now, go ahead and rewrite your next draft of *Magic Shop Gifts*.

Activity 2K   Revising Unwanted Gifts

1. Share the first draft of your advice column with your writing partner, who will help you by telling you these things:
   a. whether or not Confused would be able to understand your advice about giving gifts
   b. one more piece of advice you might give about picking out gifts
   c. whether you have answered all of the questions Confused asks in the letter
   d. an additional example to help make one of your ideas clearer
   e. a different order for your sentences to help clarify your ideas

Now, go ahead and rewrite your next draft of *Unwanted Gifts*.

Editing and Proofreading

Activity 2L   Solving Some Problems

1. Exchange your story or advice column with your writing partner. Your partner should do the following:
   a. Point out one sentence that could be written in another way and rewrite this sentence at the bottom of your page.
   b. Pick out three words, from different places in your writing, that could be replaced with words that might be more colourful and interesting.
   c. Point out two places where verbs could be replaced by more active ones that do a better job of describing movement.
   d. Check to see that you have not made any mistakes with these homonyms, which are easily confused:

there	We went *there*. (direction)
their	It is *their* house. (ownership or possession)
they're	*They're* my best friends. (contraction)
our	This is *our* answer. (ownership or possession)
are	We *are* friends. (special kind of verb: linking verb)
whether	I'll go *whether* or not you go. (states a condition)
weather	The *weather* is cold. (atmospheric condition)
your	This is *your* car. (ownership or possession)
you're	*You're* going, too? (contraction: you are)
its	The dog licked *its* paw. (ownership or possession)
it's	*It's* time to go. (contraction: it is)

Make any necessary corrections and changes to your writing and then write the final copy of your story or advice column. Give it one last proofreading, or ask a partner to do it for you.

Publishing and Sharing

Activity 2M   The Final Thing

Try some of these ideas with your finished work:

1. Use your speaking skills to share your work. Have a session in class where each person reads his or her finished story or advice column. Listen for the good points in your classmates' readings and be ready to compliment them.

2. Put together a booklet of advice about gift-giving, with a copy of each student's advice column.

3. Put together a Magic Shop story collection that includes each student's story.

4. Send away your writing to someone who lives outside your community. Maybe you can make your writing a special gift to that person.

The Gift of Writing

Each piece of writing you do is like a gift. You give yourself the satisfaction of creating something new and personal. You give your reader the opportunity to understand something about you, to find out what you think and how you feel.

Some gifts are surprises, and you may find that your own writing can surprise you. You discover ideas and feelings that you hadn't considered before.

This chapter has prompted you to use the writing process: prewriting, writing, revising and rewriting, proofreading and editing, publishing and sharing. It is a gift that will help you as you do writing tasks, both in this textbook and in other subject areas.

LINK 3 A

Details can help to communicate an idea or message clearly. A study of this cartoon will show you how details work in communication.

Cartoons are like paragraphs. They have a **main idea**, which is like the **topic sentence** of a paragraph. The rest of a cartoon or a paragraph is made of **details**, which add to this main idea.

1. Write in your notebook the topic sentence, or main idea, of the cartoon.

2. Pick out the details in the cartoon that support this main idea and list them in your notebook.

3. Is the visual message that this cartoon communicates better than your written version? Why or why not?

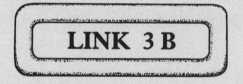

LINK 3 B

This dictation passage is called "Fog." It describes a heavy fog that has settled over Vancouver.

The topic sentence introduces the main idea of the paragraph. The rest of the paragraph develops this main idea through specific details.

Your teacher will read this passage aloud as you listen. As your teacher reads the passage a second time, write it down as a dictation.

For seven days fog settled down upon Vancouver. It crept in from the ocean, advancing in its mysterious way in billowing banks which swallowed up the land. In the Bay and the Inlet and False Creek, agitated voices spoke one to another. Small tugs that were waylaid in the blankets of fog cried shrilly and sharply "Keep away! Keep away! I am here!" Fishing boats lay inshore. Large freighters mooed continuously like monstrous cows. The fog-horns at Point Atkinson and the Lions' Gate Bridge kept up their bellowings. Sometimes the fog quenched the sounds, sometimes the sounds were loud and near. If there had not been this continuous dense fog, all the piping and boo-hooing would have held a kind of beauty; but it signified danger and warning.

Ethel Wilson, "Fog"

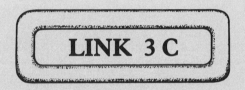

LINK 3 C

The topic sentences have been left out of the following paragraphs. Your task is to find a topic sentence that summarizes all of the supporting details provided in them. Note that a topic sentence can be placed at either the beginning or the end of a paragraph.

1. Read Paragraph A to find out what it is about.

2. In your notebook, write three possible topic sentences for this paragraph and put an asterisk (*) beside the one you like best.

3. As a whole class, place several of these first-choice topic sentences on the chalkboard. Discuss your choices.

4. Repeat this procedure for Paragraph B.

Paragraph A

The ice on the small lake was at least four inches thick. It glistened in the morning sunlight, smooth and hard. Small wisps of snow danced about on the frozen surface, driven by the gently blowing wind. As Juan's skates hit the surface, he looked forward to a hard-hitting game with his friends. _____ _____ .

Paragraph B

_____ . If you are careless about library book due dates, you may forget you have the material. It is embarrassing when librarians have to phone or write notes to remind you of your neglect. You show yourself to be a poor library customer. More importantly, though, you may be holding up someone else's work. Nothing is more frustrating than reserving a library book that you really need and then finding it has not been returned to the library on time.

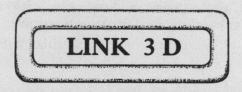

LINK 3 D

In the next chapter, you will have to do some role-playing. To prepare, you need some practice in talking aloud. A good speaker uses inflection or voice expression when talking. This activity gives you some practice.

1. Work in pairs for this activity.

2. Practise telling a funny story to your partner by using the letters of the alphabet instead of words and sentences.
   a. You may repeat the alphabet as many times as you must to finish your story.
   b. Your voice expression is the only way you have of signalling to your listener. Be sure to let him or her know about dialogue in your story and indicate the ending.

3. When you and your partner have both had a chance to tell an amusing story to each other, try some of these stories:
   - a sad story
   - a ghost story
   - a fairy tale
   - your own topic

4. As a class, listen to some of these alphabet role-playing situations. Talk about how the actors get meaning across to the audience through the inflections in their voices.

The next chapter is about listening and how important this skill is in your life. This newspaper story points out how necessary it is for people to communicate clearly.

1. Before you read this newspaper article, write a short answer to this question in your notebook: If you were at an airport and someone told you *to clear the runway*, what would you do?

2. Now read this article.

TORONTO (CP) — When a snowplow operator was told to clear the runway at Ottawa airport last March he began clearing snow, and only last-minute action by the pilot of a 737 jet prevented an accident similar to one that killed 43 people in Cranbrook, B.C.

Peter Proulx, Transport Canada's director of air traffic services, told a federal air safety inquiry Tuesday the snowplow operator understood the instruction "clear the runway" from the control tower to mean he was to remove snow, rather than get off the runway.

The pilot spotted the revolving yellow lights on the snowplow as he came in to land, pulled up and flew around again until the vehicle left the runway.

On Feb. 11, 1978, at Cranbrook, B.C., 43 people died when a Pacific Western Airlines 737 jet crashed after trying to avoid hitting a snowplow on the runway.

Proulx said an investigation of the Ottawa incident found the air traffic controller had not used standard phrases.

"The word 'clear' has two meanings — clear the runway of snow, or clear the runway of your presence. The snowplow operator took the first meaning."

Proulx nodded agreement when Mr. Justice Charles Dubin, heading the air safety inquiry, suggested the words "get off the runway" would have been understood.

Proulx said the controller is expected to look at the runway to see if there are vehicles or to ask vehicles to report after they have left the runway.

Since the incident, Transport Canada has issued a bulletin to air traffic controllers reminding them to use standard instructions.

The inquiry also heard that three aircraft, including a jumbo 747 jet, nearly crashed in mid-air over Toronto last spring because of unclear air traffic control instructions.

The inquiry continues.

3. What would have happened to you if you had been the driver of the snow plow?

4. As a class, hold a discussion to exchange stories about times when problems arose because someone did not hear accurately.

The Ferry, Quebec James Morrice

CAN YOU HEAR ME?...
WHAT?

James Morrice's painting, *The Ferry, Quebec,* presents a quiet, calm scene of the province of Quebec at the turn of the last century. It is a simple painting, made up of three horizontal lines: the wharf, the river, and the far shore. These basic lines are broken with some interesting shapes of people, animals, and things. The painting sets the mood to introduce the topic of this chapter: **listening**.

This chapter will focus upon the skill of listening. Keep in mind that this skill is basic, one which you use to support all other communication skills. Your study of listening will take you into an interesting writing task in which you will have to write a short dialogue, using the form for plays.

DETAILS ARE AN
IMPORTANT PART OF
LISTENING

You often want to remember the details of what was said after you've talked to someone. The following activity will give you practice with this kind of listening.

Activity 3A   The Ferry, Quebec

1. Study Morrice's painting for a minute or so. Think about its content or about anything closely related to the painting.

2. In your notebook, list four things that you see in the painting, or things that are closely and obviously associated with the painting. *Example:* You could compose a list such as this:
    horse, man, water, sky.

3. To this list, add another word that is not in any way associated with the painting. The example list would now look something like this:
    horse, factory, man, water, sky.

4. As each student reads his or her list, listen for the one word that does not belong in the list and write it in your notebook.

Extension: You could do the same exercise using sentences that say something about this painting, inserting one sentence that is completely unrelated to the painting.

SOMETIMES IT'S HARD TO LISTEN

You may find, at times, that you have trouble listening. This section will explore some of the factors that may cause problems when you listen. These factors are **distracting noises**, **unclear sound**, and an **unclear message**.

Distracting Noises

You have probably had the experience of trying to listen to one thing while a loud and insistent noise is going on. You try to watch television while someone is vacuuming. Or you are talking to someone at the door when the telephone beings to ring.

Activity 3B   Don't All Talk at Once

In this activity, you will experience once again the frustration of trying to listen to several messages at once.

1. Select three volunteers. These students will practice their extem-

poraneous speaking skills, while the rest of the class practises listening. *Extemporaneous speeches* are those that are not rehearsed or thought about before you begin to speak.

2. The volunteers select any one topic from this list for a sixty-second extemporaneous speech. Each volunteer must choose a different topic.

* bread
* pig
* spirals
* science fiction movies

* jam
* bank
* circles
* horror movies

* turkey
* grocery story
* trains
* submarines

3. The rest of the class will divide a page in their notebooks into three columns. Put one volunteer's name at the top of each column.

4. The volunteers will speak simultaneously, or at the same time, for sixty seconds. The rest listen to all three speeches, without taking any notes.

5. At the end of the minute, write down the points you remember each speaker making. Put each point in the correct column.

6. While this is happening, the speakers should make a list of the things they did say.

7. The speakers will read out the points that they made in their extemporaneous speeches.
   a. Check off each one that you included in your list.
   b. Find the class average of points heard and remembered for each speaker.

The point of this exercise is for you to understand how difficult it is to listen when there are extra signals coming in. The discussion questions in the next activity will help you examine how you as an individual cope with an overload of messages.

Activity 3C Distracting Signals

1. Do you have a longer list for one speaker than for the others? Why is that? Is the same true of the rest of the class? Is it the same speaker?

2. Did you feel frustrated during the sixty seconds? Approximately how far into the sixty seconds did you feel the greatest frustration?

3. Did you make a decision to change how you listened part way through? Did you stop trying? Did you listen to only one speaker? To only two speakers? Did this decision coincide with the point at which you felt the most frustration?

4. What caused you to recall those points that you remembered? Were they particularly interesting points? Were they expressed the loudest? Were they stories? Is there any pattern to the points that you remembered?

5. Did you move your attention from speaker to speaker in a deliberate pattern? Did you let your attention be caught at random? Did you try not to listen to any one speaker, but to open your ears to all of them? How did you listen?

6. Did the speakers feel frustration with the noise created by other speakers? Did they get distracted? What did they do to cope with the distractions?

Although you don't have to listen to three messages at once very often, this activity provides you with an opportunity to examine how people try to cope with too many messages.

Activity 3D   It Happens All the Time

1. As quickly as you can, make a list in your notebook of the typical circumstances in which you might be trying to listen to one message while another message is trying to get in, or while a distracting noise is occurring.

2. Form a team of three students and combine your answers to make one list.
   a. The first member reads out a circumstance, which the others add to their own list if they don't already have it.
   b. The second member reads out a new circumstance and the others note it if it isn't on the their list.
   c. Keep going until all ideas have been noted.
   d. Add any new ideas that have occurred to you.

3. On your own, select two examples and for each of them write a short incident demonstrating how your characters cope with the problem created by the extra noise.

Activity 3E   Not to Me It Isn't

This activity encourages you to listen to your incidents and to think about good listening skills.

1. One member of the class will read out one incident from question 3 in Activity 3D.

2. A second member of the class will orally volunteer an alternate solution.

3. As a class, vote on which solution is best.

4. After your class has listened to most of the incidents, you should be able to create a class list of good listening skills. Make a chart entitled *Good Listening Skills* and display it in your room.

Unclear Sounds

Another problem in listening is trying to distinguish one sound from another. For example, you will have to read these words aloud a few times to find the meaningful phrase behind them:

Ladder rat rotten hut
I love end I love end elbow your hows town

These examples show just how close or similar some of the sounds of English are.

Messages coming into your ears can be garbled if you are not able to hear the differences between two sounds. *Further* and *farther* sound very much alike, as do *jealous* and *zealous*.

This activity will give you practice in hearing the differences between sounds that seem similar. In other words, you will practise auditory discrimination.

Activity 3F   Unintelligible

1. Turn your textbook over, take out a piece of paper, and write this list in your notebook as your teacher reads it to you:

   rake, fade, cold, medal, lock, hurt, pedal, top, nail, riddle, tart, crow, made, hear, dry, heard, colt, metal, grow, tot, petal, mate, tarp, rattle, fate, ale, ear, try, rate, log.

2. Examine the words in this list to find pairs of sounds that are easily confused, such as the *ck* sound in *frock* or the *g* sound in *frog*. Write your list in your notebook.

3. As a class, talk about why each pair of sounds is easily confused. For example, the *ck* sound and the *g* sound require that you put your lips in the same position while you make the sound. It is the position of the tongue that is different.

   When you are watching someone speak you are much more likely to distinguish between two words that sound the same because you can see the different positions used to produce the sounds. This is what is meant by lip-reading.

4. You do not often sit and listen to someone read you a list of words. Rather, you usually listen to someone who is speaking in complete sentences. Name two ways that you distinguish between similar-sounding words in ordinary conversation.

Unclear Messages

In the last activity, it seemed that it was your problem if you did not receive a message clearly. You could not distinguish the sounds. But it is possible that the problem lies with the person who produces the sound, and that there is nothing wrong with your listening ability.

The final concern about listening is related to the sender of the message, the speaker, as much as it is to the receiver of the message, the listener.

This simple diagram shows how communication happens.

Sender	**Receiver**
encodes ———————→	decodes
messages	messages

The sender or speaker has a message to convey and puts it into words or **encodes** it. The receiver or listener hears the words and puts them back into a message or **decodes** it. What goes wrong in communication quite often is this: what the speaker encodes and the receiver decodes are not necessarily the same message.

For example, suppose you are hungry. You may encode this as "What time is dinner?" — an incomplete message. Your harassed parent may hear that hidden message and decode it accurately: you want to know when dinner will be ready because you are hungry now. Your parent may say, "Six o'clock but you can have a snack now." On the other hand, your parent may think you want to eat right away because you want to go out with your friends, and say, "Six o'clock but you've been out three times this week and I think it's time you did some homework."

The next activity is designed to help you see the problems involved in accurately encoding — speaking — and decoding — listening — to convey a message.

Activity 3G   What Did You See?

1. Five volunteers should leave the classroom for a few moments. Decide who is number one, two, three, four, and five.

2. The first volunteer is brought in and shown the Jim Unger cartoon on page 54.

3. The second volunteer returns to the classroom. This volunteer listens as the first volunteer describes the cartoon. The second volunteer never sees the cartoon.

4. Repeat this procedure until volunteer number five has listened to a description of the cartoon. The rest of the class should try not to laugh or make distracting noises because this throws off both the speaker and the listener.

5. The fifth volunteer makes a simple drawing on the chalkboard of what he or she thinks the cartoon looks like.

6. As a class compare the drawing to the original in your textbook.

7. Repeat this activity with the second cartoon on page 54.

To see what happens in the typical encoding and decoding situation, it is important to look at all of the differences between the original drawing and the fifth volunteer's drawing. Use these differences to answer the discussion questions in the next activity for each of the cartoons.

Activity 3H   Well, I Saw . . .

1. Is the main point of the cartoon on the chalkboard still present? If it is, what does this show you about speaking and listening?

2. Have any details been omitted? Which ones? What does this tell you about what typically happens when messages are relayed through several speakers and listeners?

"You gotta be real fast when you're painting ducks!"

". . . but, Harold, I promised the kids they could watch . . . they've never seen anyone write a letter before and put it in an envelope and put a stamp on it and take it down to the letter-box . . ."

3. Have any new details been added? Which ones? Who first added each one? What does this tell you about the communication process of encoding and decoding messages?

4. Have any details become over-emphasized? Which ones? How does this activity add to your understanding of how listening works?

5. Did the encoders or speakers use direction words such as *upper left, middle, to the right of, north of,* and so on to indicate where things were located in the cartoon? If they didn't, would it have helped if they had?

6. Did the decoders or listeners experience frustration as they listened? Could the audience tell they were frustrated? How?

What happens when one person feels something but doesn't encode it accurately, and the other person hears it but doesn't decode it accurately? The answer — a quarrel.

Here is an example of poor communication — encoding and decoding.

> Father: [concerned that the guests will think he lets his son run wild and knowing he has not time to clean his son's bedroom himself because he has to get the salad ready] Look, I don't have time to argue. Clean it up this minute — you can't go out until it's done.
>
> Son: [isn't the best player on the team and is concerned about being dropped off the team, especially if he's late] I'll do it when I get home, okay?
>
> Father: [That won't solve his problem that the guests might see it. He's also really upset now about getting the salad ready.] Not later — Now!

This same conversation with more accurate encoding and decoding of the real message might have gone like this:

> Father: [annoyed at son for leaving his room messy when company's coming] We're having company at 7:00 and here it is 6:30 and your room is a mess. Clean it up quickly.
>
> Son: [wanting to leave for basketball practice] I didn't know we were having company. I've got to get to the basketball practice by 7:00. The coach gets furious if we're late.

> Father: [concerned that the guests will think he lets his son run wild and knowing that he has no time to clean the bedroom himself because he has to get the salad ready] Look, I've got to get the salad ready so I can't clean it and I don't think it's fair for you to expect me to clean it up when it's your mess.
>
> Son: [worried about time] What about if we close the door? You can show it to them next time they come. I'll clean it up as soon as I get home. I promise. Look dad, I'm not the greatest player on the team and I'm afraid the coach will drop me for being late.
>
> Father: [The salad is calling. Knows the room can't be cleaned in time for both company and basketball practice] Well, okay. But let's take five minutes to sort some of the biggest mess away just in case they open the door. I'm counting on you to clean it up when you get home. And you owe me one, young man!

Activity 3I   That's What I Said

1. In groups of three, discuss situations you can think of in which poor communication, encoding or decoding, can cause quarrels.

2. On your own, select a situation and write two brief conversations. The first one should show how the conversation would go with poor communication. The second, how it would go with good communication.

3. Exchange papers with a writing partner to help each other complete this writing task. Read your partner's two conversations. Follow the *That's What I Said! Checklist* as you react to your partner's writing.

4. Look at your partner's comments on your dialogue. Make the changes you wish to make in your conversations.

5. Write out a good copy of your dialogues.

6. Form groups of four. Select one set of dialogues from those prepared by your group. Be ready to read your before-and-after script to your class.

That's What I Said! Checklist

1. Label one conversation ''inaccurate communication'' and the other ''accurate communication.'' Check with the author. Were you right?

2. Does the conversation sound accurate? Are the words and phrases those that the two people with those labels would actually use? Circle any that don't sound right.

3. Are both people represented as decent people with feelings that seem authentic? Put a line under anything that makes it seem as if one of the communicators is a ''good guy'' and the other a ''bad guy.''

4. Are the feelings underlying what is said the same in both cases — up to the point where the solution appears? If not, draw a square around anything that is different.

5. Is the solution a realistic one? If it's too easy or if one of the people ''wins'' by having the other one ''give in'' completely, it probably isn't. Write what you think about the solution. If you think it is not realistic, think of an alternative solution.

6. Is each speaker clearly indicated in the dialogue? If not, correct the speaker set-up to correspond to the father-son example.

7. Are there square brackets around the thoughts of the speaker and no brackets or quotation marks around what the speaker says? Make necessary corrections.

Activity 3J Afterthoughts

These cartoons comment on the place of television in your education.

1. Study both cartoons, and in your notebook write out three or four sentences to summarize what they are saying about the place of television in your life.

2. What are the implications of TV watching for the communication skill of listening?

"Use my mind? At home?"

"Do you want me to be the only nonviewer in a nation of nonreaders?"

An Encoded Message

In this chapter you learned about listening as part of communication. The first exercise had you listen for details. The main part of the chapter looked at problems that can occur with listening. Test yourself. What are some of these problems? How can good listening skills help you improve your ability to communicate?

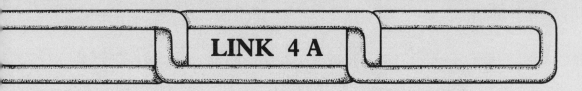

LINK 4 A

Here's a cartoon to think about.

I'll have what he's having.''

1. Practise saying the punch line to this cartoon: *I'll have what he's having.*

2. In pairs, role-play the conversation that occurs between the couple at the next table, after the waiter removes the plate.

3. Have several of these conversations presented to the whole class.

4. Ask one pair to repeat their conversation. Copy their dialogue into your notebook, using the form used in books of plays.
   Example:
   Man: [looking confused] He took my plate.
   Woman: Now, dear, don't be absurd. The waiter wouldn't take *your* plate without a good reason.

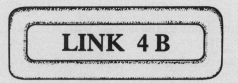

LINK 4 B

When you put dialogue into stories, you must use a different convention or set of rules: **quotation marks**. Quotation marks set off the exact words said by a speaker. This form is called **direct narration**.

The man's exact words are enclosed in quotation marks.

Note the comma following the tag phrase; he said.

Note that there is a new paragraph for each new speaker.

The waiter quickly removed the plate from the table. The man sat there, with a confused look on his face. Finally, he said, "He took my plate."

"Now, dear, don't be absurd," the woman replied. "The waiter just wouldn't take *your* plate without good reason."

"Yes," said the man, "he did!"

Note that this period inside the final quotation mark.

Note the comma used before the tag phrase.

Note the period at the end of this sentence. The next sentence begins with a quotation mark and a capital letter.

Note how to punctuate a direct quotation when the tag phrase is in the middle.

1. Turn the play dialogue that you wrote in Link 4 A into **reported direct narration**. Use this explanation of how to use quotation marks to help you write your dialogue.

2. Add words and comments to make your story as entertaining as you can.

LINK 4 C

This activity will provide you with practice in **listening for detail**.

1. With your books closed, listen while your teacher reads this passage about racoons:

2. Answer the questions in the box on page 63.

3. When you have finished answering the questions, return to these directions to find out what to do next.
   a. In your notebook, place an asterisk (*) beside the answers which you are not sure about or which you think are completely wrong.
   b. Read this passage to correct your answers.

4. As a class, discuss this question: How successful were you in listening for detail?

> A creature of twilight and darkness, the raccoon deserves its burglar's mask of black fur. It is a glutton and will eat almost anything, stuffing its belly, belching, napping and eating again when food is plentiful. It is a common evening visitor to campsites where food or garbage is available. Fish, frogs, mice, fruit, vegetables, insects and birds are all on its diet. Sweet corn is a favorite and the raccoon relishes crayfish, which it catches by dabbling sensitive paws under streambed boulders. A liking for chickens and their eggs, and raids on garbage cans often make the raccoon unwelcome.
>
> If kindness is shown to a raccoon it responds with affection, charm and endearing good manners. It is easily tamed, but authorities advise against keeping it as a pet. It has been known to bite its human friends without warning. An adult raccoon will fight bravely against great odds. Alone, a fit young raccoon can beat off two or three dogs. A mother will defend her offspring to the death.
>
> About 33 inches long and averaging 19 pounds in weight, the raccoon resembles a fat cat, the result of the excess body fat it stores in preparation for a long winter's sleep. Its stout body is clothed in a long thick coat, generally of grizzled gray, and it is easily recognized by the black mask across cheeks, eyes and nose, which gives it a mischievous appearance. It has four to six prominent rings around its short bushy tail.
>
> *Outdoors Canada*

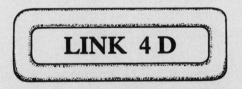

LINK 4 D

Here are some more sentences that use quotation marks. Listen as your teacher dictates these sentences and then check them as directed.

Note: Watch the fifth sentence. It contains a **quotation within a quotation**.

Hint: The inside quotation is enclosed in single quotes, like this:

He said, "I think she said, 'This is getting very confusing.' "

1. "Joe," said the coach as he chewed on a celluloid toothpick. "I want you to go in as defensive end. Get moving."

2. "I think that Mary's book is on the table," said my mother. "Will you get it for her?"

3. The engineer cried, "Watch out for that swinging beam! Do you want that head of yours cut off?"

4. "I want you to lie down quietly," said the judo expert, "and relax your body's muscles completely. Then get up, ready to move quickly."

5. "Did you hear him say, 'I'd like you to come to the movie with me?' " Janet asked.

John Farrell, *The Creative Teacher of Language.*

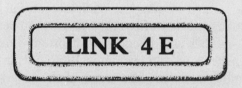

LINK 4 E

This **dictation passage**, which contains direct quotations, comes from Eric Nicol's anecdote or story, "Be It Ever So Humble, Don't Move."

Note: Quotation marks are also used to indicate the titles of short articles, short stories, and poems.

Directions: Listen as your teacher reads this passage. Then, as your teacher reads it a second time, copy the passage into your notebook. Watch for quotation marks and paragraphing. As your teacher reads the passage a third time, check your work. Your teacher will tell you how to correct your dictation passage.

"You see how easy it can be adapted to the modern style of having a live tree growing up through your living-room," said the realtor, patting a bearded conifer that had penetrated the siding of the house.

"That moss growing on the inside of the window frame is handy too," said my wife, "in case you want to know which way is north."

"Is the house insulated?" I put in.

"Sure is," said the agent. "Eight layers of wallpaper. There's enough thickness of paste alone to keep you snug. Let's take a look at the kitchen."

We moved into a square of balding linoleum.

"Lot's of cupboard space, see." The agent flapped his arms at the jutting scraggle of doors painted the colour of clotted blood. "And you can easy modernize the sink if you want."

"Oh, no, I wouldn't touch that hand-pump for the world," crowed my wife. "If I added anything it would be a chicken standing on the spout."

Eric Nicol, "Be It Ever So Humble, Don't Move,"
A Herd of Yaks.

Answer the following questions after your teacher has read the raccoon passage. Write the answers in your notebook:

1. What time of day do raccoons come out?

2. Why do raccoons visit campsites?

3. List five things mentioned that raccoons eat.

4. Why are raccoons often unwelcome visitors?

5. Why is it not safe to keep a raccoon as a pet?

6. What kind of fighters are raccoons?

7. What is the average length and weight of a raccoon?

8. Why does the raccoon have excess body fat?

9. What gives the raccoon its mischievous appearance?

Three Frigates in a Storm, John O'Brien

O'Brien's painting suggests the excitement of Canada's past. This painting shows you the majesty of history: sailing ships on wide oceans. This next chapter is about history too — the history of everyday folk. You will learn how to collect history by writing anecdotes.

CHAPTER 4

THIS IS HOW IT HAPPENED

TELL A TALE

Have you ever watched what people do when they are gathered together in a group? They tell stories. These stories are usually about things that have happened to them. Children tell about funny things that happened to them. Parents tell about funny things that happened to their children. And on it goes.

This kind of story—a story about one incident—is called an **anecdote**. You usually tell an anecdote to entertain or to give an example.

If it's an anecdote told to entertain, it will be about something strange, wonderful, horrible, or funny that happened to you. Even a horrible thing can be said to entertain in that the listener concentrates all of his or her attention on your story.

If your anecdote is used as an example, it will be because you are trying to prove a point by illustrating it with something that happened to you or someone you know.

An Anecdote That Entertains and Instructs

Here is an anecdote about someone's neighbour.

The strangest thing happened to my neighbour. She came home from shopping and she had three or four paper shopping bags in her station wagon's back seat. As she drove into the yard she heard the phone ringing. She turned off the engine and left the car standing in the driveway with the front door open. When she came outside, the car and the groceries were gone. She was astounded because she'd just left it for a few minutes and we live in a nice neighbourhood. So she phoned the police and the whole family was upset.

Well, the next morning she got up and there was the car sitting in the yard — and all the groceries were still in the back seat. On the windshield was an envelope with a note in it that said:

> I needed your car urgently because of a family emergency. Thank you for its use. I'm sorry for worrying you. Here are tickets for you and your husband to go to the next Lions game. Hope you enjoy it.

There were two tickets inside for Friday's game.

Well, last Friday they went to the game. And when they came home they found that while they were gone, some people had backed a moving van up to the front of their house and stolen all their furniture.

Shows what the world is coming to, doesn't it?

Activity 4A   *The Form of an Anecdote*

The following questions are designed to help you see how this sample anecdote is constructed. Write the answers to these questions in your notebook.

1. An anecdote entertains, and often instructs. What lesson can you learn from this anecdote?

2. An anecdote answers the five W's and an H: *Who? When? Where? Why?* and *How?* Look through the anecdote and find the answers to these questions and write them in your notebook.

3. An anecdote begins close to the central idea. This anecdote begins a few minutes before the car is stolen. If this were a poor anecdote, how might it have started?

4. An anecdote builds to a climax or high point of interest. This anecdote has two climaxes. We think the climax has occurred when the car is returned and we read the note. What is the real climax of the anecdote?

5. An anecdote closes quickly after the climax. How many sentences are there after this climax?

6. Use the information in 1 to 5 to help you determine what the characteristics of a good anecdote are. List them in your notebook.

Activity 4B Telling an Anecdote

It's your turn to tell an anecdote.

1. Tell an anecdote from the point of view of the man in the cartoon below who is carrying the two pails.

2. What story, for example, will he tell his friend as they sit down to afternoon coffee?

3. Write this anecdote in your notebook.

4. Does your anecdote entertain or instruct? How does it entertain or instruct? Is there a lesson to be learned from your anecdote?

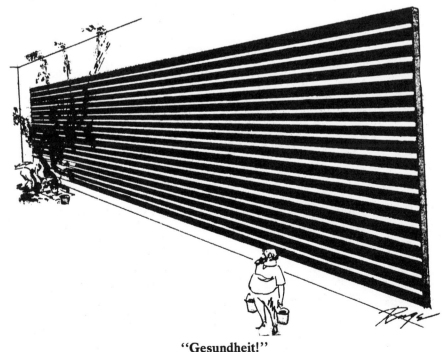

"Gesundheit!"

Activity 4C   Telling Another Anecdote

This cartoon will help you tell another anecdote.

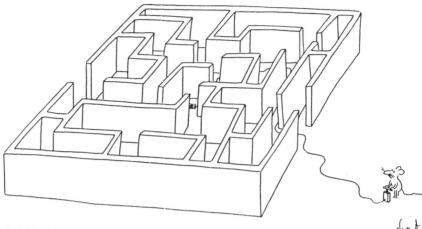

1. Use these questions to think about the cartoon:
   a. What has happened before this scene takes place?
   b. Why is the mouse doing what it is doing?
   c. What is a possible ending to this story?

2. Decide next whether your information entertains you or instructs you, or both?

3. In your notebook, write the anecdote this mouse might tell when it gets back to the mouse colony.
   Note: Decide whether your mouse anecdote instructs or entertains, and write it from that perspective.

PUT YOUR TALE IN ORDER

All stories follow some kind of order. The most common way to organize a story is **chronologically** — according to the time when the events took place.

> *Chronus* was the original Greek god of time. This explains why all words containing *chronus* refer to time.
>
> What do these words mean: chronograph, chronometer, anachroism?

There are two ways of creating chronological order:

1. by placing events in the order in which they happened

2. by showing the relationship of words with time words or phrases

When you were very small and wished to tell your mom or dad something exciting that had happened to you, you would use *and then* to string your whole story together.

"We went to the park *and then* Nathan wanted to go on the slide *and then* Linda helped him up *and then* he slid down all by himself."

Since then you have learned more complex ways of showing time in your stories.

Activity 4D   Chronological Order

This activity gives you practice arranging an anecdote in chronological or time order.

1. Stage One — Arranging an Anecdote
   a. Form groups of three people.
   b. The first person in the group takes a blank page and copies sentences one to five from the *Mystery Anecdote*, leaving three spaces between each sentence. The second person does the same thing with sentences six to ten. The third person uses sentences eleven to fifteen.
   c. Cut or tear the sentences apart so that you have fifteen separate sentences before you.
   d. Working as a group, decide upon the order these sentences should go in. Note the clue that helped you decide on each slip of paper.

The Mystery Anecdote

1. I was about four years old and every day I walked three blocks to kindergarten on even, flat roads with no traffic.

2. Each day I would walk by without running and without looking at them because I thought that if they knew I was afraid they might chase me instead of just sitting on that lumber.

3. I remember once asking my mom to go to school with me. →

4. I never told her that they threw rocks at me and called me names.

5. I can only imagine that in my four-year-old mind I just didn't think of it.

6. Why didn't I just tell her my problem so that she could make it go away?

7. And so, when my child asks me to do something, I try to remember that he may be able to talk but still be unable to explain.

8. The rocks didn't come anywhere near me, but I was startled each time by the children's hostility and their childhood taunts — "You're a baby," and "We're going to get you" would make my stomach turn.

9. She looked at me and said, "Why? You've walked by yourself for a long time. You can do it by yourself."

10. So, I never did tell my mom the one thing that would have caused her to talk to Mrs. Davidson or at least would have caused her to walk to kindergarten with me.

11. I could tell she thought I was being babyish.

12. There was one corner to turn.

13. Around that corner and just out of sight of our house was a construction site where, every morning, a boy and a girl, twins about my age, would sit on a pile of lumber in the middle of their yard and throw rocks at me.

2. Stage Two — Thinking about Your Answers
   As a small group, talk about these questions and be prepared to share your ideas with the whole class.
   a. What clues helped you piece together the fifteen sentences? List them in your notebook.
   b. Are there any sentences that seemed to fit in several places? Why?
   c. What is the climax of the *Mystery Anecdote*?
   d. What lesson can you draw from this anecdote?

Activity 4E   Time Words: A Game

Time words and phrases also help to tie together events in chronological order. Here is a chart of some time words and phrases.

Time Words	Time Phrases
after	in the morning
since	the following day
Tuesday	

1. Form teams of three or four people.

2. Here are the rules of this game:
   a. Create a chart like the one above for your group.
   b. Appoint one person as recorder for your group.
   c. Create as long a list as possible of time words and phrases.
   d. You have two minutes to add to the list of time words and phrases from the time your teacher says *Go!*

3. Here is how you score your answers:
   a. Count one point for each word or each phrase.
   b. Only the first variation of a phrase or word counts: That is, you can get one point for *Tuesday*, but you can't get seven points for each day of the week. Or, you can get one point for *in the morning*, but you can't get a second point for *in the afternoon*.
   c. The team with the most points wins the match.

Activity 4F   Telling Your Own Anecdote — Again

Now that you know more about what an anecdote is, it's time to try writing another one. This activity will involve you in some of the oral history in your community. Oral history refers to the everyday experiences of people that have so far not been recorded in print.

1. Think of an anecdote you know. Select one that your mother or father has told you, or go and talk to some people in your community to find an anecdote. Make certain that you have an anecdote in your mind before you go on with this activity.

2. Find a partner among your classmates. Listen while your partner tells you his or her anecdote. Write down this anecdote in note form — just enough so that you will remember.

3. Then tell your anecdote to your partner, while he or she takes notes.

4. Write your partner's anecdote in two or three paragraphs.

5. Take your written version back to the writing partner who gave it to you.
   a. Your partner will add any significant details you have missed.
   b. Your partner should also check the characteristics of a good anecdote, which you listed in Activity 4A, and note any concerns about your written anecdote.
   c. When your writing partner returns this anecdote to you, write a final draft.

6. Share your anecdotes in a class session.

FILL YOUR TALE WITH DETAIL

An oral anecdote is often simple in style and wording. It relies for its impact on the tone of voice of the speaker and dramatic pauses at appropriate moments. In fact, an oral anecdote with too many details can cause the listener's mind to wander off on the wrong track.

A written anecdote, on the other hand, is better when it includes important details. This section will give you practice in providing details as you write anecdotes.

Activity 4G   Adding Details to a Skeleton

This activity contains a bare-bones outline of an anecdote. This anecdote could be improved if you add details.

1. Rewrite the following anecdote by improving each sentence. You will finish this activity with a one-paragraph anecdote.

2. Use the questions that follow each sentence to help you add details to the basic sentences.

3. You may also add sentences of your own, containing details that you think improve upon this anecdote.

    a. A mother was searching the fair grounds.
- What did the mother look like?
- What were the fair grounds like?
- What are the places she searched?

    b. She asked passing strangers if they had seen her daughter, Diana, who was three and wore a red and white dress.
- Describe two people whom she asked. What did she say? What did they say? What did they do?
- Include a more specific description of the daughter.

    c. She was exhausted and nearly in tears when someone suggested the lost children's department.
- Describe her exhaustion in more detail.
- Describe the person who made the suggestion in more detail.

    d. As she came up, there was her daughter, eating an ice-cream cone.
- What did the lost and found department look like?
- Where was the lost and found department?
- Describe what the child looked like (sitting on what, standing on what, etc.).

    e. Her daughter said, "Mom, I got an ice-cream cone. You got lost."
- Keep the quote the same but try to show more contrast between the scared but relieved mom and the carefree child.
- What kind of ice-cream cone was it?

4. Exchange anecdotes with a partner and use the set of guidelines below to help you assess your partner's work.

    a. Write the number of each statement in your partner's book, and beside each number, write the words *yes* or *no*. This will tell your partner how well you think he or she followed the rules of writing anecdotes.

An Assessment Scale for a Controlled Anecdote		
Characteristic	**Yes**	**No**
1. It begins close to the central idea (which is the lost child.)		
2. It contains the five W's and an H.		
3. The climax occurs very close to the end.		
4. At least seven important details are included.		
5. At least three quotes are included.		

TELL A TALE IN QUOTES

Dialogue is an important part of many good anedcotes. In fact, some good anecdotes are almost all dialogue.

Activity 4H Writing Dialogue in an Anecdote

1. Review the rules for using quotations marks in your writing. (Look back at the activities in Link 4 if you need help with this.)

2. Read the following comic strip carefully.

3. Retell this comic strip in writing as an anecdote, making sure that you use dialogue in your retelling.

The characters in this anecdote are Ralph and you . . .

TELL A TALE THAT'S IMPORTANT

Some excellent books have been collections of anecdotes, sparked by the author asking one question of a cross-section of people. One of the best of these is *Ten Lost Years* by Barry Broadfoot, who asked this question of many people across Canada: *What is your most vivid memory of the Depression?* What surprised him was how instantly the people he asked could tell him a wonderful anecdote. Everyone who had shared the Depression was marked for life by the experience.

Here is an anecdote that appears in *Ten Lost Years:*

WORKING FOR NOTHING

"I'm not at all sure I could do it again. No, I don't think any of us could do it all over. If I went out, my mother had to stay home in slippers because there was only one pair of decent shoes in the place.

I got out of commercial school with decent marks, shorthand, typing, you know the rest of it, and this was in '32 and there was no jobs. I remember thinking I could get one over at the hospital and I very nearly did, yes, very nearly did, until some other girl got it. I found out she was the friend of a friend of the administrator's daughter. It was who you knew, not what you knew. That kind of thing. It still is today, I guess.

That winter I walked the length of Jasper Avenue (in Edmonton) about three times and I'd stop in ever place and ask. No luck. Then something happened. You want to call it luck? My uncle had told me that law offices were good places to work because lawyers always got business, foreclosures and such, and I'd tried the Jasper Block more than other places because it had the most lawyers. Anyway, I went into the lobby one morning because it was maybe 30 below out and I was warming myself when a man from one of the law offices came down those marble stairs that wind around and he recognized me from the number of times I'd been at their counter and he asked me how I was doing. I said I wasn't, rotten, or something like that and then I had this brainwave and I asked him if I could work in their office free. I couldn't stay home and listen to mother whine, and at least I'd be in a warm place and would be able to practice my typing and shorthand.

When I said free, I meant I would work for nothing. I guess it didn't sound that much out of line because young lawyers out of law school work on the same basis. He said fine, come in tomorrow, and I did. In my mother's shoes and a cousin's blouse and my own skirt, and my hair done nicely. Oh, God, but it was a good feeling. Just 18 and a real job. The first week I worked like the devils were chasing me, and at the end of the second week they gave me a dollar. For carfare, they said, although I could walk to work. Nobody said I was on the payroll and I sure wasn't going to be the one to ask. Not any way, thank you.

A month later I was doing a lot of legal work, the forms, typing them, delivering to the court house, swearing to papers at the court registry, and about the fifth week I got a pay envelope. I can remember it yet, Yellow, and my name, Margaret Evans, written across it. In red ink. I still remember it. Three dollars. I went out at noon and bought a pair of shoes at Army and Navy for a dollar, gave Mom a dollar that night, and I had the other dollar. I was rich.

In another month I got a two dollar raise and I stayed with those people for 20 years, until they sold the practice and retired, and they were the nicest people in the world. One went to the coast and retired and I still get a Christmas present from them. The other died. They were good men.''

Barry Broadfoot, *Ten Lost Years*.

Activity 4I Looking at an Anecdote

Use these question to have a second look at this anecdote.

1. How many sentences go by before the anecdote really begins?

2. What is the anecdote's climax? Quote it. How many sentences come after it?

3. This anecdote seems to be a written-down oral anecdote. What evidence from this anecdote tells you that this is so?

4. Margaret Evans seems to have taken a message from her experience. What is it? Do you draw a different message? If so, what is it?

COLLECTING ANECDOTES

Barry Broadfoot travelled across Canada with a tape recorder to collect the anecdotes that he included in his books. This final section will prompt you to become a kind of oral historian in your community and collect anecdotes of things that have happened there. The final result of this project will be a class book of anecdotes from people living in your community.

Activity 4J   A Class Project: Oral History

1. As a class, decide upon some significant even that happened about twenty years or more ago. You may find a topic that has significant memories for the people in your community, or you may choose a topic of national significance: the Depression, World War II, the Kennedy assassination, the FLQ Crisis, the first Canada-Russia hockey series when Paul Henderson scored the winning goal.

2. Each member of your class should select two informants and interview them with a tape recorder. Make certain that you select people who are old enough to have good memories of the event you are investigating.

3. Start your interview with this question: *What is your most vivid memory of_____? Then, encourage your informant to tell you all he or she can about this memory. Use your tape recorder for this interview and make notes about the interview as well.

4. Use your tape and your interview notes to construct two anecdotes, one for each person you interviewed.

5. Use writing partners and the revision chart in Activity 4F to revise and edit your anecdotes to make them ready for publication.

6. Turn your individual anecdotes into a class project. Collect all the anecdotes and make a book of them. If possible, make copies of the book and give one to each of your informants. Place a book in your school library. Or you might consider giving your book of personal anecdotes as a gift to someone special in your life.

The Tale Has Been Told

In this chapter you learned about writing a specific form: the anecdote. In addition, you studied other aspects of writing: chronological order, details, quotations. These skills will stay with you long after you have forgotten about the anecdotes you wrote for this chapter.

LINK 5 A

Charlie Brown found a rather unusual use for his dog Snoopy. This activity gives you a chance to do some creative thinking to find an unusual use for some common objects.

© 1960 United Feature Syndicate

1. In your notebook list at least *five* unusual uses for these common objects:
   a. the core of a roll of toilet paper
   b. a paper clip
   c. an empty milk carton
   d. an empty egg carton

2. In small groups of two or three students, share your answers and choose the best answer for each object.

3. Try out your suggestions or create a cartoon to explain them.

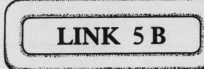

LINK 5 B

The last link activity gave your small group a specific task to accomplish. During this group activity you will discuss ideas to achieve your group task.

L'avenir en têtes ...

We have the future in minds.

1. Appoint one group member as recorder.

2. List as many interpretations for this slogan as your group can find, while the recorder makes a list of all suggestions.

3. Talk about all suggestions to make certain that everyone knows what each suggestion means.

4. Decide upon the three best interpretations of this slogan: *We have the future in minds*.

5. Choose one interpretation that the group can agree upon.
   Note: You should come to a **group consensus** about your decision. That is, you should keep talking about this problem until all group members can agree upon one interpretation. To arrive at group consensus, individual members of the group may have to give in to the opinion of the whole group.

6. The recorder should be prepared to report the group decision to the whole class.

7. Select another member of the group who will report upon the way the group went about solving its problem:
   a. How many suggestions did the group create?
   b. How much difficulty did the group have selecting the three top choices?
   c. How did the group decide on the best choice?
   d. Did any group member have to back down on his or her choice? How was this done? How did he or she feel?

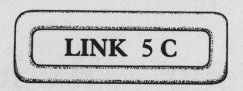

LINK 5 C

This activity gives you more practice with **group problem solving**. It takes you through a very structured exercise called **brainstorming**. Brainstorming is a technique that is especially useful if you want to find creative, unusual solutions.

Group problem: *What are some winter uses for summer things?*

Examples:
   Beach balls could become Christmas tree ornaments.
   A wading pool and an outboard motor could become a winter whirlpool spa.

Setting Up: The class should divide into small groups. Four or so students in a group is a good number. This size allows everyone a chance to talk; yet there are enough members in the group to give a number of comments and ideas.

Step 1: The first task is to select a recorder who will do all of the writing for the group.

Step 2: Define your problem clearly. In this case, the group has to come up with five creative, winter uses for summer things.

Step 3: Now comes the fun part! Think of five summer things and list them on a page. Then, think of as many winter uses for these summer things as possible. Let your imagination run.

Often the answers that seem extreme, even crazy, will end up being the best answers. Comments can come later. Right now the task is to get as many ideas from the group as possible. This step is the actual brainstorming procedure. The recorder's job is to write down all of the ideas created by the group, without worrying too much about spelling.

Step 4: The recorder reads the ideas back to the group. The group selects the *five* best solutions from the main list.

Step 5: Finalize your answer to the problem—the five best winter uses for summer things.

Step 6: The recorder reports the group decision to the class.

Afterward: Your class may wish to take all of the ideas generated in small groups and choose from them one best winter use for a summer thing.

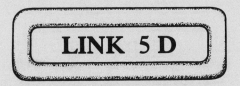

LINK 5 D

This dictation passage reviews the use of periods and commas.

The big slough! The path to it from town wound through the bush, and as we raced down it in the hot days of July we shed our pants and shirts as we ran, ready to plunge into the water as soon as we hit the shore. Then we would swim and wade out into the beautiful, black, soft, squishy muck that covered the bottom, and plaster the stuff all over our bodies, and make mounds of it on the shore. To this day I don't feel really good in water unless I can sink in nice, slippery, gooey muck up to my ankles.

Max Braithwaite, *Never Sleep Three in a Bed*.

1. Make a list of all of the nouns in this passage that are modified by adjectives.

2. Beside each of these nouns, list the adjective(s) that modify them.

3. Rewrite this passage in your notebooks. But this time, give the reader the feeling that you absolutely *hate* the muck in the slough. For most of the adjectives in this passage you will have to substitute adjectives that convey a feeling of disgust.

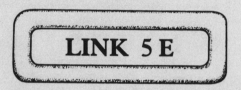

LINK 5 E

In the dictation passage in Link 5 D, Max Braithwaite uses words that are important to him in his memories of summer. Here is an outline of a **thought web** for his summer memories:

1. Reread the dictation passage in order to help you complete the thought web. You may have to add some new branches to it.
2. Copy this thought web into your notebook.

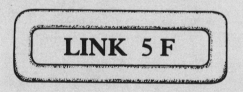

LINK 5 F

1. Think of some important things that have happened to you, things for which you have strong memories. Make a thought web from these memories.

2. Place one word from these memories at the centre of your thought web.

3. Add to this centre word, keeping related words and ideas clustered together.

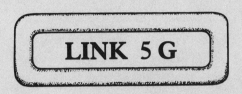

LINK 5 G

1. Use the thought web you made in Link 5 F to write a paragraph about this memory.

2. Choose the most important or dominant memory from your web and focus on it as you write your paragraph. Don't be afraid to leave out some of the branches in your web.

3. Exchange paragraphs with a classmate and read each other's work.

4. At the bottom of this paragraph, write a one- or two-sentence response. Your response should tell the writer what his or her idea makes you think about.

A Circle of Gladness

The photograph above shows an Inuit carving, a ring of people shaped from a walrus tusk. It shows the joy of people being together. The next chapter explores some of the ways you work in groups — your circle of gladness.

A CIRCLE OF GLADNESS

Working with others is an important part of many things that you do. For example, you need group skills to work well with other people in each of these situations: playing a team sport, singing or playing an instrument with a group, creating a school project. Group skills are important in school as well as in the rest of your life.

Many of the activities you are asked to do in this textbook require you to work with a group. In this chapter, you will not only look at the way groups work but plan work for your own group—to find out how to make your own circle of gladness.

THE PROBLEM

As part of a group assignment, six students were given this problem to solve: *What is this odd-shaped object and what is it used for?* Their teacher gave them fifteen minutes to find an answer.

The group was left to solve the problem. The following transcript shows you the process the group went through.

Pat: Look at this! I can't believe the stupid things they want us to do around this dumb place.

Sandy: You can say that again!

Kerry: I don't know — this thing looks kind of interesting to me. Why don't we all move over by the window so we can look at it in the light?

Mickey: The light is good right here by my desk. You can all move over here by *my* desk.

Sandy: Okay. I'll put my chair right here beside yours.

Chris: Why? Are those two chairs personally acquainted or something: I'd bring mine over too, but they say three's a crowd! (laughs)

Pat: Any place you are is a crowd, you moron.

Sandy: Yeah!

Kerry; We've only got fifteen minutes to figure out what this is for. Mickey, if you'll make notes, maybe we could all try to see what we can do with this thing.

Sandy: Good idea! Let me try.

Mickey: I'll see what I can do with it first. Somebody else can take the notes. I want to see whether it rolls if you push it.

Kelly: Try blowing through it, too. It's got all those funny little round holes on the side — maybe it's something like a whistle.

Kerry: Pat, will you take the notes? Where are you? Pat?

Pat: If I have to take any notes, I'll take them right out that door, and I won't be bringing them back either!

Chris: Say — talk about walking out — why did the chicken cross the road? Huh, Sandy?

Kerry; Never mind. I'll take the notes. Mickey, what do you think we can do with that little thing? I'll keep track of what you think about it.

Sandy: That's a good idea.

Kelly: It looks a little like something you might use to hold things. Try putting pencils through those holes and see if they balance. Maybe it's a pencil-holder for a desk.

Mickey: *I* already thought of that. I'm going to use pens.

Chris: Well, come on, why did the chicken —

Pat: You're a chicken yourself — big beak and no brains.

Kelly: If we could plug the hole in the bottom, we could use it to store smaller things inside.

Kerry:	I'm writing that down. Sandy, why don't you take a turn with it?
Sandy:	Yeah! Sounds interesting.
Chris:	Well, this is the answer — the chicken crossed the road because it was too long to go around!
Kerry:	We've only got two minutes left. Does anybody else want to take a turn?
Kelly:	Let me try one more thing. Could we use it as part of a game, like *Monopoly*?
Pat:	Two minutes is three minutes too long, if you ask me.
Kerry:	Well — let's get back to our own desks now. The time is just about up.

Activity 5A   Working Together

1. Look back at the transcript of what the students in the group said, and think about whether the group was successful or not in dealing with the assignment.

2. Pick out one thing that you think was good about the way the group worked, and write it in your notebook.

3. Pick out one problem about the way the group worked, and write it in your notebook.

4. Suggest a solution for this problem, and write it in your notebook.

5. Be prepared to share your answers with the class.

Activity 5B   Who's Who?

In every group, individuals do things that are helpful or destructive to the group's effort. Look back at the transcript of what the students in this group said to find out who's who in this group.

1. For each of the six students in the group, — Kerry, Chris, Pat, Sandy, Mickey, and Kelly — answer the following questions:
   a. Was the student helpful or destructive to the group's efforts?
   b. Explain your answer to a.

2. Decide which student was the most helpful to the group's efforts. In your notebook, write down the student's name and the reason why you feel that he or she was the most helpful.

3. Decide which student was the biggest problem for the group. In your notebook, write down the student's name and the reason why you feel that he or she was the biggest problem.

4. Be prepared to discuss your answers with the class.

Playing a Role

Working in groups is sometimes a matter of life and death. For example, when a team of doctors and nurses performs surgery, they have to work closely and carefully as a group.

Other groups have to work together to make important decisions that affect everyone. The government conducts Parliament as if it were a large group.

Because group work is so important, psychologists have studied the roles that people play when they work in groups. Here are six common roles that psychologists have discovered:

• **The Organizer**: This person is quick to see what has to be done and the best way to do it. The organizer often reminds the other group members of their responsibilities. He or she also often keeps the group on track.

• **The Blocker**: The opposite to the organizer is the blocker. The blocker places obstacles in the group's way and is often a trouble-maker. His or her negative behaviour may block the group's progress toward a solution for its problem.

• **The Joker**: This person enjoys a joke and likes to share the humour in things. The joker may not intend to be destructive or troublesome, but his or her attempts at humour may sidetrack others.

• **The Explorer**: The explorer is a creative thinker who sees unusual or unexpected solutions. This person is a little like the joker, but while the joker simply looks for fun, the explorer often contributes good ideas.

• **The Star**: This person is a little like the organizer because he or she wants to solve the problem quickly. However, the star insists on doing things his or her own way. This person likes to dominate the group and be the centre of the action. Sometimes this person helps solve the problem, but at other times becomes a problem for the group.

• **The Follower**: Unlike the star, this person goes along with what other people say. The follower may spend more time agreeing with everybody else than thinking up ways to solve the problem. The follower often agrees with the last person who spoke.

Activity 5C   Match Them Up

Each of the students in the transcript was playing a role within the group.

1. Reread the transcript to decide who played which role:
   a. List each of the six students' names in your notebook.
   b. Beside each name write the name of the role which that student was playing in the group: organizer, blocker, joker, explorer, star, follower.
   c. Next, write down your reason for matching each student with the particular role you assigned to him or her.

2. Decide on one thing that each student could do to improve his or her work with the group. Write your suggestions in your notebook.

3. Be ready to discuss your ideas with the class.

THINKING ABOUT GROUPS

Why Do Groups Get Together?

People form groups for a variety of reasons. Here are some of the most familiar reasons:

- to share fun and good times
- to do a job that cannot be done by one person alone
- to solve a problem by pooling knowledge and ideas
- to share different points of view
- to make decisions
- to overcome threats or danger

Activity 5D   How Groups Work

1. Think about examples of groups that get together for the reasons noted in the list above.

2. In your notebook, list at least one kind of group that fits each of the reasons.

3. Think about how each of these groups is set up. In your notebook, beside the name of each group, write down:
   a. whether or not the group has an official leader

b. how the leader, if there is one, is selected

c. how the group's responsibilities are assigned to other members of the group

4. Write down which one of these groups you think is the best organized and explain the reason(s) for your choice.

5. Be prepared to talk about the examples you have listed.

Keep your lists in your notebook. You may wish to refer to them when you work on other activities in this chapter.

What Are the Skills for Group Work?

How well a group works together depends on many things, such as the personalities involved and the task or problem. Sometimes a group's success might even be related to the length of time left before lunch or the dismissal bell.

One of the most important factors in successful group work is whether or not the group members have mastered certain skills. Any group will work better if its members can do these things:

- give directions clearly
- follow directions exactly
- cooperate with others

Later in this chapter, you will need these skills to complete a group project. Try practising your group skills now by working on these puzzles.

Activity 5E   Are You Listening?

1. Arrange seats so that six to eight players can see each other comfortably.

2. To begin, each player, in turn, will give his or her name. Each player must use a fictitious name, not his or her real name. Go around the group once, using these new names.

3. On the second go-round, each person adds an extra bit of information about himself or herself. For example, give the person's age, the name of the place where the person was born, his or her favourite foods, and so on.

4. Then, the first person starts introducing each member of the group to the class by telling:

a. the student's new name

b. the extra bit of information that was given

5. The first student introduces as many students as he or she can without making a mistake or forgetting something. When the first student forgets something or makes a mistake, the turn passes to the student who was being introduced. Keep going until all students in the group have been introduced.

6. When you can do this listening task easily, expand the number of students in the small group.

Activity 5F   Giving Directions

For this activity, each student will need three plain sheets of paper and a partner to practise the skill of giving clear directions.

1. Working by yourself, use one of your sheets of paper to make up a design for an object that you can create by folding your paper. *Examples:* a paper airplane, a boat, a kind of fan, or an animal shape. Be certain to keep your model hidden from your partner.

2. On your second sheet of paper, write down the steps you took to create this object. These steps should be written as directions for someone else to follow.

3. Exchange your written set of directions with your partner.

4. Using your third sheet of paper, carry out your partner's directions and fold your paper into the design your partner has created.

5. Compare your finished product with your partner's original object and notice any differences between the two.

6. Discuss with your partner why the set of directions was (or was not) clear and easy to follow with accuracy.

7. Following your partner's advice, write corrections on your own set of directions. Keep this page in your notebook.

8. Be prepared to discuss with the class what you have learned about how to give directions clearly and accurately.

Activity 5G   Following Directions

This activity asks you to practise the skills needed to follow directions. Work alone to carry out the steps you are given.

1. Read this set of directions over before you begin.

2. On a blank page in your notebook, write your name and the date at the top of the page in the right-hand corner.

3. Write the number 1 in the left-hand margin. Then, list your height, weight, and shoe size.

4. Add these numbers together. Write the total on the next line, and underline the number.

5. Write the number 2 in the left-hand margin. List your birthday, the date of your favourite holiday, and the date it will be next Monday.

6. Add together the numbers for the days of the month for these dates in step 5, and write the total on the next line. Draw a circle around that number.

7. Put the number 3 in the left-hand margin. Write down a number that is supposed to be good luck and a number that is supposed to be bad luck.

8. Add these two numbers together, and write the total on the next line. Draw a box around that number.

9. Add together the three numbers that you have underlined, circled, and boxed. Write this total at the top of the page underneath your name and the date.

10. Do not do any of the steps described in steps 2 to 9.

11. If you did what numbers 2 to 9 asked, you missed the most important step of all. Reread step 1.

12. Write down in your notebook what you have learned about following directions.

Activity 5H   Cooperating with Others

For this activity, you will work with a group of three or four other students.

1. Imagine that you are all trapped together somewhere for three hours, such as an elevator that is stuck. In order to pass the time until you are freed, you decide to do something together for entertainment.

2. Whatever you decide to do, you must follow these rules:
    a. Every member of the group must take part.

    b. Each member must agree to take part willingly. No one can be forced into doing something just to please the rest of the group.

    c. It is not possible to call for special supplies or equipment. Each group member has only what he or she might normally carry around — for example, in pockets or wallets.

    d. The group must come up with at least one type of activity.

3. Make a list of the activities that your group could do to pass the time. Then try out one of the activities as a group to make certain that it works and that you have followed all of the rules listed in 2.

4. On your own, list at least one problem your group had in deciding what to do. Do you have a solution for this problem?

5. As a whole class, share your solutions to the group task and then talk about how each group arrived at its solution.

TEAMWORK COUNTS

In the rest of this chapter, you will be asked to try out your group skills by completing at least three group projects. The first two projects will allow groups members the chance to get acquainted as a team. The third project will put the team to work. You should work on these projects as part of a group of three or four students.

Activity 5I   Getting to Know Us

How quickly can your group get the answers to fifteen questions? Your first group project is to find answers to the set of fifteen questions entitled *Who's Who?* You may wish to compete with other groups in the class or with the clock to see how quickly you can work together as a team to get all of the answers.

1. Follow these steps to get your group organized:

    a. Decide whether or not you need a leader. If you do, select someone to be in charge of your group.

    b. Decide what basic rules the group wants to follow in order to get the project done.

    c. Decide how to divide up the work among the team members.

2. Find the answers to these questions by asking students in other groups in your class, but not those in your small group, the questions from *Who's Who?*

Who's Who?

For each of these questions, find the name of one person in your class. If necessary, you may use the same name twice, but not more than two times.

Who in the class:

1. is an only child?
2. has had a broken arm or leg at some time?
3. knows how to play a musical instrument?
4. had toast for breakfast?
5. went to bed before ten o'clock last night?
6. has travelled to at least one other province in Canada?
7. owns three t-shirts with messages printed on them?
8. is wearing blue socks today?
9. is named after one of his or her parents?
10. had a birthday last month?
11. has relatives who are twins?
12. has a family member whose name begins with a *B*?
13. has a pet with wings or fins?
14. has a brother or sister who does not go to school?
15. lives in a house that has three outside doorways?

3. When the group finishes its list, record the amount of time it took to complete the set of questions. Then, discuss among yourselves the way you went about solving the problem. What worked? What didn't work? Is there another way you could have organized your group?

4. As a group, decide upon the answers to these questions. Then each group member should write responses in his or her own notebook.

   a. Was a leader necessary? If so, what should the leader have done to be sure that the group completed the project efficiently?
   b. What basic rules were helpful in getting the group to work well together?
   c. Was the division of work appropriate and efficient?
   d. What problems, if any, did the group have? What should the group do in order to overcome these problems next time?

Activity 5J   Getting to Know Us Better

At times you will need to work with others to find out information from books. Work with your group to find answers to the ten questions that follow. Look for the answers in reference books such as dictionaries, thesauruses, and encyclopedias.

1. Follow these steps to help your group work efficiently:
   a. Decide whether or not you need a leader. If you do, select someone to be in charge of the group.
   b. Decide what basic rules the group wants to follow in order to get the project done.
   c. Divide up the work in an appropriate way.

2. Find the answers to *Ten Questions* by working with your group and using reference books.

Ten Questions
1. Where would a person who delivers *epistles* work?
2. Which part of your face contains an *iris*?
3. Would you describe yourself as a *quadruped*?
4. If your arms are *akimbo*, where are your hands?
5. If the label on a bottle says *corrosive*, would you rub its contents on your skin?
6. If someone says you have a *bovine expression*, would you be flattered?
7. Would you give your best friend a *penumbra* for a birthday present?
8. Which would your grandmother be most likely to give you, a *buss* or a *blunderbuss*?
9. Were the people of Crete powerful during the *Cretaceous Period*?
10. Would your family be surprised if you invited a *naiad* home for dinner?

3. When your group finishes its list, discuss the way you went about solving the problem. On your own, write in your notebook any suggestions you have on these points:
   a. Was a leader necessary? If so, what should the leader have done to be sure that the group completed the project efficiently?
   b. What basic rules were helpful in getting the group to work well together?
   c. Would the work have gone more smoothly if the tasks had been divided up differently?
   d. What problems, if any, did the group have? What should the group do in order to overcome these problems next time?

PUTTING THE TEAM TO WORK

Your major group project for this chapter allows your group a choice of activities. It asks you to communicate something to others as a group.

For each of the descriptions of major projects, your **audience** is your class. Keep their interests in mind as you work.

Project 1

Think up a future invention, something that will be common in fifty years but that doesn't exist now) and decide how it will work. Either build a model or draw a diagram of it. Display the model or diagram to the class. As a whole group, explain how your invention will work and what it will do.

Project 2

Make up a new group game or sport. Decide on the equipment, rules, number of players, and scoring system. Demonstrate the game or sport to the class, and explain the equipment and rules so that others can play it.

Project 3

Write and perform a short script showing a humorous, suspenseful, or exciting situation. Everyone in the group should be involved in the performance, either acting in the scene or creating sound effects and special effects. Include props and costumes to help build up the dramatic effect.

Project 4

Design and make a poster that represents your group. Include details to show the individuals in the group and the things the group does best together. Display the poster to the class. As a whole group, explain how the poster represents your group's interests, activities, and achievements.

Activity 5K   The Grand Project

Form groups of three to five students. Then follow these directions to create your major project:

1. Discuss the four projects and choose the one that the group agrees to work on together.

2. Decide whether or not the group should appoint a leader.

3. Make up a list of the tasks the group should do in order to complete your major project.

4. Make a list of any equipment or supplies you will need to complete the project.

5. Decide how to divide the tasks among the group members, and plan the group's work.

6. Aim for a deadline when everyone will have finished his or her share of the group's work on the project.

7. Make plans to share your project with the rest of the class.

Closing the Circle

In this chapter, you have talked about the way small groups work together and the importance of small groups in your life. You have also had the experience of working in small groups.

Look once again at the picture of the Inuit carving at the beginning of this chapter. Think about the carving for a few minutes as a record of the achievements of a society. Think about the ways humans have learned how to work together to achieve their goals. Your ability to work with others is an important skill, one that is basic to all societies.

LINK 6 A

In the last chapter you learned how to write directions. The writing of directions was a part of group work. You had to learn how to communicate with others so that they understood you easily. This cartoon provides you with an unusual set of directions.

1. Think about this cartoon and then write your answers in your notebook.

2. How would this sign read if it were the office of:
    a. a football manager?
    b. an orchestra conductor?
    c. a quiz-show announcer?
    d. a mathematics teacher?

Extension: Try your hand at designing a cartoon to suit one of your answers.

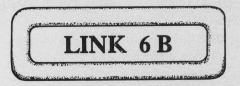

LINK 6 B

When you write directions, you often use sentences that give commands. In this activity you will look at command sentences, as well as three others kinds of sentences.

This chart shows you what these sentences are like and what the purpose of each one is.

Types of Sentences

Sample	Kind of Sentence	Purpose of Sentence	Punctuation at End of Sentence
The 1956 Thunderbird is a classic car!	Exclamation	makes an excited or emotional statement	Exclamation mark (!)
What is a classic car?	Question	asks for inform-ation or opinion	Question mark (?)
A classic car has shape, has style, is unique, and appreciates in value.	Statement	provides inform-ation or opinion	Period (.)
Buy one if you can.	Command	gives order or directions	Period (.)

The command sentence does not have a subject. (This sentence is sometimes called an imperative sentence.) The subject is implied; it is the person the writer is talking to. Instead of saying, *You buy one if you can*, the writer leaves out the subject — *you. Buy one if you can.*

In writing, you can give variety and liveliness to your style by using all four sentence types. In sentences giving directions, many sentences will be commands.

1. Examine the following sentences. Decide which are (1) exclamations, (2) questions, (3) statements, or (4) commands.

2. Write the letters a to k in your notebook. Beside each, note what kind of sentence each of the following is. Then rewrite it, making sure that you have the correct end punctuation mark.
   a. How do you throw a frisbee
   b. Hold the frisbee waist high
   c. The concave surface is the one that curves up
   d. Hold the frisbee with the concave surface facing the sky
   e. Put your thumb over the surface and your four fingers around the edge
   f. Put the frisbee up to your elbow, as far back as it will go, held horizontal to the ground
   g. Fling it
   h. Twist your wrist out away from you as you throw
   i. When you do, let go
   j. When your arm is extended as far as it will go, let go
   k. Try again until you get it right

3. Using the directions for 2, rewrite these sentences in your notebook.
   a. Do you know what the recipe for a perfect teacher is
   b. Begin with someone who is strict but not mean
   c. Spice with a sense of humour
   d. A good teacher has well-prepared lessons
   e. Fair tests are critical
   f. Stir in the ability to challenge the talented
   g. Top it off with caring about those who find it hard to learn
   h. How long do you bake perfect teachers
   i. Keep cooking until they're done
   j. Enjoy them
   k. They may not last long
   Serves 30 at a time.

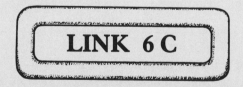

LINK 6 C

The next chapter is about the words you use and some choices you have to make between words. This activity is a warm-up for the next chapter, *Good Words . . .And More Good Words*.

Discuss your responses to these questions as a whole class:

1. Which sentence is about a cow with no sense of smell?
   a) The cow smells bad.
   b) The cow smells badly.

2. Which sentence describes sensitive fingers?
   a) I sure do feel good.
   b) I sure do feel well.

3. Which sentence signals that the speaker is jealous?
   a) My father likes skiing better than me.
   b) My father likes skiing better than I.

LINK 6 D

This activity is about speaking and enunciation — just in case you have not been practising your speaking skills.

1. On your own, try reading these tongue twisters. Read them slowly at first. Increase your speed only after you can say them clearly.

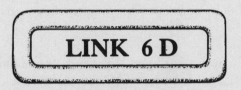

Three free things set three things free.

That bloke's back brake-block broke.

Ted threw Fred three free throws.

Six thick thistles stick.

The sixth sheik's sixth sheep's sick.

2. Try these tongue twisters in small groups:
   a) Say them to each other.
   b) Say them as a group, in unison.

3. Add your own tongue twisters to your repertoire or collection of tongue twisters.

4. Finally, try reading your tongue twisters as a whole class.

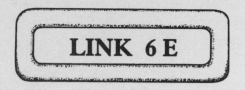

LINK 6 E

This activity provides you with more practice in listening for details.

1. Close your book, and listen as your teacher reads the following passage.

2. Each time you hear a word that is a colour, or a homophone (a word that is pronounced the same but has a different meaning) for a colour, write the word in your notebook.

Note: There are seventeen colour words in this passage.

Once there was a young girl named Rose. She read her horoscope in the newspaper. Picking up a mauve pen, she wrote strong marks on the white paper.

"How dare they blacken my family tree!" she exclaimed, as she read on. "I'll tan their hides! I'll cream them, I will!" Her face crimsoned in anger.

She thumped her hand on the brown table. Her hand turned black and blue from the beating. Purple with rage, she continued to skim the paper.

"What's this?" she muttered. "In dig o?"

As the yellow fire died out in the fireplace, she blew on her hands to warm them. Aunt Violet called her to dinner.

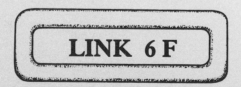

LINK 6 F

You have been hired by a detective agency to get information about a person living in a hotel in Ottawa. It is suspected that this person is a spy, getting classified secrets out of Canada and selling them to a foreign country. No one knows who this person is nor to whom the secrets are being sold.

Disguised as a service person, you have managed to get inside this *spy's* hotel room. But you have to be quick. The person may return and become suspicious. You have only ninety seconds to survey the room for clues. Now you must get into action.

1. Study the details of the contents of the spy's writing table. You have ninety seconds and no longer. (Your teacher will be the time keeper.)

2. Close your textbook and list in your notebook all of the items from the writing table that you can remember.

3. Compare your list with the picture in the text to see how many of the items you could remember.

4. As a whole class, talk about this spy. What do the clues on the writing desk tell you about this person?
   a. Is this spy male or female?
   b. Where has the spy been and where is he or she going next?
   c. Has this spy been out of this hotel room very long? Did he or she leave very suddenly?

d. In what foreign countries does this spy have contacts?
e. What information might this spy be offering to a foreign power?

5. Now that you have all of this information about our spy, you are in a good position to write one of the following thrillers.
   a. The spy flies to Amsterdam. And you are on the plane, too.
   b. You go back to New York and Chicago to put the pieces of the puzzle together.
   c. The spy flies to a country south of the equator and you are there.
   d. You phone the RCMP in Ottawa to help you capture the spy at Mirabel Airport in Montreal.

This Norman Rockwell painting was the cover of a magazine called *The Saturday Evening Post*, April 3, 1943. It was published as an April Fool's joke. How many things can you find that are wrong with this painting?

CHAPTER 6

GOOD WORDS . . . AND
MORE GOOD WORDS

Have you ever found yourself in the same situation as the owl Frederick: *someone corrects your English*? Why does this happen?

There is a simple answer to this question. As a child you were learning the language and you needed help to master it.

But the situation is more complex than this answer suggests. Some words seem all right in one situation, and no one will mind your using them. But try to use them in another situation — and they seem totally wrong. This experience can be confusing.

This chapter will look at what is meant by good words and incorrect words. It will help you look at the problem of the use of words and give you some practice using the right words at the right time.

ABOUT IDIOLECTS AND DIALECTS

For many reasons, people speak differently. The same person speaks differently on different occasions and in different situations. Let's find out about these differences.

Idiolects

This activity will help you find out more information about the language of individual people.

Activity 6A   Me . . . Unique?

1. **Three members of the class will have to be blindfolded so that they cannot see the speakers, but still hear them. Let's call these students the *blindfold team*.**

2. **Four speakers, in turn, talk with the blindfold team for about one minute each. The speakers should be careful not to give away their identity by what they say.**

3. **After the last speaker, the blindfold team will identify the students with whom they are talking.**

4. **Repeat this experiment two or three times, with different blindfold teams and different speakers.**

5. **As a class, discuss this question: *How were the members of the blindfold teams able to identify the speakers?***

You are a *unique* person. No one is exactly like you. You have your own name, your own appearance, and your own mind. No one has had the same experiences that you have had. You are truly one of a kind.

As a speaker of English, you are unique as well. It is this uniqueness of each class member that allowed the blindfolded students in Activity 6A to identify the speakers.

Each person has a unique way of speaking. This unique way of speaking is called his or her *idiolect*.

Your idiolect is yours alone. It makes you different from every other speaker of English. Activity 6A helped you identify what these individual characteristics are.

Dialects

Activity 6B   A Canadian Quiz

This quiz is about Canada. Write the number of the best answer for each question in your notebook.

1. The population of Canada is:
   a. about 10 000 000   c. about 15 000 000
   b. about 20 000 000   d. about 25 000 000

2. The distance from Victoria, British Columbia, to St. John's, Newfoundland, is:
   a. 7600 km   c. 5000 km
   b. 1900 km   d. 2250 km

3. The ancestors of non-Native Canadians came from:
   a. Great Britain only   c. France and a few other countries
   b. a great many countries d. South America only

4. After English and French, which language is spoken by the largest number of Canadians?
   a. German   c. Ukrainian
   b. Italian   d. Cree

5. The Indians of Canada speak about how many different languages?
   a. one   c. five or six
   b. twelve   d. a great many

6. The language spoken by the Inuit is:
   a. Algonkian   c. Inuktitut
   b. Wakashan   d. Montagnais

7. Canadians work at about how many different kinds of jobs?
   a. about 100   c. about 500
   b. about 1000   d. a great many

The correct answers to this quiz tell you that:

• Canada is a big country.
• Canadians have come from many different countries.
• Native People speak several different languages.
• Canadians work at a great many jobs.

Because of the great differences among Canadian people, they have tended to live and work in groups. Certain groups of people, each with a unique idiolect, have much in common with each other. And they tend to speak in the same way.

> This common way of speaking among groups of speakers is called a **dialect**.
>
> Dialects that are unique to certain areas or regions are called **regional dialects**.
>
> Dialects that indicate such things as how much education people have or what job they work at are called **social dialects**. A person may have several different social dialects.

Regional Dialects and Social Dialects

This section will give you more information about regional and social dialects.

Activity 6C   Regional Dialect Quiz

This activity will test to see how much you know about regional dialects in Canada. Write the letter of the answer that correctly completes each statement in your notebook.

1. **In Newfoundland, *brewis* is:**
a. a fish   c. something to eat
b. a boat   d. a plant

2. **On the Prairies, a *bluff* is:**
a. a grove of trees   c. a cliff-like bank
b. a field of oats   d. something to harvest

3. A *Calgary redeye* is:
a. a fish
b. a drink
c. a flower
d. a newspaper

4. The phrase *It's some hot today* is frequently heard in:
a. British Columbia
b. Ontario
c. the Yukon
d. Nova Scotia

5. In Alberta, a *chinook* is:
a. a game
b. a type of cattle
c. a warm wind
d. a coniferous tree

6. If you went to a *Gaelic Mod* in Cape Breton Island, you would attend:
a. a summer picnic
b. a rock concert
c. a drama festival
d. an event with sports, music, and dancing

7. In New Brunswick, a *bogan*, which is an Algonkian word, means:
a. a little toboggan
b. a berry with purple juice
c. a sun flower
d. a marsh where a creek joins a river

8. In the Maritime region, a *gaspereau* is:
a. a small fish
b. a short street
c. a lamp
d. a small house

9. In Kitchener, Ontario, if you order *Kraut Wickel*, you would eat:
a. a sugar cookie
b. cabbage rolls
c. doughnuts
d. sauerkraut

10. The word *shanty*, from the era of the lumber trade in Ontario, meant:
a. a hut
b. a raft of logs
c. a pole to guide logs
d. to cut a tree

11. On the Prairies, a *pool* could mean:
a. a cooperative
b. a grid road
c. survey technique
d. an early school house

12. A *black blizzard* on the prairie is:
a. a storm at night   c. a hail storm
b. a swarm of grasshoppers   d. a dust storm

13. A *lobstick* in northern Canada is:
a. a kind of candy   c. a spear
b. a trail marker   d. a lead dog in a team

14. In the Klondike gold rush, a *cheechako* was:
a. a newcomer   c. a colourful song bird
b. a sled with a curved back d. a brownish coloured dog

15. In northern Canada, the word *chimo* is used:
a. to start a dog team   c. to call for help
b. to cheer at a contest   d. to offer a toast before a drink

16. If a boy were called *skookum* in British Columbia, he would be thought of as:
a. short and quiet   c. jolly and fun
b. big and strong   d. silly and witless

This quiz gives you some idea of the nature of regional dialects in Canada. There are a few words that are understood only in a specific region of Canada.

The major English dialect regions of Canada are: Newfoundland and Labrador, the Maritimes, Quebec and Ontario, the Ottawa Valley, the Prairies, British Columbia, Eastern Arctic, Western Arctic. Yet Canadians speak a general Canadian English and people from one end of the country to the other are able to communicate with each other.

Activity 6D   Some Social Dialects

1. In your notebook, list the different groups which you *or* an adult member of your family belongs to or did belong to.

2. Use this list to help you think of some groups:

   • a religious group
   • a business group
   • a social group or club
   • a neighbourhood group
   • a union

- a professional or work group
- a group of people the same age

3. Choose one group from your list and write it in your notebook as a title for the next question.

4. For this group, list five different words or expressions that are unique to this group, and that are not generally used by people outside this group.

Activity 6E   More Social Dialects

What does this cartoon tell you about social dialects?

Activity 6F   Still More Social Dialects

Discuss these questions in class:

1. What does this *Archie* cartoon tell you about social dialects?

© 1984 Archie Comic Publications, Inc.

2. **In the *Peanuts* cartoon on the next page, Linus is thinking about differences in *ideas* between one generation and another. Are there *word* differences between generations as well? If so, what are some of them?**

Attitudes Towards Dialects

People react to the *meaning* of the words you use as well as to the *choice* of your words. For example, if you were to meet someone who is about your age, would you use this greeting? *How do you do?* Not very likely! But why?

The choice of words — *how do you do* — just doesn't fit with this situation. Two young people don't talk this way. This greeting is not **appropriate**, or right, for the situation.

The problem of choosing the appropriate word becomes more complex, as this next activity shows.

Activity 6G   What About Ain't?

Discuss these questions as a whole class.

I ain't gonna go! is a good enough sentence. It tells us that *I intend to stay*!

1. Would you use this sentence on the playground to tell your friends that you are not going to their hockey game? Why or why not?

2. Would you use it in a formal speech, in front of all the students in your school? Why or why not?

Words cannot be right or wrong. Instead, words are right or wrong in the situation or context in which they are spoken. *I ain't gonna go!* is all right on the playground, but not for a formal speech in class. Here is the same thing expressed in another way, this time more formally. *Words are correct if they are appropriate for the situation in which they are spoken.* Words not used correctly are inappropriate for the situation in which they are spoken.

Does it matter to you if you use a word in an inappropriate situation? The next activity will help you consider this question.

Activity 6H   Attitudes to Words

1. Read the conversation and answer the following questions in your notebook.

> "I ain't gonna go!" said Leslie.
> "You must," said Robin. "It's absolutely necessary for you to go."
> "Who's big 'nuff to make me? Ain't no one nowhere who's gonna push me 'round."
> "Now, Leslie," said Robin. "Calm yourself. You and I *have* to go. There just isn't any other way."

1. Look at the words in the box on the next page. Which ones seem to describe Leslie? Which ones seem to describe Robin?

2. Make a chart like the one below and write down the words that seem to you to best describe Robin and Leslie.

Example

Leslie is . . .   Robin is . . .
honest   bossy

3. Now look at the words you chose for each of the speakers. As a class, discuss your choice of words to find out why you answered the way you did.

Exercises like the one you just completed often tell us a great deal about ourselves. Your feelings about Leslie and Robin came from the way they used language in speech. Neither way of speech is incorrect, yet readers and listeners often make judgements or assumptions about people by the way they write or speak. Often the words you use to describe someone tell more about you than they do about the one you describe.

Extention: Divide into small groups of four or five students and role play the conversation between Robin and Leslie. How can the tone change the impression a listener gets about them?

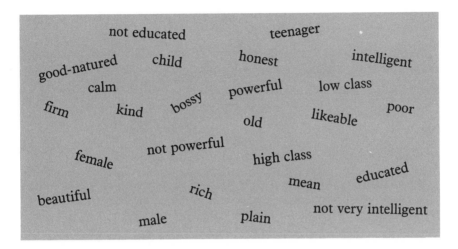

STANDARD AND NON-STANDARD USAGE

People determine the right-ness or wrong-ness of words. Words themselves are not wrong. For example, the word *ain't* is not incorrect by itself. People decide that it is wrong. The reason for this kind of decision is very complex. It involves people's attitudes and beliefs.

If people, or society, decide that words are right or wrong, then you will find it necessary to know the right time and place to use them. It is quite possible for you to use a word in one situation but not in another.

Words may be classified into two categories: **standard usage** and **non-standard usage**. Standard usage is the language spoken in most classrooms or written in most textbooks. It also tends to be the language of radio and TV, particularly news broadcasts. Written standard usage tends to be slightly more formal than spoken standard usage.

Non-standard speech is used by subgroups of people. It may be the spoken language of a particular community. Children may use non-standard usage on the playground. Or, to cite another example, sports announcers, describing an exciting moment in a game, may slip into non-standard usage. There will be many other examples of non-standard speech in your world.

Activity 6I   Looking at Standard Usage

This activity will give you practice in separating standard usage from non-standard usage.

1. Decide which sentence would be appropriate in each of these situations:

   Situation A — Standard Usage: You are giving a formal talk to your class as the first stage in an oratory contest.

   Situation B — Non-standard Usage: You are writing a play about a group of workers, who are meeting very informally over a cup of coffee.

2. Copy the letter of each sentence in your notebook, and write either Situation A or Situation B beside each letter.
   a. I ain't seen a more beautiful horse.
   b. Does iron expand in winter?
   c. We was going to tell you the secret.
   d. I knowed the answer to that question.
   e. Them books belong to the school library.
   f. The collie dog was an inspiration to all of us.
   g. Me and my father went to the football game.
   h. The ballerina practised her dance for six hours.

Activity 6J   The Language of Ads

1. Which word is an example of non-standard usage in this advertisement?

2. Why did the ad writer choose to use this word and not a more formal, standard word?

3. Make a collection of ten ads in which the ad writers have used non-standard usage and explain why they used these words.

"I figure I'm part of it."

PETRO-CANADA It's ours!

Activity 6K   Listening for Standard Usage

This activity requires you to listen to distinguish between standard and non-standard usage.

1. Write the letters a to j in your notebook.

2. With this book closed, listen as your teacher reads these sentences to you.

3. Decide whether each sentence uses standard or non-standard usage.

4. Then write the word *standard usage* or *non-standard usage* beside each number.
   a) Lucien and me were picked to start the game.
   b) Danielle, please take Allan and me skating.
   c) The teacher sent for Marc and me.
   d) Why won't you let we girls play hockey?
   e) He has ran a good race!
   f) No one has learned the new card tricks.
   g) I haven't had no lunch today.
   h) Gina divided her money between Shane, Miriam, and me.
   i) Last holidays I seen a CFL game when I visited Montreal.
   j) One of the eleven rookies were hurt during spring training.

THE EFFECTIVE COMMUNICATOR

You have learned to classify words as non-standard usage or standard usage and not as correct or incorrect usage. What is the importance of this difference? The answer lies in the term **appropriate usage**. A word, then, is judged on the importance of its use in certain situations. If a word communicates effectively, it is the right or correct word. In some communities, most speakers will say *I seen the dog*. In this situation, the word *seen* is appropriate—even though it is an example of non-standard usage.

Does this mean that every word is correct, no matter what — that there are no rules for using words? The answer is *no*, quite decidedly. The answer goes back to the issue of attitudes towards words, as you explored in Activity 6H. Because people have attitudes towards words and attach value to how they are used, it is necessary for you to know how to use them—to know when it is appropriate to use standard usage and when to use non-standard usage.

Here are some examples of this statement about words. *I seen the map* may be appropriate when you are talking with your friends. This usage would be inappropriate for a written report in social studies. Or, you could say *Him and me went to the movies* when talking with one of your friends, but not when you are being interviewed for a job.

The **effective communicator** is the person who knows what kind of word to use for each occasion.

Activity 6L   Standard Usage for Reports

This activity is also concerned with standard and non-standard usage. It contains sixteen sentences written for a social studies report on Madeleine de Verchères, the heroine from Quebec.

1. If the sentence is written in standard usage, write standard usage beside the number of the sentence.

2. If the sentence is written in non-standard usage, rewrite it, using standard usage.

Note: Think very carefully about the sentences that contain direct quotations.

1. Madeleine de Verchères, a fourteen-year-old girl, lived in the wilderness on the Richelieu River.

2. Her father and mother had went to Montreal on a trip.

3. Her and a servant girl led the cows out of the fort.

4. The cows drunk from a quiet stream.

5. "I ain't got nothing to do," Madeleine said to the servant girl beside her.

6. Suddenly a band of Iroquois warriors appeared in the clearing.

7. She and some others escaped into the fort.

8. "We don't have no soldiers here," cried an old guard.

9. Madleine took command of the fort because all of the soldiers were away.

10. All of the children clumb the bastion of the fort where the cannon was mounted.

11. They wore helmets and pretended to be soldiers.

12. The Iroquois thought that there were many soldiers inside the fort.

13. "We don't got a chance to live," cried one child.

14. "This here is no way to talk," said Madeleine.

15. They was happy to have Madeleine take command.

16. She defended the fort with just a handful of women and children until help came.

Madeleine de Verchères

This poem is about words and some other things:

> **Motto**
> I play it cool and dig all jive,
> That's the reason I stay alive,
> My motto, as I live and learn,
> Is: Dig and Be Dug in Return.
>
> Langston Hughes,
> *Panther and the Lash.*

Langston Hughes is a well known poet who grew up in a Black community in a large American city. Let's examine Hughes's poem to find out what he is saying.

Activity 6M   *Motto*

1. In your notebook, write down in your own words what you think Hughes is saying in his poem.

2. In small groups of three or four students, share your thoughts about Hughes's poem.

3. When you have finished sharing your thoughts, write out a group statement about the meaning of the poem.

    This statement should include the ideas and point of view of each member of the group and note the sameness or differences among members of the group.

4. Share these small group statements with the class.

5. Discuss the poem and your statements about it and comment on what the poem has to say about the way people use words.

6. Return to your notebook and write out a new statement about what the poem means.

7. Write your own motto. You might use words from your own idiolect or dialect to express your meaning.

EXAMPLES FROM AUTHORS

Authors may write in more than one dialect. They may use both social and regional dialects. This skill is particularly important for those authors who include dialogue or conversation in their works. The following examples show some authors flipping back and forth in their writing from standard usage, which is really a standard dialect, and non-standard usage, which includes social and regional dialects.

Janet Lunn's *The Root Cellar* describes the adventures of three Canadian children who became involved in the American Civil War during the 1860s. This is a fantasy that joins people living in two different times. Rose, a girl from the twentieth century, goes back in time to join Susan and Will, who live in the nineteenth century. To distinguish the speech of these children, Ms. Lunn uses standard usage for the twentieth century, and non-standard usage for the nineteenth century.

In the following passage, Will describes his feelings about the American Civil War:

"It's part mine [my war], Susan, it's part mine. My ma come from the States. Her country needs soldiers bad. The war's been going on for three years and things is desperate. Steve [a cousin from the United States] told me last time he come here that him and Aunt Min and them all went down to New York City when Abraham Lincoln was there and they seen him. He says Lincoln's all but a saint and I believe him. Lincoln freed the slaves from those rich people in the South — and you know yourself how some of them black peoples come across the lake to get away from being slaves and the terrible things they told about being beaten and put in chains and made to work like animals. Well, after the war there ain't going to be no more slaves and, what's more, them states in the South ain't going to be able to quit the United States just because they happen to feel like it.

[Handwritten annotations in margin:]
came
badly
are
came
all of them
he
saw
said
those
came
people
isn't
any
those
aren't

In this next quotation, Ms. Lunn provides an encyclopedic description of the Civil War. Note the formal, literary style of this passage:

> The American Civil War, also called the War between the States, the War of the Rebellion, and the War for Southern Independence, was a war between the eleven states of the south and the states and territories of the north. The causes of the war were many and complicated but, although emotions ran high on both sides on the issue of slavery, the basic cause was economic. The issue was the right of the states to their own government. Abraham Lincoln was elected president in 1860 as an advocate of strong central government. . .

standard usage handled very formally, becoming legalistic in its tone.

Ms. Lunn has used words appropriately. Her words are the right words for the occasions she created in her book.

Activity 6N Understanding Dialects

Edna Staebler, in *Cape Breton Harbour*, uses standard usage for her descriptions of Cape Breton, but non-standard usage, or regional dialect, to report the conversation of Cape Bretoners.

1. In your notebook, write the numbers 1 to 16.

2. Read the following passage and then write the standard usage for each of the non-standard forms used in this quotation.

> "Some warm today," a very old codfisherman   *1*
> said as he landed, "hottest day we ever had in   *2*
> our loife."
> "You should wear shorts," I teased him. He   *3*
> laughed and said, "We always wears fleece-lined,   *4*
> summer or winter, never changes 'em. We sweats   *5*
> but it soaks in and dries off; when snow comes we
> stop sweatin' but we don't feel the cold; weather's
> all the same to we, never feels it through our   *6*
> clothes."   *7*
>
> Five young boys in bathing trunks, their legs and
> bodies white as foam, forearms and faces brown,
> emerged from a stage near the dock. One of them

standard usage for description

was Tommy Seaforth; seeing me, he crossed his
arms over his bare chest and ducked behind a pile of
lobster traps. The rest screamed as they splashed
each other in the shallow water near the shore.
"You supprised them can't they swim?" Big Jim
asked me. "Not many in Harbour be swimmers. Ain't
no one to learn 'em. I ain't been in water for
ower twenty year myself."
    "Why don't you go?" I asked.
    He gave an embarrassed laugh, "We used to go
in our bare buff but when tourists started comin'
in cars it weren't never the same."

standard usage for description

8
9
10
11
12
13
14
15
16

Activity 60 Non-Standard Usage in Books

1. Look for examples of non-standard usage in the stories you are reading.

2. Make a classroom display of examples of standard and non-standard usage taken from the same story.

STANDARD USAGE — WHY?

Now that you have examined language usage, how do you feel about the statement: *a word is correct if it is appropriate for the situation in which it is used*.

If you agree with this statement, then you should be able to handle language usage easily. You have to learn to fit the words you use to the situation you find yourself in. It is natural, then, for you to use different expressions and words when you are with a gang of kids than when you talk with your school principal, just as it is natural for you to use different words and phrases when you write a poem than you do when you write a science report.

You don't need help to learn the words you use with your friends. You probably do this very well. As you go through *Bridges 2*, you will find that you occasionally have to write or speak the way you talk among your friends — with some non-standard words. These instances will give you practice following the rule: the appropriate word for the situation.

Something that you may find more difficult to write is standard usage. This is the English that you use for more formal situations: a letter to the editor, a science report, an English essay. Indeed, this is the usage that is most common in Canada, the usage, or dialect, used by the greatest number of people.

Standard usage is used commonly because it makes communication between different groups easier and more accurate. At the same time, there is a tendency for people who use the standard dialect to be critical of those who don't use this dialect. You will often be expected to speak with standard usage, or you will suffer the consequences of people's attitudes towards the words you choose.

One of the main purposes of this textbook is to give you the opportunity to learn to write and speak in the standard dialect. For some of you, this skill will be easy because you tend to use standard usage in your home. For others, this skill will be more difficult because you will have to learn a word usage that is different from your usual way of saying things.

The Rockwell Painting

You began this chapter by looking at a Norman Rockwell painting. Rockwell's painting is very different from the others presented in this text. His use of the visual medium is different, but it is not wrong.

Words, too, can be used in many ways. This chapter has given you a glimpse of this. Although words are used differently by different people, non-standard usage is not wrong, just as Rockwell's painting is not wrong, but merely different.

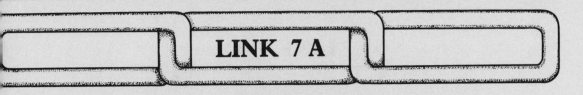

LINK 7 A

1. Look at the cartoon below. What does the speaker mean when he says that he has an **indigenous cultural dialect**?

2. Once you know what these words mean, do you agree with what he is saying?

"Of course it's misspelled. I'm preserving my indigenous cultural dialect."

LINK 7 B

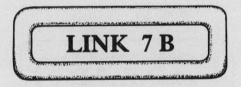

The king is writing in his journal. Right writing, no doubt.
  By the way, how are you doing with your journal writing?
  Let the king inspire you to spend a week with your journal.

"Reigned all day . . ."

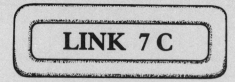

LINK 7 C

Here is another activity that makes you look carefully for differences between words. Talk about these sentences in class.

1. In which sentence does Marika appear to put other people first?
   a) Marika has done good with the money she earned.
   b) Marika has done well with the money she earned.

2. In which sentence do *I* have a more relaxing time?
   a) I lay about the house all day.
   b) I lied about the house all day.

3. In which sentence is the man dishonest?
   a) The man lay in that room.
   b) The man lied in that room.

4. In which sentence is Claudette being watched?
   a) Claudette looked careful.
   b) Claudette looked carefully.

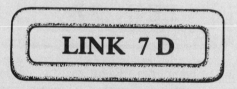

LINK 7 D

These sentences are ambiguous. Just by looking at them, you cannot tell what meaning the writer intended.

Your reading of these sentences shows the importance of stress in oral communication. **Stress** refers to the emphasis you place upon certain words as you speak a sentence. A change in stress may change the meaning of a sentence.

1. Read each of these sentences aloud. Experiment with the stress you place upon different words. You should be able to get at least *two* entirely different meanings for each sentence.
   a) Melissa gave her rabbit pellets.
   b) Why do you want to read Laurence?
   c) Bruno showed the pretty baby pictures.

d) A French teacher reported that junior high students are revolting.

2. As a class, compose several sentences that are ambiguous in their written form but are clear if the stress is correct.

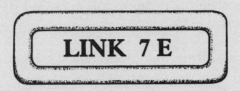

LINK 7 E

This activity tests once again your skill as a listener.

1. Send one member of the class out of the room.

2. While this person is out, make up a list of five actions you want him or her to do upon returning to the classroom.

3. Read this list of actions to him or her — all five at one time.

4. The person who was out of the room performs all five actions, in order. If five actions are too hard, reduce the number. Try to build up the number of actions that you can hold in mind. Perhaps you can reach seven.

Example:
- Walk to the front, left corner of the classroom.
- Scratch the back of your neck.
- Return to the door of the room and knock three times.
- Go to the teacher's desk and place your left hand on it.
- Return to your desk and say, "The rain on the Canadian plain comes mainly in May."

Review: What purpose do the sentences in the example serve? What is the name given to this kind of sentence? What are the names of the other three kinds of sentences, and what is the purpose for each one? If you need help, look at Link 6B.

LINK 7 F

This task will prompt you to do some creative thinking.

1. Make a list of impossible things to do or accomplish.

2. Form groups of four or five people and share lists.

3. Choose one impossible feat from the combined list.

4. Brainstorm among the group members to find ways to solve the impossible task.

5. As a whole class, share your problems and solutions.

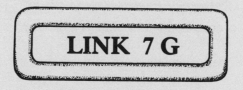

LINK 7 G

Here's another task to encourage your originality.

1. Make a poem by writing a word in such a way that you describe its shape.

Examples: U ^P   ^DO_W_N   O^VE_R   A^R_O_D_N^U

2. Try these words: *under, fire, pole, chair.*

3. Now add a few words of your own, and make poems from them. These kinds of poems are called **concrete poems**. You will be examining ideas like this one more fully later on in this book.

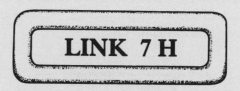

LINK 7 H

In the next chapter, you will be practising letter writing. See if you can complete this quiz about the postal system. If you do not know the answers, ask your school secretary or someone from your local post office for help.

Post Office Quiz

1. How much does it cost to mail a post card in Canada?

2. What is the First Class postal rate for letters under thirty grams?

3. What is the First Class postal rate for letters under thirty grams mailed to the United States?

4. What is the postal rate for an International Letter under thirty grams?

5. What is the cost of mailing a letter to the United States that weighs between thirty grams and fifty grams?

6. What price units do Canadian postal stamps come in?

7. What does Special Delivery mean?

8. What is a registered letter?

9. What is the design on the stamp that has been released most recently?

10. Who makes up and prints stamps?

This map of Canada shows the allocations of the first character of the postal code. Look through a *Postal Code Directory* to see how this system works.

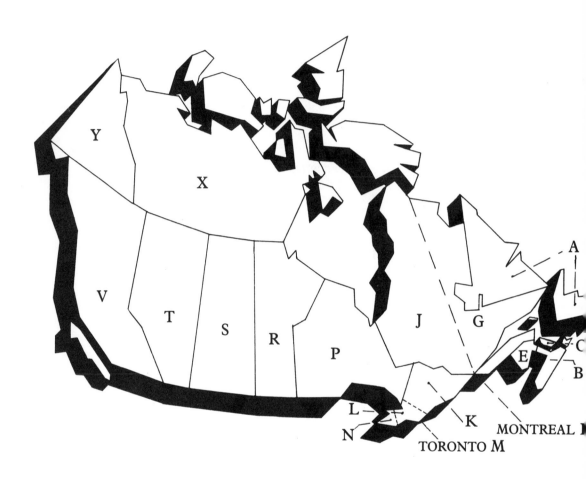

A	Newfoundland/Terre-Neuve	N	Southwestern Ontario/
B	Nova Scotia/Nouvelle-Ecosse		Sud-Ouest de l'Ontario
C	Prince Edward Island/Ile-du-Prince-Edouard	P	Northern Ontario/Nord de l'Ontario
E	New Brunswick/Nouveau-Brunswick	R	Manitoba
G	Quebec East/Est du Québec	S	Saskatchewan
H	Montreal Metropolitan/Montréal Métro	T	Alberta
J	Quebec West/Ouest du Québec	V	British Columbia/Colombie-Britannique
K	Eastern Ontario/Est de l'Ontario	X	Northwest Territories/
L	Central Ontario/Centre de l'Ontario		Territoires du Nord-Ouest
M	Toronto Metropolitan/Toronto Métro	Y	Yukon

CHAPTER 7

TO WHOM IT MAY CONCERN

TRUE OR FALSE?

Take this quiz to see how much you know about letter writing in Canada. Write your answers in your notebook under the title *Post Office Quiz*.

1.	Telex machines and long distance telephone calls have replaced business letters.	T	F
2.	People generally no longer write personal letters.	T	F
3.	The Canadian Post Office is having serious problems because of a decrease in the volume of mail.	T	F
4.	In Canada today, people really don't need to know how to write letters.	T	F
5.	Business letters always must be typed.	T	F
6.	It costs only 10 cents to send a letter to your Member of Parliament in Ottawa.	T	F
7.	Businesses that once used the mail to advertise have now turned to television.	T	F
8.	The electric typewriter has had very little influence on letter writing.	T	F
9.	It doesn't matter how you say things in a letter as long as you get the message across.	T	F
10.	There used to be set formats for laying out letters, but these are no longer used.	T	F

Activity 7A A Post Office Quiz

1. Did you find any of the answers to the questions in the Post Office Quiz surprising?

2. As a class, discuss any answers you find unusual or you would like to dispute.

Writing business letters involves knowing how to use a few basic matters of **format** and **style**. In this chapter you'll also explore some facts about letter writing and some reasons why people write business letters. You'll also have an opportunity to write a letter of your own, mail it, and await a reply. Letters can make things happen!

The following letter was written for you. So was the reply. Let's take a look at them:

```
                                              6626 Kingsway
                                              Burnaby, B.C.
Mr. R. Michael Warren                         V5E 1H1
President and Chief Executive Officer
Canada Post Corporation                       84-03-31
Ottawa, Ontario
K1A 0B1


Dear Sir:
I am preparing some material to help students learn more about writing
business letters. I feel that letter writing is still a very important part of
Canadian life and that students should learn to conduct business in an
acceptable way through the mail.                                        →
```

I would be very grateful if you could send me some current information on letter writing in Canada. In particular, could you please supply some facts on such matters as

1. the volume of mail passing through Canada Post now compared to five and ten years ago;
2. the current trend in the use of mass advertising mailings by businesses;
3. the extent to which devices such as Telex machines and computers are affecting or will affect letter writing as a part of business and industry.

Any other pertinent information you have for students would be welcomed.

Thank you for your cooperation.

Yours truly,

Stephen D. Bailey
Head, English Department
Burnaby South Secondary School

And the reply . . .

Canada Post Corporation
Ottawa, Ontario
K1A 0B1
84 09 30

Mr. Steve Bailey
1404 Dansey Avenue
Coquitlam, B.C.
V3K 3H8

Dear Mr. Bailey:

Please excuse the delay in replying to your letter requesting information about Canada's postal services. I certainly agree that letter writing is an important skill students should acquire, and my description of Canada Post's growing mail volume will confirm that letter writing, in particular business letters, is very much a part of Canadian life.

The volume of mail handled by Canada Post is steadily increasing compared to five and ten years ago. In 1973–74, we handled 4.68 million pieces of mail (not counting unaddressed third class mail); by 1978–79 that figure had increased to 5.09 million pieces. In 1982–83, we processed 5.3 million pieces of mail — quite a mailbag!

You asked about the current trends in the use of mass advertising mailings by businesses. Several factors can be identified as trends in this important area of our operation. For example, our addressed admail sales volumes have shown a definite upward trend, except in years when there have been work stoppages which have seriously hampered our ability for continued growth. In the area of unaddressed mail, too, our sales volumes have increased by about 10 per cent a year. When we look at the performance of the United States Postal Service in the area of advertising mail, we see a potential for even greater growth in the future.

It is true that telex machines and other electronic means of communication are becoming increasingly popular in the business world, but they are not expected to have an immediate or great effect on mail to and from householders. Canada Post's electronic mail services allow businesses to send information electronically to destination centres, where the messages are

Thank you for making this information available to Canadian students. We hope your students will use with satisfaction some of the many services offered by one of Canada's largest and busiest Crown corporations.

Yours sincerely,

R. Michael Warren
President and Chief
Executive Officer

As you can see, letter writing is an important part of Canadian life and business. You will probably write many business letters during your lifetime. If you are to be an effective communicator, you have to learn the conventions of writing business letters.

Activity 7B   The Format of a Business Letter

Look again at the two letters. Remember that the purpose of a business letter is to give information or place a request quickly. Also, keep in mind that you probably do not know the person to whom you are writing.

1. In groups of three or four, discuss these questions:
   a) What are the parts of a business letter?

b) **Is the language of these letters standard or non-standard usage? Explain your answer.**

c) **What do you notice about the size of the paragraphs in these letters?**

2. **Choose one group member to report your conclusions to the class.**

3. **Summarize your findings in your notebook.**

Writing business letters involves the same basic process you use in other writing situations. You must decide who your *audience* is, what your *purpose* for communicating is, and which *form* you wish to use.

TAKING A CLOSER LOOK

Formats and styles for business letters vary slightly depending on the writing handbook you consult. The following example is a widely used style you might want to consider. It is written in **block style**.

As you look over this letter, notice the information about the parts of the business letter.

50 Grassington Crescent
Bramalea, Ontario   (1)
L6S 1Z6

85-03-29

Postarama Limited
P.O. Box 370
Station "C"   (2)
Montreal, Quebec
H2C 4K3

To Whom It May Concern: (3)

I am responding to your special offer outlined in your letter dated 85-03-05.

Please send me the stamp sets indicated on the enclosed order form. Also, please find full payment enclosed.   (4)

Yours truly,   (5)
Mark Wong
Mark Wong   (6)

encl.   (7)

The parts of Mark's letter are as follows. You will want to include the same parts whenever you write a business letter.

1. **Heading:**
   - your street address, city, province, postal code
   - the date, spaced appropriately (the year, the month, the day)

2. **Inner Address:**
   - name of the person and/or company to whom you are writing, address, and postal code

3. **Salutation:**
   - punctuated by a colon
   - if you know the name of the individual you are writing to, use it (e.g., "Dear Ms. Bentley:")

4. **Body:**
   - single spaced with two spaces between paragraphs
   - keep paragraphs short and to the point
   - maintain a formal business style
   - use a new page for the second page of your letter (do not write on the back of the first page)

5. **Complimentary Close:**
   - first word only is capitalized
   - followed by a comma
   - leave four spaces for written signature

6. **Signature:**
   - a written signature is included above the typewritten one

7. **Reminder:**
   - some letters need reminders; "encl." is a reminder that something is enclosed with the letter
   - the abbreviation "cc." indicates a "carbon copy" (nowadays often a photocopy, but cc. is still used) of the letter will be sent to someone else (e.g., "cc. Mr. M. Gonyou")
   - initials at the bottom of the page are a reminder that someone other than the writer has typed the letter. For example, if an office worker named James Richmond had typed Mark's letter, he might put the following at the bottom of the page: "MW/jr"

Activity 7C   Practice with Format

Practise writing parts of the business letter in your notebook. Check the model letters for proper spacing and punctuation.

1. Heading
   a. Write a heading using your personal information.
   b. Write a heading using the address of a friend.
   c. Write a heading for a fictitious person who lives in a different province.

2. Inner Address
   Write these two inner addresses, complete with postal codes:
   a. You are writing to Mr. Pierre Jardin, who lives at 3629 Porteau Avenue in Montreal, Quebec. His postal code is H3A 1V7.
   b. You are writing to Ms. J.T. Sandhu, who is sales manager of the Canadian Motorcycle Corporation. The address is 3325 Portage Avenue, Winnipeg, Manitoba. The postal code is R3J 0E5.

3. Salutation:
   Write salutations for the two inner addresses you wrote for 2.

4. Body:
   Write a three-paragraph body for a business letter to the Canadian Motorcycle Corporation, using the following details:

   Paragraph 1:
   • On a recent visit to a motorcycle shop, I picked up some information about your company.
   • I would like to build a minibike.
   • I need more information about the minibike kits you have available.

   Paragraph 2:
   • Please send me your brochures numbered 1605 and 1607.
   • If you have any further information that might be useful to me, please forward it also.

   Paragraph 3:
   • I have included $2.00 to cover the cost of the brochures and of mailing.
   • Please forward this information at your earliest convenience.

5. Complimentary Close
   • Write three complimentary closes you might use in a business letter. Be sure to use punctuation and capital letters properly.

6. Take the appropriate parts you wrote for 1 to 5 and put them together into a letter to Ms. Sandhu at the Canadian Motorcycle Corporation. Use today's date for this letter. Use the "encl." abbreviation to indicate you have enclosed your cheque for $2.00.

As you work, remember to space the parts of the your letter properly and "frame" your letter on the page. This guide will help you:

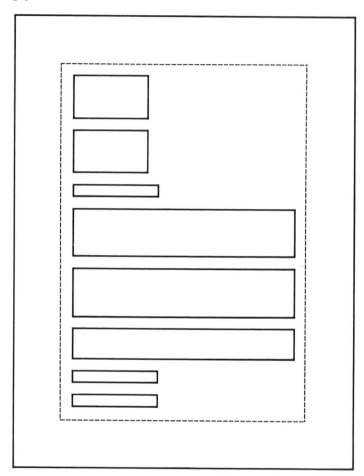

Format for a Business Letter

Activity 7D   Thoughts About Business Letters

How many purposes can you think of for writing business letters?

1. Brainstorm with two or three other students, using the following outline to guide you.

2. Appoint someone in each group to record the suggestions for each of these categories:

   a. Letters to businesses:
        purposes:
   b. Letters to newspapers and magazines:
        purposes:
   c. Letters to government officials:
        purposes: ·
   d. Letters to clubs or groups:
        purposes:

Activity 7E   Your Own Business Letter

Look at all the suggestions for writing business letters on this page.

1. Choose a situation that appeals to you.

Write to the Canadian Cancer Society, 200 Melrose Avenue, Ottawa, K1Y 4K7, asking for information on the dangers of smoking.

d. Write to the Prime Minister of Canada, House of Commons, Ottawa, K1A 0A6, and let him know how you feel about nuclear power, acid rain, money spent for space exploration or for foreign aid, or . . . another issue that concerns you.

f. Write to your favourite author and ask any questions you may have about the book he or she has written. If you do not know her or his address, try writing her or his publisher, or ask the Writers' Union of Canada, 24 Ryerson Avenue, Toronto, Ontario M5S 1M5 to forward your letter to the author.

Write to the Philatelic Service, Canada Post, Ottawa, K1A 0B5, asking how you can receive First Day Issue stamps.

c. Write to your Member of Parliament, House of Commons, Ottawa, K1A 0A6, asking for information on an issue of importance to you.
Remember: letters to Members of Parliament do not require any postage!

e. Write to your local radio or television station to express your views on programming, or to request publicity for an upcoming school event of community interest (include a brief written announcement the announcer can use). Find addresses in the telephone directory.

2. In your notebook, write down as many ideas as you can that could be included in your letter.

3. Share your ideas in groups of two or three. Help each other by suggesting additional ideas that could be included in the letters.

4. Think about the person(s) to whom you are writing. What kind of business letter will this person or persons expect to receive?

5. Make a first draft copy of this letter, keeping in mind the purpose and intended audience.

6. When you have drafted this letter, work on revising with a writing partner:
   a. Exchange letters and read each other's letter.
   b. Has your partner:
      • used the correct format: heading, inner address, salutation, layout of the body, closing and signature?
        If not, add your corrections.
      • expressed the purpose of the letter clearly in formal, businesslike language?
        If not, make some possible changes.
      • kept the paragraphs short to help the reader process the information quickly?
        If not, show your partner how to change the paragraphing in the letter.
      • used proper business letter punctuation? This includes:
        — periods with abbreviations such as St. and Ave., Mr. or Ms.
        — commas between city and province in the address and after the complimentary close
        — hyphens (or periods) in the dates
        — a colon in the salutation
      • Write notes in the margin of the letter to point out two things about this letter that you believe your writing partner did well.

7. When you get your own letter back, look first at the notes that tell you the good things you did in writing this letter.

8. Next, look for any suggestions or corrections your writing partner added.
   Do these suggestions and corrections make your letter better? If so, use them. If not, forget about them. After all, you are the owner of this letter and you must make the final decision about what goes in it.

9. Write a finished draft of your letter, putting it in final form for mailing.

10. If necessary, ask your writing partner to proofread your work. If you are still in doubt, ask someone else to proofread it.

11. Don't forget the envelope! The proper format for an envelope is shown in the one used for Mark's letter to Postarama Limited. For business letters, use *business* or *legal* size envelopes.

```
M. Wong
50 Grassington Crescent
Bramalea, Ontario L6S 1Z6


                    Postarama Limited
                    P O Box 370
                    Station "C"
                    Montreal, Quebec H2C 4K3
```

Remember to space the information on the envelope properly:

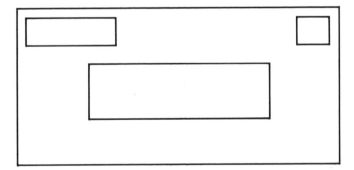

When these letters are completed and before they are mailed, you may wish to make copies of them for a classroom display. It would also be interesting to display answers to these letters as they come in.

Winding Up

Now that you have had practice writing business letters, you will find it much easier to send away for the information or items you want. Remember that the more clear and well-written your letter is, the more likely you will be to get a useful response to it.

LINK 8 A

In Chapter 5, you learned about some group discussion skills. This activity helps you look at the role the **leader** plays in a **group discussion**.

A group leader may be appointed to that job. Or a leader may emerge from a general group discussion, as someone capable of giving direction and purpose to the group.

1. In a small group of four or five students, appoint someone to take on the role of discussion leader and appoint another student as a recorder.

© 1974 United Feature Syndicate

2. In the role of leader, one student will guide a group discussion of the above cartoon:
   a. Help the group decide what question(s) it would like to discuss about this cartoon.

Suggestion: What message does this cartoon give about modern society? Do you agree with this message?

b. Call upon a group member to make the first comment about the question(s) defined in a.

c. Ask another group member what he or she thinks of this first comment and what might be added to this comment.

d. Continue asking and receiving responses to this first comment as long as group members have something to say.

e. Ask a group member to make a second comment about the question being discussed.
   Note: This second comment could be the opposite point of view from comment 1.

f. Continue to ask and receive comments and ideas about comment 2, until the group runs out of ideas.

g. Continue until all ideas have been given to the group.

h. Ask a member or members of the group to summarize the ideas presented in this discussion.

3. Ask the recorder to prepare a summary of the group discussion for the whole class.

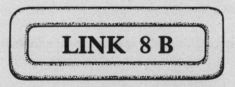

LINK 8 B

As a small group, repeat the procedures outlined in Link 8 A, with another student appointed to the role of group leader.

1. Discuss the meaning of the following cartoon and what it says about modern society.

© 1967 United Feature Syndicate

2. Report the group's ideas to the whole class.

LINK 8 C

Continue with your small group discussions, with still another student taking the role as a leader.

1. As a small group, discuss the meaning of the following cartoons and determine what they say about the modern world.

2. Be prepared to report your ideas to the whole class.

"How are you going to explain 'counterclockwise' to a kid who has seen only digital watches?"

Suggestion: Continue with these small group discussions until all members of your group have had a chance to practise the role of group leader. You might use the following ideas as sources for discussion topics: current events, a literary selection, television, movies, sports teams.

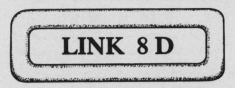

When you are speaking, you often use **inflection** to communicate meaning. Inflection refers to the rising or falling sound of your voice as you speak.

Example: A rising inflection suggests a question.

I walked a mile?

A falling inflection suggests certainty.

I walked a mile.

1. Work at these sentences in pairs.
   a. Person A says the first sentence, with rising inflection, to ask a question.
   b. Person B says the same sentence, with a falling inflection, to make a statement.

   Sentences:
   • I got the correct answers
   • My mother believed you
   • You think he's guilty
   • You have the correct answer

   c. Reverse roles and practise the sentences again.

2. In pairs, play a game of **word tennis**.
   a. Person A serves a question, with rising inflection.
   b. Person B returns the serve by providing an answer, with the appropriate inflection, as quickly as possible.
   c. Person A then asks another question, and so on.
   d. The server has three seconds during which to ask a new question once the second player has returned the answer. If the server fails to return the question within three seconds, then the serve changes sides.

e. If the receiver takes longer than three seconds to answer the question, or if the receiver uses the wrong inflection, the server earns a point.

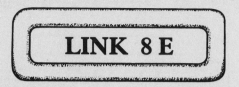

LINK 8 E

Another concern involved in speaking is that of **pronunciation**. You are expected to use **standard pronunciation** in most situations in which you give a speech.

Try saying these words, using the rhyming guides to help you:

Word Often Mispronounced	Correct Rhyming Word	Incorrect Rhyming Word
1. just	must	fist
2. get	let	lit
3. for	more	lure
4. again	men	bin
5. any	Benny	skinny
6. poor	sewer	more
7. sure	sewer	fur
8. can't	ant	faint

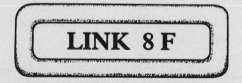

LINK 8 F

Here is a more difficult task with **standard pronunciation**.

1. One student will say one of the following pairs of words.

2. The other students in the class will decide which of the two words was given.

Column 1	Column 2	Column 1	Column 2
a. weather	whether	f. what	watt
b. ate	hate	g. ladder	latter
c. wandered	wondered	h. win	when
d. adapt	adopt	i. madder	matter
e. wear	where	j. accept	except

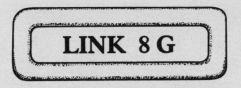

LINK 8 G

Here is a discussion topic. The British novelist Joseph Conrad is credited with this quotation:

Give me the right word and I will move the world.

1. What does Conrad mean in this quotation?

2. Has anyone ever found the right word?

3. What are some examples of people who have found the right word and have moved the world, or at least part of the world?

   Hint: Start your discussion with some of the slogans used to advertise products on television.

20 cents

The Universal Star

16 Marz 2014.11

Weather: METEORITES WITH SOME RADIOACTIVITY. ICE CLOUDS ON MARS II. OTHERWISE ALL SPHERES CLEAR.

MOON CAUSES WAVES & QUAKES

At 3:00 PM today, Jupiters' 3rd moon Europa, suddenly and mysteriously pulled away from the orbiting planet resulting in near catastrophe. The planets southern half was flooded in mass tidal waves, the northern half devastated with numerous Jupiter quakes. The estimated death toll is over 9000 and all the planet jupiter is considered a disaster area. This has been the worst disaster in this planets history. Each planet of the galaxy will give Jupiter a grant to help in the rehabilitation. Noted scientists of Jupiter do not know why the moon was pulled out of orbit, but they believe the moon is floating around in space. No foul play is suspected.

Jupiters 3rd moon Europa, before it left Jupiters orbit mysteriously. The scientists of Jupiter don't know where the moon went or how it got there. Intercepters were sent to find it.

-PX PRESS

TARNUCKS WIN

After trading Don Lever and Brad Smith to Saturn for Ivan Boldirev and Darcy Rota, the Tarnucks have finally won a hockey game. They beat the Martians 4-1, in a spectacular show of teamwork. Thomas Gradin and Stan Smyl had one goal apiece while Rick Vaive pulled a hat trick. Rick MacLeish scored the only goal for the Martians. Coach Harry Neale of the Tarnucks was quoted as saying, " This is only the beginning of a winning spree".

The next Tarnuck game will be aired at 7:00 pm Tuesday, Marz 23, on Channel T of your video screens.

SHIPS INTERCEPT MOON

The moon has recently broken away from Jupiter. It is a danger to surrounding planets and a threat to all space travel. At any time the moon could collide with a space shuttle or even a planet. The United federation has taken action to send three space shuttles equipped with lasers and photon torpedoes to intercept the moon before it causes any damage. The shuttles left early today. At departure Captain Rogers was heard to say, "It will be a tough job, but we can handle it".

-PXP

BAD SLOPES NO HOPES

Skiing on Mars is the worst it has ever been. To date the total snow fall is 89cm and that is barely enough to cover the rocks. Investors say they are losing $2600.00 per day because so few people are taking to the slopes. Rumor has it the mountains will be closed down completely unless there is an abundant snowfall.

★ INDEX ★

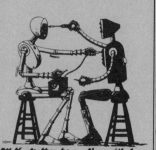

★ Celestial Trivia ★

FAMOUS QUOTES

We used to think that if we knew one, we knew two, because one and one are two. We are finding out that we must learn a great more about "and". Arthur Stanley

He uses statistics as a drunk man uses lamp posts for support rather than illumination. Andrew Lang

All the better to see you with!

EDITORIAL

Dear Editor,

We did not like the sarcastic humor in last weeks paper. The jokes your paper made about our planet were distasteful. We hope your paper doesn't print any more jokes of that nature, or we will stop buying it. D. T. WERT Mars

Dear Editor,

I would like to see more stories on the technology of earth. I realise that earth is a bit behind, but I would like to know just how far behind they are. F. R. Smart galaxy X

Dear Editor,

It was a dark and stormy night, suddenly a shot rang out. A door slammed, a maid screamed, a pirate ship appeared on the horizon. A king lived in luxury while millions of people starved. Meanwhile, on a small farm in Kansas a boy was growing up. A light snow had fallen and the girl in the red tattered shawl had not sold a violet all day. At that very moment, a young intern at City hospital was making an important discovery. The mysterious patient in room 213 had finally awakened. She moaned softly. Could it be that she was the sister of the boy in Kansas who loved the girl in the tattered shawl, who was the daughter of the maid who loved the King that escaped from the pirate?? The Intern frowned........

That was a story my younger sister wrote. It won her a trip to the moon. I think it is a great story. How about you? DP Gills - VENUS PRESS.

Thanks for all letters & cards.
David Allsop -EDITOR-

THE EARTH PLANE, TOTAL LUXURY, FUEL EFFICIENT, BUT SLOW.

EARTH NEWS

Earth's transport trends will veer away from the latest technology, and will turn back to the slower and more graceful travel era of airships and sailing vessels. The universal idea of seeking progress from the past belongs to three noted naval architects. They have been given a grant of $20,000. from the government of Earth to develop their Super-schooners. "We are confident we can design commercial sailing ships superior to modern vessels in many respects" said Joe Madison one of the architects.

Madison, who headed up the first sailing project, adds that the sailing ships could save four millions barrels of fuel that is now used by motorized cargo ships per day. With the rapid increase in the cost of air travel, one new design which is being considered is a throwback to the days of gracious travel aboard huge luxury airships which glide smoothly across the ocean. "We had the neccessary technology to do this in 1974, but noone had put it into use" says Morris Francis, an aerospace engineer. He sees the airship as a luxury liner, 1,000 ft. long and equipped with every item requires for comfort from sleeping cabins to swimming pools. It could fly across the Pacific Ocean in one and a half days giving the passengers two full nights sleep. The airship

would use one tenth the fuel of a jetliner and this would cut the price of fares. The airship would be equipped with non-flammable helium airbags to keep it afloat.

Not all travel looks to the past. Already in the making is an incredible laser-like train which will tear across the continent at a scorching 14,000 miles per hour. The Planetran is designed to whisk passengers along a electro-magnetic wave from Vancouver to Halifax in just 21 minutes.. Riding on a cushion of air that suspends it just six inches off the surface of an enclosed tunnel system, it will shoot through a tube as if it were caught up in a vacuum. However, for the immediate future, travellers will still have to rely on the jetliner, which will become larger and slower. New jets are already in the air for tests. The emphasis on these new jets will be on fuel economy........ © TY PRESS.

CHAPTER 8

DATELINE 2100

No one needs to tell you how quickly the world is changing. Each day you hear of new discoveries and of new ways of doing things. Many of these new things affect you personally.

In order to keep track of what is going on in the world, you talk to people around you, watch television, listen to the radio, and read magazines and newspapers. The **mass media** — such things as television, radio, magazines, and newspapers — give you information and provide you with entertainment. They help you think about the present and the future. And they, too, continue to change as new and more efficient communication methods are developed.

For example, what might a newspaper look like two hundred years from now? How will it arrive at your home? Will newspapers even exist two hundred years from now? As you study this chapter you will have an opportunity to think and talk about the future of newspapers. Working together, you will learn about writing news stories and about laying out material for newspapers.

HERE COMES THE FUTURE

Taking the Future Seriously

People have become so interested in the future that English has develped a new word — **futurology** — to describe the study of it. Futurologists make predictions based on a knowledge of the present. They suggest ways our society can or should change.

Here are some predictions for the twenty-first century and beyond made by futurologist Gordon R. Taylor:

— Improvement of intelligence in people and animals
— Prolongation of youthful energy as people grow older
— Control of aging and extension of life
— Direct links between human brains and computers
— ''Cloning'' or copying of individual animals and persons
— Indefinite postponement of death

Taylor's Predictions Gordon R. Taylor

Activity 8A   Predictions for the Future

1. **Form a discussion group with two or three people in your class.**

2. **As a group, talk about each of Taylor's predictions:**
   a. **What would be the *advantages* of each of these things?**
   b. **What would be the possible *disadvantages* of each (if any)?**

3. **Now discuss the predictions:**
   a. **What would be the effects of each of these things on our society?**
   b. **If you could choose to live in a world with only three of these possible future realities, which ones would you choose? Why?**

4. **On your own, write a summary of your group's responses in your notebook.**

5. **Choose one member of your group to report your findings to the whole class.**

6. **Listen carefully and write down any interesting insights the other groups came up with.**

Storytellers Like the Future Too

Science fiction writers study the future in their own way. They provide you with stories and films that stimulate your thinking about what the world might be like a hundred or more years from now.

Here is a day in the life of Joe Schultz:

In Lambeth, Ontario, it was one of a lifetime of identical days for everyone, including Joe Schultz. Having finished his work at the antique furniture plant, Joe decided that he wanted the company of an autoteria rather than the drab silence of his bachelor roomette. Prices were the same whether you slipped your ID card into the slot at homes or at the autoreria — the main difference was that you could see the actual rows of offerings rather than mere pictures, and there was life, such as it might be, around you. Moreover, there were opportunities for an enterprising man like Joe. He had punched his choices, picked them up at the robo-cashier's desk, and noted with some discomfort that his receipt was blue, though it was still nearly a week till "pay day" rolled around. Well, he thought, often enough he was on the red by this time, and had once or twice even had to go through the lengthy routine of securing extra credit to be placed against his account a few days before pay day. And he was one of the fortunate ones: he actually performed physical work of a certain specialty, thereby gaining a little higher credit in his account.

Adapted from H.A. Hargreaves, "Dead to the World," in *North by 2000.*

Edmonton should have seemed relatively small and uncomplicated, with a mere million inhabitants, yet Jason found his apprehensions had been at least partly justified. He had come in by monorail from Red Deer, near the school, and the trip had been pleasant until the last few minutes, when he'd watched the gap narrow between himself and the motorway stretching back to Calgary. The hairs had risen on the backs of his arms and neck, under his new swagger suit, as he watched northbound traffic beneath, moving nearly as fast as their own 200 kph. Even moving along the pedexpress to Leacock Manor, his new home, he felt vaguely uncomfortable, as if after all this time he should still be somewhere prowling the sub-levels. The lobby of the Manor was no help either. He'd been escorted to the office by a supercilious and disapproving manager, obviously put out at having to come and open to his ring.

H.A. Hargreaves, "Cain n," in *North by 2000.*

Activity 8B   The World of the Future

1. Write answers to these questions in your notebook.
   a. There are three words in the previous selections that describe possible future inventions. Write down one and give a brief description of what it does and what it might look like.
   b. In four or five sentences, describe the kind of world Joe Schultz lives in.
   c. Explain why Jason was nervous about his trip from Calgary to Edmonton.

2. Discuss your answers in class. Listen carefully and write down any additional points that arise in class discussion.

3. End your class discussion by deciding whether the future worlds that Joe and Jason live in have solved all human problems. If there are any problems, what are they?

Now It's Your Turn

You can construct your own picture of the future just as these writers and cartoonist have done. Think of all the movies you have seen and books you have read that are set in the future. You can use some of the ideas from them to help you create your own unique view of the future.

Activity 8C   *2100 A.D. — A Day in the Life of . . .*

1. Working with your writing group, discuss what a day in the year 2100 might be like. Be sure to appoint a recorder to write down your ideas. Choose a group leader if necessary.

2. Use the following questions to help you, but don't let them restrict you. They are only a guide:
   a. What will Canadian cities be like in 2100?
   b. What kind of homes will Canadians live in?
   c. What will education be like?
   d. What will people do for sport and entertainment?
   e. What will be the chief means of transportation and of communication?
   f. What inventions will make life easier?
   g. What will Canadians eat and wear?
   h. What issues and news might interest Canadians in 2100?
   i. What will it be like to live in the world in 2100 A.D.?

3. Choose a spokesperson for your group and join forces with one other group to talk about your ideas.
   a. When both spokespersons have presented each group's ideas, allow all students to join in the discussion.

4. When your discussion is finished, return to your original discussion group and have your recorder make notes as your group summarizes the discussions you have had.

5. Get a copy of this summary from your recorder so that you can keep the information handy. You will need it later.

NEWSPAPERS NOW AND IN THE FUTURE

News From the Future

More than any other **mass medium**, the **newspaper** reflects day-to-day life and people's interests in a way that can be easily preserved for future study. You can go to the public library and, through **microfilm** or **microfiche** — a method of reducing print for easy storage and retrieval — drop in on any day in the past, or at least for as long as newspapers have been published.

Right now, you are going to use the newspaper to drop in on the future. Producing a future newspaper from a typical day in 2100 will enable you and your work group to express your ideas about the future.

Think of what a future newspaper itself might be like. Today's newspapers present news, comics, advertising, pictures, classified advertising, and articles and letters from three major sources: newspaper staff reporters, freelance writers, the newspaper's readers, and wire services such as Canadian Press (CP) or Associated Press (AP). These wire services send news from different parts of the world to newspapers over teletype machines. Material is laid out in different sections, printed, and then delivered to your home or to your local store. Some newspapers, such as *The Globe and Mail*, are national. Satellite transmission allows them to be beamed to printing presses in different parts of the country, where they are printed and sent out for distribution.

Satellites beaming whole newspapers to presses around the country represent the latest newspaper technology. But how might newspapers change by 2100?

Activity 8D Newspapers of the Future

1. Get together with a discussion group and choose a group leader and a recorder.

2. Discuss how newspapers might be assembled, printed, and distributed in the year 2100.

3. Use the following points as discussion starters.
   a. Will computers affect newspaper production?
   b. Will newspapers need to be delivered door-to-door?
   c. Will readers be able to assemble their own newspapers using computerized information sources?

4. Store your group's ideas with your notes on the future from this activity.

Newspapers Today

As a basis for producing your newspaper of the future, you should be familiar with today's newspapers. You will probably use many of the current characteristics of newspapers to produce your future newspaper.

Like all kinds of communication, newspapers are directed at specific audiences and fulfill definite purposes. For example, *The Financial Post* gives business people information they need about the economy. The *Saskatoon Star-Phoenix*, the *Halifax Chronicle-Herald*, or the *Victoria Times-Colonist* are published daily and they inform, entertain, and try to appeal to a broad spectrum of readers, young and old. *The National Enquirer* is directed at readers who like to be entertained by off-beat stories about famous people and stories of strange occurrences. It is an example of a **tabloid**. Tabloids are printed on newsprint cut to one-half the size of regular newspapers.

Activity 8E Newspapers of Today

1. Think of as many newspaper titles as you can and list them in your notebook.

2. Beside each title, write down that newspaper's intended audiences and the communication purposes you think that newspaper aims to fulfill.

3. If you have the opportunity, visit your public library or newsstand so you can add to your list.

a. Spend some time looking at newspapers with which you are not familiar.

b. Try to determine what the intended audience and communication purposes for these newspapers are.

c. Add these newspapers to the list in your notebook.

Daily and Weekly Newspapers: What Can You Find?

When you put together your future newspaper, you may wish to include a variety of articles and features. Since most daily and weekly newspapers are aimed at a wide audience, they try to present a variety of material to meet different needs and interests. The newspaper, perhaps more than any other mass medium, tries to be all things to all people.

Activity 8F   Inside a Newspaper

1. Bring a copy of a daily or weekly newspaper to class.

2. Working with your discussion group, make a list in your notebook of all the sections and different kinds of material represented in your newspapers.

3. Discuss and make a note of which kinds of material your group would like to include in its newspaper of the future.

Newspaper Layout

Newspapers have to be assembled and printed quickly. Deadlines are very important because news soon becomes old. For this reason, newspapers are laid out in columns to give editors flexibility. Some articles are laid out one column wide while others may be double-column. Pictures may be one or even four or five columns wide in a standard six-column newspaper.

Activity 8G   Parts of a Newspaper

1. Look at the newspaper front page on the next page.

2. Match the letters on the newspaper page with the definitions given below. Write the answers in your notebook.

The **banner** supplies the name of the paper and information about where and when the newspaper is published.

_____ **Ears** are boxed-in pieces of information near the banner.

_____ A **banner headline** stretches right across the front page.

_____ A **headline** is the title that usually accompanies each story.

_____ A **kicker** appears just above a headline and is usually underlined. It provides additional information about the story.

_____ A **cut** is a photograph, chart, or illustration.

_____ A **cutline** appears near a cut — usually below it — and explains its content.

_____ A **byline** gives the name of the person who wrote the article. If no byline appears, the story may be identified by wire service and place of origin (e.g. Ottawa (CP)).

DATELINE 2100

Writing News For Your Future Newspaper

News stories usually begin with the most up-to-date or important information and go on to provide background details and points of lesser importance. Unlike stories that build to a climax and hold you in suspense, news stories give away the main story in the **lead**, the first one or two paragraphs. The rest of the story explains the lead. This method of writing is sometimes compared to a "pyramid." The story below is organized in this way and has been purposely shaped like a pyramid to remind you of its organization.

There are two main reasons why news stories are organized in this way. One reason is that editors have to make stories fit the available space in a newspaper. By placing facts of lesser importance at the end of a story, a writer makes it possible for an editor to shorten it without eliminating the most important facts. A second reason is that newspaper readers tend to skim stories. They want news quickly. A lead that gives all the important facts makes for easier newspaper reading.

Leads usually answer some or all of what reporters call the five *W's and the H: who, what, where, why, when, and how.* Here is a story from one student's future newspaper presented as an example of the pyramid style of writing. As you read it, consider its organization or structure.

MEDICAL BREAKTHROUGH
TO INCREASE LIFE EXPECTANCY

by Phyllis Watts

Scientists
at the Medical
Research Centre in
Toronto have announced a
breakthrough in their study of the
human aging process.
The breakthrough involves a reversal in the
hormone sending function of the pancreas and
and could ultimately lead to immortality.
Dr. A.J. Hakkinen, director of the Centre, said that "this
development could result in an increase of between 10 to 15 years in
human life expectancy." Life expectancy currently averages 125 years.
Researchers, while admitting that complications could arise, hope to begin treatments on volunteers as early as 2112. The Centre reports that it has enough funding
for this project to last until 2125. By then the hormone reversal treatment should be perfected.
Dr. Hakkinen reported that he would like to be one of the first people to undergo the treatment.

Activity 8H   A Look at a News Story

1. Answer the following questions in your notebook:
   a. Which of the five W's and the H does the lead of "Medical Breakthrough to Increase Life Expectancy" answer?
   b. What do you observe about the length of the paragraphs in a news story?
   c. What does the use of a direct quotation add to a news story?
   d. Why has the writer arranged the facts of the story in the way she has?

2. In your notebook, comment on "Flings Found to Cause Skin Disease."
   a. Note which of the five W's and the H are identified in the lead.
   b. Note which details are most important to the writer and which are of lesser importance.
   c. Suggest places where an editor could cut this story if there wasn't enough space to run all of it.

New Findings Confirmed

FLINGS FOUND TO CAUSE SKIN DISEASE

Montreal — The jet-propelled, knapsack-like flying devices that people have used for over 15 years have conclusively proved themselves dangerous.

Many reports have come in regarding the heated air expelled from the jet-propulsion engines. This dry heat often produces a terrible skin disease even if a safety suit is worn.

Many fling owners have been interviewed and have been found to have a rare skin disorder on their lower back and legs. They wore their safety suits, but somehow the gases penetrated the urethane-coated leather. All of these people need to have major skin grafts.

The signs of this skin disease include enlarged glands, a red rash, and large egg-shaped bumps on the skin.

The company that produces the 'tested' safety suits is being sued for millions of dollars because of this situation.

Scientists claim to be developing a new extra protective spray to coat the safety suits. Soon you will be able to use your fling, provided that your safety suit is well coated with protective spray.

Activity 8I   Space Probe — A News Story

1. Write a news story in your notebook, using the information below.

2. As you work with this information, be sure to do the following:
   a. Construct a strong lead using some or all of the five W's and the H.
   b. Keep paragraphs short.
   c. Feel free to add details of your own.
   d. Arrange details from most to least important.
   e. Indicate the end of your story by writing "-30-" after it, as newspaper reporters do. This number is a signal to the layout people that the story is finished and is omitted when the story is laid out in the newspaper.
      Here are the facts:
   - An object found only six hours ago on Mars is believed to be a space probe sent from Earth over one hundred years ago.
   - The find prompted a study of the scientific knowledge of Earth society one hundred years ago.
   - The object was discovered by engineers when the area was being made into a new supply station.
   - The probe is a crude machine assumed to be typical of the technology of one hundred years ago.
   - All records of Earth's scientific knowledge one hundred years ago were destroyed in the tragedy of 2006.
   - This is the first indication that humans have been anywhere except on Earth.
   - Scientists plan to continue their investigation.
   - "This is a tremendously important scientific find, ranking with the discovery of our solar system's fourteenth planet," said Professor Fred Lepkin of the University of Canada.

3. When you are satisfied with your story, trade with another student so that you can make suggestions to improve each other's work. Be sure to check the lead, paragraph length, and order of the details.

Your Own Newspaper

You are now ready to write some future news of your own. Working with the information gathered for Activity 8A your group should be able to put together an interesting look at a typical day in 2100.

Activity 8J Today's News: 2100 A.D.

1. Get together with your work group to plan your writing.

2. Review the ideas for the future that you created during your brainstorming sessions.

3. Divide up writing tasks among members of your group.
   a. You should each write two new stories dealing with one aspect of life in 2100. Here are some areas from which you might choose: world events, Canadian events, education, inventions, sports, entertainment, foods, fashions.
   b. Everyone should also choose one or two additional kinds of newspaper writing to work with: advertising, classified advertising, letters to the editor, an entertainment schedule, comics, a crossword puzzle.

4. Write a draft of your stories and the additional material.
   a. For news stories, review the guidelines for writing news stories.
   b. For the additional material, look at the format in the newspaper you brought to class for Activity 8G.

You don't have any wire services to work with, but you make one of your stories look as if it came to you over a news wire such as CP or AP. Invent a future wire service, if you wish. As you write, try to get a feeling for what reporters must go through each day: **gathering** material, **drafting** stories and features, and then **revising and editing** according to the wishes of the editor.

After you have finished drafting, you can each take on the role of editor and prepare your material for publication.

Activity 8K Work Party: Putting a Newspaper Together

1. Read your draft material aloud to another member of your writing group and make any necessary changes.

2. Read each other's material silently, making suggestions for revising and editing.
   a. *Revising:*
   Could anything be done to make the news stories more interesting or informative?
   • Does the lead arouse a reader's interest?
   • Does the lead directly state the appropriate parts of the five W's and the H?

- Are details arranged from most to least important?
- Are paragraphs short?

b. *Editing:*
- Are sentences well constructed and punctuated properly?
- Are words well chosen and spelled properly?
- Do all parts of the story fit together well, or does the flow from paragraph to paragraph need to be strengthened?

3. Return the material to the writer, along with your suggestions for revising and editing.

4. When the editor returns your material, read over the suggested changes or corrections and do any rewriting you think necessary.

Now that you have written your material and taken it through the important stages of revision and editing, you are ready to put it into a newspaper. Here is a chance to explore and create your own newspaper layout. As a group, you can make decisions about what your newspaper will look like and then plan the format you will use.

If you have poster board at your school, you may wish to use that for your newspaper pages. It comes in the size of a regular newspaper page (54 cm by 35 cm). You can type or print your material on paper in newspaper-column format and then glue the material to the poster board. It is probably best to lay out a page in four columns, each eight cm wide with a little space between each one.

If you do not have poster board, you might do your layout on long white typing paper in three columns of 6 cm each. If you want to make a smaller tabloid format, fold long typing paper in half lengthwise and turn it sideways. You then have four pages that you can lay out. Use smaller columns and type or print your material, gluing it to the layout sheet once you have finished arranging it.

Since future newspapers may be computer printouts printed right in your own home, you may simply wish to print out your stories on your school's computer or on a computer at home and lay them out in an interesting way. Your group can decide.

Activity 8L   Newspaper Formats

1. With your group, study the two pages from a student-made future newspaper on page 162 and on page 148. Discuss the following questions:
   a. How many columns do these students use?
   b. What kinds of pictures and illustrations do they use?
   c. Identify the ears, the banner, a banner headline, and cutlines.

d. How have the students written the headlines in their newspaper?

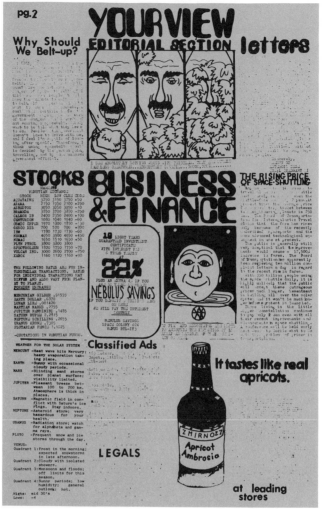

2. Gather your materials and plan your layout.

   a. Print or type your edited stories and other material in columns. For some things, you may wish to use double columns or even wider columns. See examples in a newspaper.

   b. Proofread your material very carefully and correct any errors.

   c. Write appropriate headlines or titles for your material.

   d. Draw or find appropriate cuts (pictures or illustrations) and write cutlines where necessary.

   e. Design a banner.
      • Give your paper an interesting name.
      • Don't forget other banner information such as the date. Choose a date in 2100.

   f. Lay out your material into pages.
- For your first page, decide on your lead story and whether or not to include a banner headline.
- Keep to news on the first page, and lay out remaining news and material on additional pages.
- Don't forget to provide space for your headlines and your cuts and cutlines.

   g. If you need any filler material to complete a page, write something or find a cut to fit the space to be filled.

3. When all the material is arranged, glue it to the layout sheet and then write your banner and headlines onto the layout sheet in the proper places. You might like to do one final proofreading to ensure everything is correct.

Enjoying Your Hard Work

The best part of producing a newspaper is getting other people to read it. The next activity provides you with some suggestions for distributing your newspaper.

Activity 8M   Extra! Extra! Read All About It!

1. Trade papers around the classroom and read each other's efforts. Talk about them as a whole class:
   a. Consider each group's ideas about the future as expressed in the news stories and features.
   b. Note how each group has made use of the newspaper format.

2. Send your newspapers to another class in your school and ask students in that class to write you a letter to the editor commenting on something in your newspaper.

Back to the Present

Dateline 2100 has taken you into the world of the future. It's time now to return to the world of the present and sign -30- to this chapter.

But first, a quick review of what you have learned. This chapter has given you some information about newspapers and how they are written. You have also learned the skills involved in writing for newspapers, particularly how to organize news stories. To do this you have had to work in groups and practise some group processes. To top it all off, you have done some thinking as a futurologist.

LINK 9 A

We are often in the position of wanting to record the details of an event or someone's talk. Let's practise taking notes.

You are standing on a sidewalk on Rose Street, and see the accident illustrated in the drawing.

1. Look at the drawing for one minute. Your teacher will tell you when to start looking and when to stop.

2. Try to remember as many of the details of the scene as you can. Be ready to answer these questions: Who, What, When, Where, Why, How — five W's and an H.

3. At the end of one minute, open your notebook and write down answers to the five W's and the H — *without looking back at the picture.*

4. In groups of two or three, compare the details you remembered. Did you all see the same accident?

   Extension:
   a. Look again at the scene and make a list in your notebook of all of the nouns you can find in this picture.
   b. Make a second list of all the verbs or actions you can see in this scene.

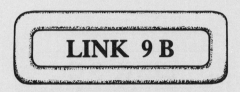

LINK 9 B

In Chapter 7 you learned that business letters should use standard rather than non-standard language. Chong has written this letter to the Chamber of Commerce in Edmonton, requesting some brochures and pictures of Edmonton for a social studies report.

1. Help Chong out by editing his first draft.

2. Feel free to change anything in the letter that you think could be improved.

3. Put in proper punctuation.

Mr J C Low
President
Edmonton Chamber of Commerce
689 Fourteenth St
Edmonton Alberta
T5R 1C7

322 Souris St
Saint John New Brunswick
E2K 1J3
85 04 22

Dear Mr J C Low

I have this here social studies project to do. I don't want to do a crummy job, so I thought maybe I would ask you if you have any brochures or pictures you could send me to help out my project.

If I could get some far out shots of good old Edmonton. I could →

tell my class what an awesome place it is. Y'know. I was there once, but it rained so much, I didn't get to see too many things.

Well, I guess I better go now. Thanks for the help.

Yours truly

Chong Huang

LINK 9 C

You have probably already learned how to write **friendly letters**. This activity reviews the format for friendly letters and also gives you a chance to do some creative thinking about how to mail a friendly letter.

This is a true account of someone who got some interesting results from letter writing.

PEN PAL IN A BOTTLE

For the past five summers, eight-year-old Christian Matossian of Montreal, Que., has been holidaying in Maine. And each summer he has been stuffing a note saying who he is and where he lives into a bottle and tossing it into the Atlantic. Nothing happened until last autumn when the bottle Christian threw into the sea in 1980 finally washed ashore on a beach 25,000 km away in Queensland, Australia. It was found by a very surprised tourist who immediately sent Christian a postcard, promising to write again. Christian can hardly wait to launch his next note-in-a-bottle. Who knows where his next pen pan might be!

Owl Magazine February 1982.

Christian has found a unique way to mail a letter.

1. Can you think of some novel or different ways of mailing a letter and getting a response? List as many of them as you can in your notebook.

2. Try out one of your methods and see if you get a response.

3. Make a classroom display showing your letter, telling about your mailing method, and showing the response if you receive one.

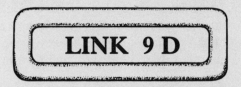

LINK 9 D

This activity reviews some of the basics of the structure of a paragraph. Words like *next*, *then*, *afterwards*, *second*, *third*, *later*, and *finally* show the order in which things happen.

1. Use these **order** or **transition** words to help you unscramble the following sentences and put them in proper order in a paragraph.

2. Look first for the sentence that starts the paragraph: the **topic sentence**. This sentence, like the title, should comment on or describe everything that happens in the paragraph.

3. Write your answer in your notebook.

Aunt Martha Goes Swimming

a. Then she would place her little toe in very slowly to test the water.

b. Finally, she would take the plunge and swim for a half hour without stopping.

c. When she went swimming, Aunt Martha was a sight to behold.

d. If the temperature was all right, she stepped in up to her ankles.

e. First she would come out of the change house and breathe deeply three times.

f. Then she stood for a long time before walking in up to her knees.

g. Later, when she came out, we would all laugh at this ritual of hers and she would always blush.

h. When she got to the edge of the lake she would look to her right and to her left to see who was near her.

i. Next she would strut like a mother hen toward the water.

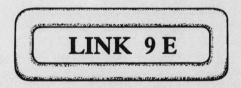

LINK 9 E

This activity gives you practice listening when there are distractions.

1. Four students go to the front of the classroom. Two students carry on a conversation. The other two try to distract them.

2. Student A has two minutes to communicate an idea to Student B. Student A should choose a topic that is quite simple and easy to talk about: the last book I read; last night's hockey game (or some other sport); why I hate/like something; last night on my favourite TV program . . .

3. Student B may help Student A with this conversation. But, *Student B can only ask questions.*

4. Students C and D try to distract Student B. They can use *only their voices*, but not in such a way that Student B has trouble hearing Student A. Here are some possible ways to distract Student B: carrying on a conversation; asking Student B a question; adding information to what Student A has said.

5. At the end of two minutes, Student B gives a summary of the information that Student A has provided. Student B is not allowed to include in the summary anything that students C and D have said.

6. The class watches this activity, and makes certain that Student B provides a complete and accurate summary.

Class Discussion

When you have done this activity several times, discuss these questions:

1. How hard is it for Student B to concentrate on Student A's message?
2. How hard is it for Student A to communicate with Student B with all of the distractions?
3. How do Students C and D feel about their roles?
4. Are there similar situations in real life?

LINK 9 F

To speak well, you must articulate or pronounce words clearly. Tongue twisters can help you to practise your articulation.

1. Work on these tongue twisters.
   a. As you repeat each one over and over, don't go for speed until you have accuracy.

b. Once you have a good amount of speed and accuracy, try repeating each one, stressing or emphasizing different words each time you say it.

Tongue Twisters

**The Shah saw Suzie's shoes
slogging so slowly she sought
to sink.**

**The skunk thunk the stump stunk,
but the stump thunk the skunk stunk.**

troy-boat (try repeating several times)

2. Have a class *twist-off*.
   a. Your class should divide into small groups.
   b. Each group should find a tongue twister that has not appeared in this textbook and choose its champion twister.
   c. The champion twisters from each group can compete for the class championship.

   Note: Marks should be awarded for these factors:
   • skill in delivering the twister
   • level of difficulty of the twisters
   • originality in selection of tongue twister
   • speed in delivering the twister

St Paul's Church, Halifax William Eager

This painting was completed about 150 years ago. Many interesting things have happened to this church over the years. One incident occurred during the Halifax explosion, December 6, 1917. Read this chapter on report writing to find out about ''the explosion window.''

CHAPTER 9

TELL ME ALL ABOUT IT

You may not write a short story or a poem after you leave school. But chances are fairly good that you will have to write a report of some kind. You will have to tell someone all about something in order to get some information across.

This chapter is about report writing. It outlines a method for doing this kind of writing task.

Report writing can be an enjoyable and informative activity. Writing a report enables you to learn a lot about your topic. You'll find new information, or you may look at old information in a way that you hadn't thought of before. And, of course, your report will provide someone else with information, and that person will learn something about your topic and something about you.

AN OVERVIEW

Let's imagine the worst possible thing that could happen to you. A two-headed monster from the depths of the ocean crawls out on the shore and says to you: "*Student, write a ten-page report about the mountain ranges on the floor of the ocean.*"

You stand there, by the edge of the ocean, watching the waves curl up on the shore. But you hear nothing. You are shocked. Dumbfounded, even. You cannot think. You can scarcely breathe. You must write a report. Ten whole pages. About mountains on the floor of the ocean. You've never seen these mountains. And what's worse — you don't even know where to look for them.

But, have no fear. Help is on its way. Out of the black clouds above you comes your benefactor, your means of salvation. In a quiet, gentle, confident voice, this benefactor says, "*Student, have no fear. We can solve your problem easily. All you need is — the system.*"

"*What system?*" you ask, with a quavering voice.

"*The system,*" says the benefactor with the same quiet, gentle and confident voice, "*that is in the universe. It pervades all. It is throughout, above, below, and in between.*" And then the benefactor's voice becomes more firm. "*The system will help you get this report written.*"

Here is the system that will help you with the task of writing a report.

The System

task	how to do it
1. *finding* information	read, talk, view, listen
2. *organizing* information	classify
3. *interpreting* information	think
4. *presenting* information	write

The first step in this sytem — finding information — gives you a choice of what to do. To collect information you can do two basic things: **ask about it** and **read about it**.

ASK ABOUT IT

If you want to find out information, you can do the logical thing: ask someone who knows. This method is a common way to collect information for report writing.

The more official name for the ask-about-it technique is the **questionnaire**. You are probably quite familiar with this technique. People who report the results of public opinion polls use it. They prepare a questionnaire and then use it to survey the opinions of many people. They collect the results of the questionnaire or survey and report their conclusions.

You will often hear information about our government reported in this way: 40% of the people surveyed agree with the government; 31% of the people disagree; 29% are undecided. Advertisements also use surveys to promote products.

It is important to know how surveys are conducted. If a survey reports that 59% of the people surveyed said that they preferred Brand X red toothpaste to Brand Y blue toothpaste — and the people in the survey have never used anything but red toothpaste, then the conclusion does not really tell you very much about how good Brand X is.

This problem of interpreting survey data will not be considered in this chapter. Rather, it will concentrate on the problems of creating and conducting a survey and reporting the information from it.

A Sample Questionnaire

Let's try out a questionnaire. Here is a question about the origins of the students in your classroom: *Does your class have a mainly rural background or a mainly urban background?*

To answer this question, and to provide some commentary about it, you can construct a questionnaire and survey the students in your classroom. This next activity takes you through the steps.

Activity 9A   A Questionnaire

Your teacher can conduct this survey, as you raise your hand to give your answer. Another way to conduct this survey would be to give each responder a copy and then tabulate the information when the forms are returned.

Responder's Name _____

QUESTIONNAIRE

Directions: Please use the following code to answer these questions —

rural community	100 people or fewer	small city	5000 to 75 000 people
village	100 to 500 people	large city	75 000 to 500 000 people
town	500 to 5000 people	major city	over 500 000 people

1. In what kind of community were you born?
   (a) rural community (b) village (c) town
   (d) small city (e) large city (f) major city

2. In what kind of community was your mother/female guardian born?
   (a) rural community (b) village (c) town
   (d) small city (e) large city (f) major city

3. In what kind of community was your father/male guardian born?
   (a) rural community (b) village (c) town
   (d) small city (e) large city (f) major city

4. In what kind of community was your mother's mother born?
   (a) rural community (b) village (c)town
   (d) small city (e) large city (f) major city

5. In what kind of community was your mother's father born?
   (a) rural community (b) village (c) town
   (d) small city (e) large city (f) major city

6. In what kind of communtity was your father's mother born?
   (a)rural community (b) village (c) town
   (d) small city (e) large city (f) major city

7. In what kind of community was your father's father born?
   (a) rural community (b) village (c) town
   (d) small city (e) large city (f) major city

The next step in conducting a questionnaire is to collect the information. The easiest way to do this is to construct a chart and record the answers from the questionnaire.

Activity 9B   Organizing Information

Make a copy of this chart in your notebook, and enter the results from the questionnaire in Activity 9A.

You might want to use a tally system like the one on the top of the next page to collect your answers.

Then make a final copy of the chart and enter the information or data in Arabic numbers.

ESULTS FROM QUESTIONNAIRE

	Students	Parents	Grandparents
(a) rural community	///	++++	++++ //
(b) village			
(c) town			
(d) small city			
(e) large city			
(f) major city			

Now you have your information organized and collected in a handy chart form. You can easily read your results. The next step is to interpret the information and provide conclusions from it.

Activity 9C Interpreting Information and Reaching Conclusions

Use these questions to examine the information you collected in Activity 9B.

Note: These questions are a guide only. You may find other questions and other answers in your information.

1. Where were most of the students born? parents? grandparents?

2. Were students and parents born in the same kind of community? students and grandparents? parents and grandparents?

3. What pattern(s) do you see in the kind of community students, parents, and grandparents were born in?

Does your information show any change from one generation to the next in the kind of community in which people live? (For example, you might notice a shift from one generation to the next from rural or small communities to larger urban communities.)

The final step in the system is to write up a report on your interpretations and conclusions.

Activity 9D   Presenting Information

Use this paragraph model to provide a short report on your survey. Copy this model into your notebook, completing the blanks.

Our class conducted a survey to find out what kind of community students were born in. In addition, we collected information about our parents and our grandparents.

We found that _____ percent of our students

were born in _____ . The other

students in our class were born in _____

_____ .

We found out that our parents _____

_____ . Our grandparents

_____

_____

From this information we conclude that there has (or has not) been a change in the kind of community in which people live. Our

survey shows _____ .

Activity 9E   Ask About It: Some Practice

Conduct a questionnaire on one of the following topics. Then organize your information, interpret it, and present it in a short report.

Suggested Topics

1. The similarities and differences in the number of books read by people in various age groups:
   under 8 years; 9 to 12 years; 13 to 15 years; 16 to 18 years; over 18 years.
   Note: You should try to get a sample of ten people from each age group. And you will have to put some time limitation on your

questionnaire, such as the number of books read during the past two weeks.

2. The number of people in various age groups who are dog lovers and the number who are cat lovers.

3. The favourite colours of people of various age groups.

4. Your own topic.

READ ABOUT IT

The second way you can find information for a report is to read about it. With this technique, you read from your source(s) and make notes. Then you think about your information and put together your report.

Making Notes

Most students have developed their own way of making notes for a report. Some use complete sentences, for example. Others just jot down key words from the passage that they read.

The technique in this section will help you get started. You should remember that it is only one way to make notes. Use the aspects of it that you find useful and add them to your own style of note-taking.

On Making Notes

1. Skim all of the material that you intend to make notes about. Then divide it into sections so that it is easier to work with.
   Note: Most books and other print material are already divided into sections, with headings or the spacing of the material on a page.
2. Read the first section of your source.
3. Write down the heading of the section if there is one. If there is no heading, you may want to make one up yourself.
4. Write words or phrases on your note paper to outline the information in the material you have just read. This information will include the ideas that are important to you.
5. Repeat this step for each section in your source material.
6. Repeat this step for any other source material you are using.

When you have collected all of the information that you want from your print sources, you are ready to begin to think about it.

The next activity will give you some practice in taking notes. The skills you develop here will help you in other subjects too.

Activity 9F   Making Notes

Follow the pattern for making notes for this passage about "The Explosion Window."

1. Read the entire passage through.
   Note: It is divided into two sections: (1) the explosion and (2) the church.

2. Read the first section, and write a one-word, or short heading for this section in your notebook.

3. With your textbook closed, write down words or phrases in your notebook that give the content or ideas from the first section. These should be your own words, not the words from the article. (If necessary, reread the section and close your book. Then write down in short phrases the ideas from the section.)

3. Repeat this procedure for the second section.

4. Next write a short paragraph in your notebook, using your notes, with this title: *The Explosion Window*.

THE EXPLOSION WINDOW

On December 6, 1917, two ships collided in the Halifax Harbour. One of the ships was loaded with ammunition . . .

For some reason best known to her captain, the Mont Blanc was not flying the red flag of warning for explosives. The Imo, a much larger ship, did not alter her course when signalled by the Mont Blanc. With collision imminent, the Mont Blanc cut her engines and tried frantically to alter course, but her load was so heavy she was slow to answer her helm. For a few seconds it seemed the collision might be averted; then, with a grinding crunch, the bow of the Imo struck the Mont Blanc and tore through the plating of her hold. Sparks showered everywhere and, under the horrified gaze of the Mont Blanc's captain, same drums of benzole burst open, spilling their deadly contents over the deck and through the gash into the hold. A sheet of flame swept across the deck. Stricken, the captain watched the fire spread. He gave the order to abandon ship and the Mont Blanc, with her lethel cargo, drifted helplessly toward Pier 6.

Unaware of the terrible danger, spectators gathered in rooftops and in the street to watch the flaming ship. The Mont Blanc hit the jetty and set fire to the wooden pilings and pier sheds on Pier 6. Then an horrendous explosion rocked the harbour, so savage and devastating in force that it was likened to the "thundering staccato roar and violence of a hundred typhoons." In an instant one square mile of Halifax — churches, schools, factories, stores and houses — was erased in a cloud of flying wreckage! 1,500 people died and over 7,500 were injured. Property damage to the rest of the city was extensive and hardly a window remained unbroken.

A wide crevice had opened in the roof of St. Paul's Church, but the stout oak and pine timbers — brought from Boston in 1750 — stood firm. When damage to the church was finally inspected, the strange phenomenon in the window was discovered.

In the disaster, the glass had shattered in such a way as to show the silhouette of a human head, an astonishing likeness of Abbe Moreau, an assistant minister of "Old St. Paul's" in 1750! So detailed is the remarkable "portrait" that ruffled strands of hair on the forehead and surplice collar can clearly be seen!

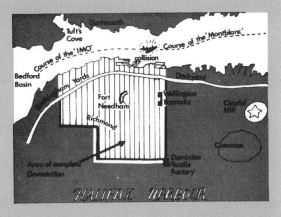

In striking contrast to the beauty of the stained glass windows adorning the west wall of the church, the Explosion Window is a pale and awesome souvenir, preserved and protected by a pane of plate glass. Each year hundreds of people come to visit the church. They stand on the sidewalk immediately below the window, or halfway up the aisle that leads to the Chapel, and gaze in silent wonder at the shape of a man's head in the glass, a tragic souvenir of a city's encounter with death and terror!

Betty Sanders Garner,
"The Explosion Window"

Organizing Your Material

Once you have made your notes, you must organize your material or give it a structure. You can begin to do this by looking for any patterns that emerge from your notes. This procedure is called **classification**.

The next few activities give you practice in classifying information. This will make it easier for you to classify or find a pattern in your own notes.

Activity 9G   Classifying: Some Easy Practice

1. Look at the socks in the picture below. Only two of them match. Which two are they? In order to do this exercise, you have to use your skill in classifying the attributes or characteristics of the socks.

Discussion: What attributes of the socks did you consider to find your answer? How did you go about finding the answer?

2. Find the *family name,* or the *classification,* which is included in each of these sets of words:
   a. ash, elm, tree, spruce
   b. jazz, music, classics, rock, pop
   c. cats, Persian, Siamese, Maltese
   d. childhood, stages, adolescence, middle age, maturity

3. Provide two words that classify each set of words:
   a. paper, papyrus, slate, screen
   b. horse, donkey, mule, pony
   c. Bach, Beethoven, Sibelius, Strauss

You have been classifying sets of words. That is, you have used your knowledge and understanding to organize groups of words by finding what is common among them. This one common word or idea has helped you to organize sets or groups of words and thereby given you some control over these words.

You do the same thing when you write a report. You classify ideas, and not just words. Classification gives you order and order gives you control over the ideas. If you have control over the ideas, you have accomplished an important step in report writing.

Activity 9H   Classifying: Harder Practice

1. Find as many ways as possible to classify the following list of items.
   Use the chart as a model to set up your answer.

wagon	train	airplane
canoe	car	toboggan
ship	rickshaw	horseback

Classification	Set of Words
water vehicles	canoe, ship

2. Look at the following list of words. Divide them into groups. Be prepared to explain the reason or reasons for your classification. Set your answer up using the same chart you used for 1.

province	ocean	date
history	waltz	border
wall	lacrosse	war
lake	government	treaty
plum	jazz	economics

   Note: The challenge is to see how many different ways your class can find to classify these words.

When you classified these groups of words, you chose the classification that seemed most logical to you. In other words, you found your own way of organizing these ideas. By ordering ideas in a way that makes sense to you, you are more likely to be able both to remember them and to make them do what you want them to.

Trying out the Read-about-It Method

This section gives you some practice with the **Read-about-it Approach** to report writing.

The information provided here is about Thanadelthur (Tǎn ə dĕl′ tər), a Chipewyan (Chip′ ə wī ən) Indian who lived about 250 years ago. It was the time of the beginning of the Hudson Bay Company in Canada, and its bid to establish the fur trade west of Hudson Bay.

Thanadelthur had been captured by the Cree Indians, who lived south of the Chipewyans, and had learned to speak their language. At this time, the white traders in the forts could understand Cree but not Chipewyan. Thanadelthur acted as an interpreter, connecting the European fur traders with the Chipewyan people. Here is an excerpt that describes her adventures.

THANADELTHUR

By Sylvia van Kirk

One of the few women to have been accorded a place in the history of the Canadian North is Thanadelthur, a remarkable Chipewyan Indian better known as the Slave Woman. Her fame rests on the successful outcome of an arduous journey undertaken for the Hudson's Bay Company in 1715–16. Several authors have told the story of how Company servant William Stuart with the aid of the Slave Woman negotiated a peace between the Cree and Chipewyan tribes which paved the way for the establishment of a fort at the mouth of the Churchill River. Little attention, however, has been given to Thanadelthur as a personality in her own right or to her position at York Factory after the conclusion of the peace mission as Governor James Knight's 'advisor.'

In the journals of York Factory, Thanadelthur is always referred to as the Slave Woman. She, along with others of her countrywomen, had been captured by the Crees in a raid upon the Chipewyans in the spring of 1713. The Crees, being the first to obtain guns from the traders, had gained the ascendancy in this tribal conflict and so devastating had their attacks been that one branch of the Chipewyans came to be known as Slaves. According to Chipewyan oral tradition, the Slave Woman's real name was Thanadelthur which meant 'marten shake'. The explorer Samuel Hearne, an astute observer of Chipewyan society in the later 18th century, recorded that girls were usually named after some part or property of the marten.

Although inaccurate in specific detail, it is notable that the story of Thanadelthur as handed down by the Chipewyans emphasized her youth and attractiveness. If Chipewyan women, in general, failed to conform to the Englishman's ideal of beauty, Hearne conceded that many were of 'a most delicate make' and 'tolerable' when young. Owing to her difficult way of life, a girl's beauty was particularly

old governor of York Factory, James Knight.

In the fall of 1714 when James Knight reclaimed the fort from the French under the Treaty of Utrecht, he was anxious not only to re-establish English trade but to extend it northward. The existence of the Chipewyans or Northern Indians was known, but their fear of the Crees prevented them from venturing to the Bayside. Knight's only contact with the Northern Indians was through his chance meeting with female captives held by the Crees. Thanadelthur was not the first 'Slave Woman' to seek refuge at York Factory. That fall another Chipewyan woman had escaped and made her way to the fort. The information she had given Knight about her country sealed his determination to establish a trade with the Chipewyans. This first woman sickened and died on 22 November. Knight was lamenting his loss when two days later, Thanadelthur was brought in 'Allmost Starv'd'.

She had a harrowing tale to tell. Earlier in the fall when camped on the north side of the Nelson River, Thanadelthur with another of her countrywomen had escaped from their Cree master, hoping to make it back to their people before the winter set in. They had only the catch from their snares to subsist on and when cold and hunger finally drove them to turn back, the two women clung to the wild hope that they might find the traders whose wondrous goods they had seen in the Cree camps. Only Thanadelthur survived. Several days after her companion had perished, she stumbled across some tracks which led her to the tent of the Company's

fleeting. Given in marriage when very young, the care of a family added to her constant hard labour rendering even the best-looking woman old and wrinkled before she was thirty. It is probable, therefore, that Thanadelthur was in her teens when captured by the Crees. Strong, young women constituted a valuable prize in Indian warfare since female labour was of such importance in a nomadic society. Apart from being 'a handsome young woman', Thanadelthur possessed a forceful and intelligent character — a combination which captured the interest of the doughty goose hunters at Ten Shilling Creek.

Knight was immediately impressed with his new informat who spoke encouragingly of her people and their rich fur resources. Even though her present knowledge of the Cree language was indifferent, she would be of 'great Service to me in my Intention' he wrote enthusiastically. To ensure the success of his plans, Knight realized that he must first endeavour to establish peace between the Crees and the Chipewyans. Early in June 1715, the Governor gave a feast for his 'Home' Crees and persuaded them to send a peace delegation to their enemies. They were to be accompanied by one of the Company's servants, William Stuart, and the Slave Woman. Bands of 'Uplands' Crees coming in to trade were also encouraged to join the peace mission, so that the party which set off on 27 June numbered about one hundred and fifty. Knight entrusted Thanadelthur, who was to act as interpreter, to the special protection of Stuart: he directed him to 'take care that none of the Indians abuse or Missuse the Slave Woman'. He gave the Chipewyan woman a quantity of presents to distribute among her people, instructing her to tell them that the English would build a fort on the Churchill River in the fall of 1716.

Thanadelthur, who readily appreciated the importance of her position, soon became the dominating spirit of the expedition. Stuart was amazed at the way she kept the Crees in awe of her and 'never Spared in telling them of their Cowardly way of Killing her Country Men.' Disaster stalked the enterprise, however. Slowed by sickness and threatened with starvation on the long trek across the Barren Grounds,

the party had to break up to survive. Most of the bands turned back, leaving only Stuart, the Slave Woman, and the Cree captain with about a dozen of his followers determined to find the Chipewyans. Failure seemed certain when Stuart's party stumbled across the bodies of nine Northern Indians, slain by one of the other Cree bands. Fearing the revenge of the Chipewyans, the remaining Crees now wanted to abandon the search.

At this juncture Thanadelthur seized the initiative. She persuaded the Crees that if they would wait ten days she would be able to find her people and return with them to make peace. She left the Crees to fortify their camp in case of attack and within a few days she came upon a large band of her countrymen. It required all her powers of persuasion to get them to return with her; she had to make herself hoarse 'with the perpetuall talking' before the Chipewyans would be convinced of the pacific intent of their enemies. In true epic fashion on the tenth day, Thanadelthur and two emissaries came in sight of the Cree camp. When Stuart came out to meet them and conduct them to his tent, she signalled to the rest of the delegation, over a hundred strong, that it was safe to approach. According to oral tradition, Thanadelthur was placed on a raised platform, 'so that her people could see her and have confidence. When she beheld her people coming, she sang with joy'.

With the help of the Cree captain, Thanadelthur once again assured her people that their party bore no responsibility for the recent unfortunate raid upon the Chipewyans and that the Crees were most anxious for peace. With those who remained doubtful, this forceful diplomat had no patience:

> she made them all Stand in fear of her she Scolded at Some and pushing of others . . . and forced them to ye peace.

William Stuart was full of admiration:

> Indeed She has a Divellish Spirit and I believe that if thare were but 50 of her Country Men of the same Carriage and Resolution they would drive all the Northern [Southern] Indians in America out of there Country.

Stuart's party arrived back at York Factory on 7 May 1716, accompanied by ten Chipewyans one of whom appears to have been Thanadelthur's brother. The Englishman emphasized that the mission owed its success to his remarkable Chipewyan ally who had been 'the Chief promoter and Acter' of it.

Activity 9I   Thanadelthur

Here is your writing task: *What kind of person was Thanadelthur?*

1. Read the excerpt from *The Beaver*.

2. Make notes as you read. Jot down any words you can find or think of that tell you about Thanadelthur.

   Note: You might consider using the thought web technique here, with the word *Thanadelthur* at the centre of the web.

3. Examine your notes and classify them. You should have about three major classifications, with the rest of your words included as part of these major classifications.

4. Write your report to provide a character sketch of Thanadelthur. Use these questions as a guideline to develop your report:

   Paragraph 1:
       What interesting way can you introduce the subject of your report?
   Paragraph 2/3:
       What information do you have about Thanadelthur that you found from your readings?
   Paragraph 4:
       What is your own personal comment about Thanadelthur?

REFERENCES

When you write a report, you are expected to include a **list of the sources** that you have read during your research. Another word for a list of references is a **bibliography**.

Here is an example of what your list of references might look like:

List of References

Crowe, Keith J. *A History of the Original Peoples of Northern Canada*. Montreal, Quebec: McGill-Queen's University Press, 1974.

Van Kirk, Sylvia. "Thanadelthur," *The Beaver* (Spring 1974) pp. 40–45.

Note

1. The references are listed in alphabetical order.
2. The second line, and all following lines, are indented so that the author's name stands out in the list.
3. The titles of books and magazines are underlined.
4. Quotation marks are used to note short articles such as those found in magazines.
5. A list of references is punctuated very exactly. Examine these two entries to look at the way they are punctuated.

A FINAL REPORT

You now know two methods to find information about a topic for a report: the survey and information from books. This activity provides you with the opportunity to put these two methods together to write a major report.

Activity 9J   A System for Writing a Report

Here is your writing task. Use a System for Report Writing to help you with your report. Remember that you don't have to follow it exactly. Feel free to make modifications to suit your particular needs and problems.

1. Write a report on one of these topics:
   a. The Value of Sport to Society
   b. The Value of Music (or Art) in Society

    c. Pets: Their Value

    d. Your Own Topic — with your teacher's approval

2. Use at least two sources to get information for your report. One of your sources should be a print source. The other may be a questionnaire.

3. Prepare your report and present it in written form.

A System for Writing Reports

Step 1:

    Choose your topic and decide how you can get information about it: print, questionnaire.

Step 2:

    If necessary, prepare and conduct your questionnaire. Choose your print source(s) and make notes on it.

Step 3:

    Organize the material from your questionnaire, if necessary. Organize the material from your print source(s).

Step 4:

    Interpret your information.

    Think about your information. What conclusions do your facts lead you to?

Step 5:

    Use the writing process to compose your report.

    1. Write a first draft of your report.

    2. Exchange reports with a writing partner.

       Read your partner's writing.

       • Write a short paragraph that could be used as the beginning paragraph for your partner's report.

       • Write another paragraph that could be used as the concluding paragraph.

       • Make up three titles your partner could use for his or her report.

    3. When you get your partner's writing back, examine it. Use from it what you like.

    4. Write the final draft of your report.

    5. Ask someone to proofread it for mechanical errors.

    6. Prepare your report to hand in to your teacher.

So, now if a two-headed monster crawls out of the depths of the ocean and challenges you to write a report, you know exactly what to tell it.

But even with the system, you may find that you have other problems writing reports . . .

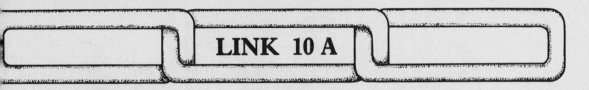

LINK 10 A

This activity provides you with another opportunity to hold a **discussion**. In Link 8A and 8B you used small group discussion to respond to some cartoons. This time, look at the *Cathy* cartoon below and hold a similar kind of discussion with the whole class participating.

1. What is Cathy's problem?

2. In what other situations might Cathy have the same problem?

3. Have you ever been in a situation where you couldn't get "the human element" to work?

4. To what extent is this kind of problem becoming a concern in society?

5. What are some solutions to this kind of problem?

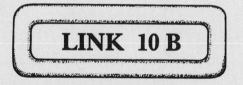

In Chapter 8, you learned what the abbreviation (CP) in a news story means. Here is a story taken from the CP wire service.

1. Read this article to find out about migraine headaches.

2. In your notebook, list as many words as you can to describe pain.

3. In small groups, brainstorm to create a list of words to describe each of these situations and write these words in your notebook:

   • how you feel when you are alone in your house at night
   • the taste of food that you don't like
   • the joy of winning a sport event or a music festival competition
   • the anger you feel when someone won't let you have your own way

4. Group or classify your word lists into types, as the doctors in the migraine vocabulary study have done.

Migraine 'vocabulary' studied

OTTAWA (CP) — Thousands who suffer from migraine headaches say there are no words to describe the pain, but psychology researchers at Carleton University here are trying to find some.

Blurred distinctions between various types of migraines often make it difficult for doctors to diagnose and prescribe effective treatments, says Dr. Jim Campbell.

But Campbell and graduate student Robert Schnurr are surveying more than 100 Ottawa-area migraine victims in hopes of devising a list of key words that could offer doctors some clues.

"People who suffer from migraines know how they feel," Schnurr says. "But it's hard to go into a doctor's office cold and just explain exactly what you're experiencing.

"If, however, they could key into a precise word on a prepared list, they and their physicians would be further ahead," he says.

There are three main migraine types: common, classic and cluster, says Campbell.

"A patient might says he has a throbbing pain, or a pulsating pain . . . we're hoping to put together a vocabulary common to the different headache types," Campbell says.

The university's "pain project" is still seeking volunteers.

Statistics indicate they should have plenty to choose from. The World Health Organization estimates 20 per cent of the population suffers from "migraine experiences."

SASKATOON *STAR-PHOENIX.*

Discussion: In class, list other situations for which it would be helpful to have accurate words to describe what is happening.

Reread a paragraph you wrote recently. Decide how you might have used words more accurately in it. Rewrite the paragraph in your notebook, changing at least twelve words so that they more accurately convey what you want to say.

HAVE YOU THOUGHT ABOUT USING A DICTIONARY OR A THESAURUS?

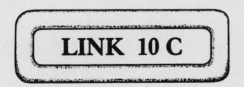

LINK 10 C

This activity will limber you up for some poetry writing in the next chapter.

1. Write in your notebook the name of a familar object. This object should be something you find interesting: a video arcade, a sports car, an old sneaker.

2. Describe your object in a thought web, using all five of your senses: taste, touch, smell, feel, sight.
   Example:

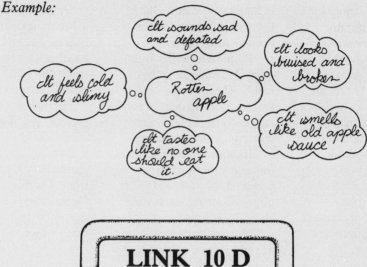

LINK 10 D

Maybe you have played a game called **word association**. This procedure can help you think of all kinds of words and ideas.

1. Your class should divide into small groups.
   a. Each person in the group takes a turn saying a word.
   b. The person on his or her right must respond with as many words or phrases as possible associated with that word.

2. Continue the game until everyone has had one turn giving the word and doing the word association.

3. Take notes while one pair is doing the association game and list all of the words suggested. Then arrange these words on a piece of paper to make a poster poem.

   Example:

   roller coaster

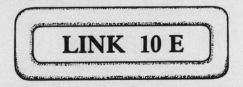

LINK 10 E

This activity will help you use word association and description to create images. **Images** are word pictures that describe something through comparisons. Here are some images in the form of similes. **Similes** are comparisons that use *like* or *as* to show how things are alike.

Example: The rain is *like* small silent hands.
The sun on the pond is *like* the shimmering of a million diamonds.

1. Write some sentences that contain images in the form of similes, using *like* or *as*.

   a. Arrange the words so that they become simile poems.

   > The rain
   >   is like
   >   small
   >   silent
   >   hands.

   b. After you have written several poems like this one, with a single image or simile, try poems that contain two or more similes.

2. Create some more comparisons using similes.

   a. Follow this model, using *as . . . as:*

   Examples:

   as slow *as* a snail going up the down escalator
   as jittery *as* a candle flame in a windy room

   b. Try these as simile starters, then write several more of your own

   as tired as . . . .
   as sparkling as . . . .
   as lifeless as . . . .
   as embarrassed as . . . .
   as slippery as . . . .

LINK 10 F

1. Using the example as a model, write your own simile poems about the picture below:

Example:

> They lept
> for joy
> like
> Slim gazelles
> and ran like furies
> into the wind

2. Write a simile poem that expresses your response to this photograph.

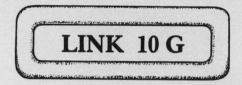

LINK 10 G

Sound words, as well as images, can help you create new and interesting effects with language. Some words make the sound of the actions they describe, like *swoosh* or *bang*. These words are called **echo words** or **onomatopoeia**. They can add vividness to your writing.

1. List as many words as you can for the following sounds:
   a. water sounds
   b. car sounds
   c. air sounds
   d. factory sounds

2. Create some of your own words for these sounds:
   a. rain on glass
   b. sucking through a straw when the milkshake is gone
   c. a motorboat running out of gas
   d. biting through hard macaroni
   e. chewing sticky toffee

3. Can you think of other sounds to imitate through words? List them.

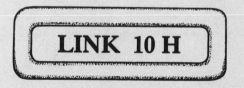

LINK 10 H

Another interesting language sound effect comes from alliteration.
   Alliteration occurs when words fairly close together begin with the same consonant sound.

   Example:

   The saws were shrieking
   and cutting into
   the clean white wood
   of the spruce logs

   W.W.E. Ross

The words *saws*, *shrieking*, and *spruce* alliterate, as do *white* and *wood*.

1. Write five descriptive sentences that use alliteration to help create their effect.

   Examples:
   The *long* and *level* desert stretched onward to the *lonesome* sky.
   How helplessly she felt as she *heard* the *haunting howl*.

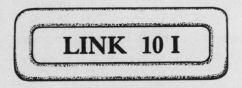

LINK 10 I

Another kind of image, in addition to the simile you practised in Link 10 E, is called the metaphor. **Metaphors**, like similes, create an image through comparison. But the comparison is more direct — without using like or as. Examples of common metaphors include such phrases as *He's a chicken* or *The villain in that movie is a real snake*. When you call someone a chicken, you don't mean that he or she is really a chicken. Rather, you associated chickens with showing fear. This is how metaphors work. They create vivid images:

The road was a ribbon of moonlight
   — Alfred Noyes

(Ribbons suggest something long and narrow.)

The black bat night has flown
   — Lord Tennyson

(Bats are associated with things many people fear at night and so the image creates a negative view of night.)

The pale, pale moon, a snow white doe
   — Isabella Valancy Crawford

(Does are soft and gentle, so the image creates a positive view of the moon.)

Each metaphor helps the writer create a clear word picture.

1. Try making some metaphors of your own for five of the following ideas.

Example:
love — a blooming, fragrant rose

a. hatred
b. love
c. loneliness
d. anger
e. peace
f. a tall tree

g. life in a big city
h. a baby
i. a flashy new sports car
j. an unexpected gift
k. a terrible storm
l. the moon

2. Write each of your metaphors into a sentence, and then turn it into a metaphor poem.

Example:
love — a blooming, fragrant rose
> Love grows
>> in me —
>>> a
>>>> fragrant
> blooming rose.

3. Use the example on the next page to help you write a metaphor poem about the picture on this page.

The snow-covered
 forest was a
  garrison of
   bare, lonely
    sentinels
     guarding the
      cold
       silence

4. Write two metaphor poems to describe your reactions to the picture
   on this page.

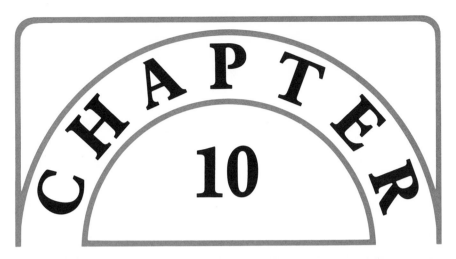

HERE YOU ARE IN A POEM!

PLAYING WITH WORDS

Poetry is special. It uses language to create patterns of sounds and images or word pictures. The pattern of sounds and images you create in making poetry lets you express your own thoughts and feelings about things in your own special way.

Poetry, more than most of the writing you do, lets you be a **word sculptor**. You can shape words into patterns as a sculptor molds clay or metal. In this chapter, you will have an opportunity to play with words and make your own poems. After you write your poems, you may work with your classmates to plan a poetry presentation so that you can enjoy your collective efforts.

Warming Up

In Link 10, you had an opportunity to do some word play activities that are good *warm-ups* for writing poetry. Continue to warm up your poetry power by exploring interesting things you can do with words.

Activity 10A   Sound-Word Webs

1. Make some *sound-word webs* in your notebook by thinking of as many words as you can with particular sounds:

| soft words | fast words | wet words | slow words | hard words |

Example:

2. Turn one of your sound-word webs into a poem by using your words to describe an object and save this poem in your writing folder.

Suggestions: a soft cat

a fast sportscar

a wet newspaper

Example:

> **The Weasel**
> **Cornered, it stood on its hind legs**
>   **hissing, a scratchy sound**
>   **slapping at the air**
>   **inflamed to fury,**
>   **finally growling until a full scream**
>   **boiled in its throat as it made**
>   **a dash for freedom.**

Activity 10B   Alphabet Poems

1. Read the following alphabet poem by Stephen Scobie.

> and apples
> and boats
> and ceilings
> and drums
> and evenings
> and feathers
> and golfballs
> and hilltops
>
> and islands
> and jesters
> and kisses
> and lots and lots of
>   marmalade
> and nonsense
> and orbs
> and poems
> and quizzes
>
> and raindrops
> and seahorses
> and trees
> and umbrellas
> and voices
> and waterfalls
> and X's on letters
> and yesterday
> and zoologists

2. Write your own alphabet poem, using different words. You may use *and*, as Stephen Scobie does, or you may use a different joining word, or coordinator, such as *or*, *but*, *either . . . or*. Save your alphabet poem in your writing folder.

Activity 10C   Thought-Web Poems

1. Choose one of the following as the centre of a thought web:

   I wish   **I dreamed**   **I used to be/Now I am**

2. Turn your thought web into a poem where each line begins with the word you placed in the centre of your thought web. Keep this poem in your writing folder.

   Example: *I wish* I had a fire red Ferrari
   I wish I could drive it down the winding road.
   I wish I could feel the wind stinging my eyes.
   I wish I could round the curves and feel the tires
      hugging the pavement
   I wish I could hear the squealing of rubber.
   I wish I could see the world whizzing by forever.
   I wish I could have you beside me.

Activity 10D   A Cat and Mouse Poem

Here is a real cat and mouse game.

1. In your notebook, create a thought web that suggests one of the following:
   a. what the cat is saying to the mouse
   b. what the mouse is saying to the cat
   c. a description of this moment of truth

2. Use your thought web to create a poem:
   • Try to capture interesting sound patterns.
   • Create an interesting rhythm with your words.

3. When everyone has written a poem, trade poems around the room to see the different *points of view* that have been created.

More About Words and Sounds

Now that you have had a chance to warm up by writing a few poems, continue to build your poetry power by taking a closer look at what you can do with words and their sounds.

Activity 10E   Sound Patterns

Poems are made up of sound patterns. Playing with sound patterns can help you hear new possibilities when you sit down to write.

1. Your class should divide into three groups.

2. Each group should choose one type of sound:
   a. Shushing, lulling sounds (*swoosh, zoom, droopy, shoes, sleek, slate* — lots of *l* and *o* sounds).
   b. Harsh, crashing sounds (*crack, clang, bam, pow*).
   c. Thin sounds that seem to spit from the mouth (*blip, ditty, clipper, tip*).

3. Working as a whole class, write these three categories on the board and suggest more words for each one.

4. When you have enough words in each category — preferably one for each person in each group — begin a *word sound orchestra*. Each group will act as a separate section, saying their list of words.
   a. Choose a conductor and establish some conducting signals to.
      • bring each group in or take it out
      • indicate *louder* or *softer* to each group
      • indicate *higher* or *lower* pitch to each group
   b. Let several people take turns being the conductor.

5. After performing together, choose *duets* and *trios* to perform. You could try mixing the words to make contrasts.

Activity 10F   Word Sound Orchestra

1. Try constructing a *word sound orchestra* based on different types of sounds: a haunted house, a snowstorm, a rusty gate.

    Select appropriate sound words for each idea. How about a word symphony of a rusty gate opening in a haunted house on a stormy night?

2. Use your orchestra to create joyful sounds or sad, wailing sounds.

Activity 10G   Chants

Create some chants with your orchestra. Chants are a very ancient kind of language word and sound play.

Here are two examples from songs that were popular a few years ago:

oo ee oo ah ah	pa pa oo mau mau
ting tang walla walla bing bang,	pa pa oo mau mau
oo ee oo ah ah	pa pa oo mau mau
ting tang walla walla bing bang.	(repeat . . .)

1. Try these chants in class, using various rhythm patterns.

2. Make up a series of interesting sounds and string them together into a chant that you can recite together.

3. You may wish to do further work in small groups, making up chants for the whole class to perform.

The point of these activities is this: *language has sound and rhythm patterns that writers can use to express themselves.*

Shapes as Well as Sounds

The poems you have looked at so far have used different **visual patterns** in addition to **sound patterns**. Let's experiment with some interesting ways of arranging words visually.

Activity 10H   Poster Poems

Try making some *poster poems* in your class:

1. Bring some old newspapers and magazines to class.
   Find a subject that interests you and cut related words out of the newspapers and magazines.

2. Experiment with different arrangements of the cutout words and decide on one arrangement that best communicates your thought or feeling.
   a. Choose words that sound good together.
   b. Focus on a particular thought or feeling.
   c. Arrange your words in an effective visual pattern.

3. Paste your arrangement of words on a piece of paper. Voila! You have a poster poem.

4. Share your poems by passing them around the classroom or by displaying them on your bulletin board.

Hot, dry weather

Walking through the

forest

Escape

roaring

furnace!

Jubilant   to   wet

crystal   air

Sometimes you don't have to look far for poetry. You can find poems. Here is a poem that was found in a sentence in a short story:

> *The sentence:*
> It was a very beautiful white pony, and as
> it went round and round the stage of the village
> theatre the two clowns would leap
> over its back or whistle to it and make it
> flap its ears and shake its long white mane.
>
> Morley Callaghan, ''The White Pony.''

Watch what happens when you give this sentence a new shape. It turns into a *found poem:*

```
        It was a
           very
             beautiful
                white pony,
                    d
                    n
                    a
     as it went   round and round
     the stage of the village theatre
     the two clowns
            would leap oᵛᵉr    its back
  or           w-h-i-s-t-l-e to it
                       d
                       n
                       a
             make it flap its ears
                       d
                       n
                       a
            shake its
                long
                  white
                      mane.
```

Activity 10I   Found Poems

1. **Take a novel or a book of short stories and find an interesting, short descriptive passage that might lead itself to being poetry.**

2. Arrange the passage into a visual pattern and create your found poem.

3. Share your found poetry in small groups. As you pass pieces around the group, note the variety of visual arrangements your classmates have used.

4. Your class may wish to make a bulletin board display for found poetry.

Another kind of visual word play you might enjoy is **concrete poetry**. To write concrete poetry, arrange letters and words so they create a picture or design that reflects the context of the words.

Here are some examples of concrete poems by students:

a. Concrete Words

b. Concrete Ideas

A Pine Tree

```
              A
            pine
                tree
         is a dark
            green, whisp-
        ering, resin-
                   ous home
          for squirrels
                   and birds,
           standing tall
                    to clear, blue
emptiness.

              A
              p
              i
              n
              e

              t
              r
              e
              e

              r
              e
              a
              c
              h
              e
              s

              u
              p
              t
              o

              G
              O
              D
              'S

              L
              I
              G
              H
              T
```

Time Running Out

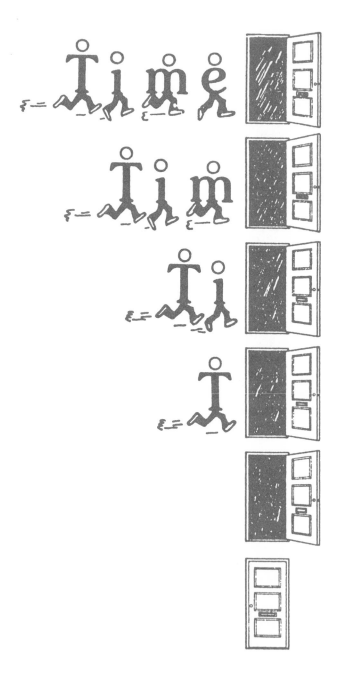

Activity 10ʃ   Concrete Poems

1. Get together with one or two of your classmates and brainstorm some ideas for concrete poetry.

2. Choose some of your ideas and work together to write some concrete poems.

3. Check your poems for effectiveness:
    a. Do they create an interesting shape or pattern?
    b. Does the pattern fit the thought or idea?

4. When you are satisfied with your products, share them with the rest of the class through a display or by putting together a class Concrete Poetry Book.

Adding Images to Sounds and Shapes

Look at these short poems that use lush, descriptive words to create one clear image or word picture. They are called *Dylan Thomas Portraits* because the Welsh poet Dylan Thomas often used this pattern.

> Did you ever feel a rotten apple?
> squishy-soft, jam-slimy, slippery to the core.

> Did you ever see a golden sunrise?
> pink-wonder, horizon-brightening,
> earth-changing, creating new day.

Notice how each poem begins with a question that asks how something looks, sounds, smells, feels or tastes:

> Did you ever see a prairie gopher?

The rest of the poem answers the question through a word picture:

> Lightning-quick, tan streak of furry nerves.

Notice also that each poem uses *double-barrelled*, or hyphenated, descriptive words for added effect:

> squishy-soft, jam-slimy, earth-changing, lightning-quick

Activity 10K   Dylan Thomas Portrait Poems

1. Working with one or two classmates, brainstorm ten questions that could form the first line of a Dylan Thomas Portrait.

2. Working alone, choose five of those and write the second lines.

3. Save your *Portraits* in your writing folders.

The *Ezra Pound Couplet* is another kind of short-word picture poem. The American poet Ezra Pound perfected the pattern. Here are two examples:

> A lost child in a department store
> A small boat in an unknown sea.

> A big delicious pizza for me alone
> A feast for the gods on Mount Olympus.

The first line of the poem makes a statement while the second presents an image or word picture. The juxtaposition (or putting together) of the two lines gives the reader a sense of a simile or metaphor. Just imagine the words *looks like* or *reminds me of* between the two lines.

Activity 10L   Ezra Pound Couplets

1. Think of ten statements that could be the first line of an Ezra Pound Couplet.

2. Take five of those lines and complete the couplets, remembering that *looks like* or *remind me of* are *understood* between the lines.

3. Keep your couplets in your writing folder.

Some word pictures or images are based on a comparison between two things. You practised writing such comparisons in Link 10 when you wrote **similes and metaphors**. Similes use *like* or *as* in their comparisons while metaphors directly combine two different images.

Example: Like a reflector his
body casts away the
sun beams which plunge
and attack him   (simile)

His flight is a
continuous
ribbon in the
sky   (metaphor)

Lynn Bennett   from "The Seagull"

Activity 10M   Simile/Metaphor Poems

1. To what things is the seagull and his flight compared in the simile
   and metaphor in "The Seagull"?

2. For each of the following pictures, write a simile and a metaphor
   that capture the subject and mood of the picture. You should end
   up with short verses like the ones from "The Seagull."

Atlantic
Storm

The Goalie

3. **Take turns reading your simile and metaphor poem to the class. Be prepared to explain why you chose the kind of comparison you did.**

HERE YOU ARE — IN A POEM

A Picture of Yourself

It's time to put together the things you've been practising. You now have the tools to make an interesting word picture of yourself.

Here's what one person wrote about herself:

> I am a play,
> With all the laughter and tears
> hidden backstage:
> I am all the characters —
> The heroine that I want to be,
> The villain that I sometimes stoop to,
> and the scenery,
> the sun and the stars,
> and the dingy slum buildings:
> I am the brilliant scenes
> and the clumsy, ashamed mistakes:
> I am a play.

Activity 10N   Me in the Middle

1. Make a list of all the words and phrases you can think of to describe yourself.

2. Now think of a comparison you can make between yourself and some of the words that appear on your list. For example, you may wish to compare yourself to a type of weather or a season of the year or a time of day. Perhaps a certain colour — or an object of some kind — best describes you.

3. Try writing your portrait using your list and your self-comparison.
   a. Start with some trial sentences.

      Example: I am like the weather, I can turn from hot to cold.
      I can be stormy and calm.
      I am . . .

   b. Select three or four of your best sentences and create your poem.

4. Check your draft to make sure you have what you want. If not, make any necessary changes. These questions may help you:
   - Does the shape of your poem please you?
   - Do the sounds of the words and the rhythms satisfy you?
   - Does the image you have created through your comparison express the idea and feeling you want to create?

5. Save your *Self Portrait* in your notebook.

You're Really On Your Own: Some Poetry Writing Ideas

The remainder of the chapter will provide you with more opportunities to write poetry. All the activities are set up to help you explore yourself — your dreams and realities — through poetry.

One way to get started writing poetry is to imitate the work of other poets. Read the following poems. The original is on the left; on the right is a student's imitation of it.

This Is Just To Say	**This Is Just To Say**
I have eaten the plums that were in the icebox	I have worn the new dress you were hiding in the closet
and which you were probably saving for breakfast	and which you were probably going to wear to the dance
Forgive me they were delicious so sweet and so cold William Carlos Williams	Forgive me it was so elegant so *très chic* and so dazzling. Steve Bailey

Activity 10O   This Is Just to Say

1. Do your own imitation of "This Is Just To Say" based on some similar experience you have had.

2. Save your poem in your folder.

Some people like to write poems about their dreams and wishes. Here's what two students did:

A Painting

If I were a painter. . . . .
I'd paint this lake
and its surroundings,
in blues, greens and browns.
The orange-purple layers of the sun setting.

The small white sail boats,
cutting through the blue-green water,
and leaving a trail of white spume.
I can feel the quietness of the foam,
breaking onto the pale golden sand.
If I were a painter. . . .
I would paint the scene as lovely as it is.

but I'm not a painter.
I'm just a poet.

Paula Miguel

The World's Greatest Baton-Twirler

I want
to be the
world's greatest baton-twirler
I want
to lead the band.
I'll wear a
shimmery costume
and sparkling boots,
and my baton will be
the finest
in the world.
I'll strut and kick
so high
and twirl my baton
with such expertise
that the crowd will stand
in awe of my magnificence.
Yes! I'll win
all the ribbons
and have trophies galore!
And after a
long day of
competitions and public appearances,
the World's Greatest Baton-Twirler
will go to bed.

Susan Foster

Activity 10P Dreams and Wishes

1. List as many things as you can beginning with *I would like* or *I wish*.

2. Choose one of your statements and write your own poem beginning *If I were* or *I want to be*. Don't imitate the structure of the sample poems you have just read. Let your poem take on its own shape and sound patterns; let it be *you*.

3. Keep your poem in your notebook.

You are probably surprised that you are such a rich source of poetry. There are all kinds of poems inside you. You might like to try writing a poem that captures a special feeling you have had or a special time that stands out in your memory. Here is one boy's memory of hitch-hiking in the country on a warm summer morning.

Highway 6, Ten A.M.

Beautiful day
To recover from last night's
Rock concert madness

The fat man in his Caddy
    Turns off onto
The winding dust clouded road
Leaving Timmy the hitch-hiker
All alone with Highway 6

alone

Except for this fresh country green and
the grey withered ghosts
of hayseed's barns

So I walk on
And greet the cows in the fields
(Cows, I now conclude, are good listeners)

The road draws on
So get ready, (out thumb)

Here comes another wind racing sucker

Activity 10Q A Time in My Life

1. Write down a list of specific times in your life about which you could write something.

2. Choose one occasion from your list and make a list of words and ideas you could use in a poem about that special time in your life.

3. Use your list to help you draft your poem, and when you are happy with your poem, save it in your writing folder.

Activity 10R A Poetry Portfolio

1. Form a work group of three or four people and read several of the poems from your writing folders.

2. Help each other by making any suggestions you can think of.
   a. Can sound or visual patterns be improved?
   b. Is the use of images effective? If similes or metaphors are used, are they suitable?
   c. Are thought and feeling clearly communicated?

3. When you get your poems back, read any comments and decide if you wish to revise anything.

4. Make final copies of your poems for your *Poetry Portfolio*, your own special book of poetry.

Poets take part in poetry readings from time to time. After all, poetry is made to be heard as well as seen. A poetry reading in your class would give you an opportunity to hear each other's work. You might even like to invite another class to hear your poems.

Activity 10S A Poetry Reading

1. Choose some of your poems to present during a classroom poetry reading.

2. You might like to present your poem along with some things to dramatize your reading.
   a. Choose slides that picture the scenes or people you are reading about.
   b. Find some music to enhance your poem.
   c. Try creating a mood-setting for your poem. Use vegetable oil and food colouring in a glass dish with an overhead projector to throw visual patterns on the wall behind you.

3. Choose someone in your class to draw up the program for your class poetry reading and to act as a host or hostess to introduce each reader.

Who Said You Couldn't?

You've done it. You've written some poetry! Poetry is a kind of communication that gives you lots of room for creativity because it encourages you to treat language flexibily.

The things you have practised as you have explored poetry can make *all* your talking and writing more descriptive and interesting. You may not grow up to be a poet, but writing poetry helps you to become a good communicator.

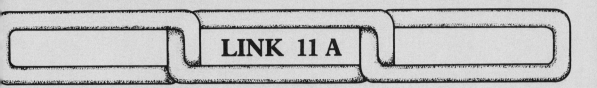

LINK 11 A

This link activity gives you practice in finding information in a cartoon.

1. In groups of three or four, study the sports cartoon below.

2. Make a list of the details that provide you with clues to the event behind this cartoon.

3. Put your clues together to see if you can name the event:
   a. What is the sports event featured in this cartoon?
   b. Where did it occur? When?
   c. What unusual occurrence happened at this event?

   Note: If you know the answer, don't give it away. Give your classmates time to work out a solution.

"Grey" Cup Game

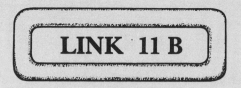

This activity will provide you with practice in reading aloud.

1. Look at the *B.C.* cartoon below and on your own, think about these questions:
   a. How should the quote in the first speech balloon be read? Why?
   b. What can you do to make the words in the second and third speech balloons contrast with those in the first balloon?
   c. Which words in each speech balloon should be emphasized when you read them aloud?

2. Now look at *Hagar the Horrible.* On your own, think about these questions:
   a. What can you do with your voice to make the kids' voices sound realistic?
   b. How do you want to make Hagar sound? Why? How can you do this?

3. In reading the caption for the cartoon opposite, where do you think the word stress should be placed:
   - on *Gladys?*
   - on *telephone?*
   - on *you?*

4. Divide into pairs and practise reading the print statement for each cartoon in 1, 2, and 3. Try reading them in several ways.
   a. Decide on the best way to read each cartoon.
   b. Talk about why you made the choice you did for each cartoon.

5. Select several pairs to do a reading.
   a. Listen for the different ways each cartoon is read.
   b. Talk about what each pair does with their reading of the cartoons.

Gladys, telephone for you.

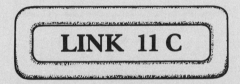

LINK 11 C

This dictation passage is from a novel called *Fly Away Paul*. As you take it down, listen for the five hyphenated words. Be sure to use capital letters where necessary.

> Paul was lucky. He suffered nothing more serious than a moderate concussion. Rushed semi-conscious in Old King Cole's late-model Buick to the Montreal Children's Hospital, his scalp was shaved and stitched, and his skull x-rayed for possible fractures. Paul lay in a dark room for twenty-four hours and complained of a sickening headache. He was kept in hospital for observation for seventy-two hours.
>
> Paul Davies

1. Rewrite these sentences so that the italicized words are placed before the noun they modify. Be sure to hyphenate these modifiers when you place them in front of the noun they describe. →

Example:
She won the race that was *fifty metres*.
She won the *fifty-metre* race.

a. Aldo made a jump of *three metres*.
b. Hilda went on a trail ride for *two days*.
c. Leena made her dress, which was *pale and yellow*.
d. Ira built a brick retaining wall which was *three metres*.
e. The plane, which was *made in Canada*, won the competion.
f. The ship, which *went on the ocean*, docked for repairs.
g. Lucien won first prize with his dog, which had *blue eyes*.
h. A cocker spaniel is a dog that has a *good nature*.
i. Ingrid's hair, which is *brownish red*, glowed in the sunlight.
j. Helmut painted his bedroom a colour that is *light yellow*.

2. Make up one sentence of your own, using three of the hyphenated words (or hyphenated compounds) you created in 1.

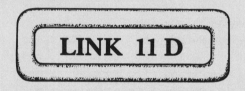

LINK 11 D

This activity will test to see how well you listen.

1. As a whole class, list on the chalkboard sounds that can be made in your classroom by using objects that are already there.

Examples:
a book dropping on the floor, a fist banging on a desk, a book slamming closed, a door closing.

2. Choose a *soundmaker* who, when the class is ready, takes five of the sounds from the list and makes them for you as quickly as possible.

3. Members of the class should listen to these sounds with their eyes closed.

4. When the soundmaker says "Go," students open their eyes and write down the five sounds in the order in which they occurred.

5. If the class did not do too well, choose another soundmaker to repeat this activity with new sounds. If you do well, increase the number of sounds, first to seven, then to ten.

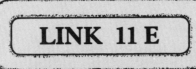

LINK 11 E

This dictation passage comes from the short story "One Small Spike." In this story Billy, a fourteen year old from Newfoundland, runs away from home to join the work gangs that were laying the first railway track through the Rocky Mountains. He is small; the rough men in the camp pick on him, especially the foreman, Big Jay. Billy finds friendship with the camp cook, Hey Wong, who has just arrived in Canada from China.

Billy and Hey Wong put up with rough treatment from the camp until the very last day before shutting down for the winter . . .

It was the clatter of stove lids that awakened him next morning. He lifted himself from the pile of rice sacks and rubbed his eyes. Looking through a tiny square of window, he could see mists hanging low down the mountains. In some ways, it was not too different from the mist that had so often swirled around the fishing shack that had been his home in Newfoundland. But here the kitchen small was different.

He was prepared for more work in the cookhouse but: "Boy!" A shout from outside rattled the glass and Big Jay stood in the dim light, holding onto a contraption of wheels and boards. On a sort of platform, kegs and water cans and pails were stacked. The foreman gestured vaguely behind him where a small stream ran.

"Fill these and keep them filled!" he snapped and turned back to the boarding car.

Mary Daem, *One Small Spike*

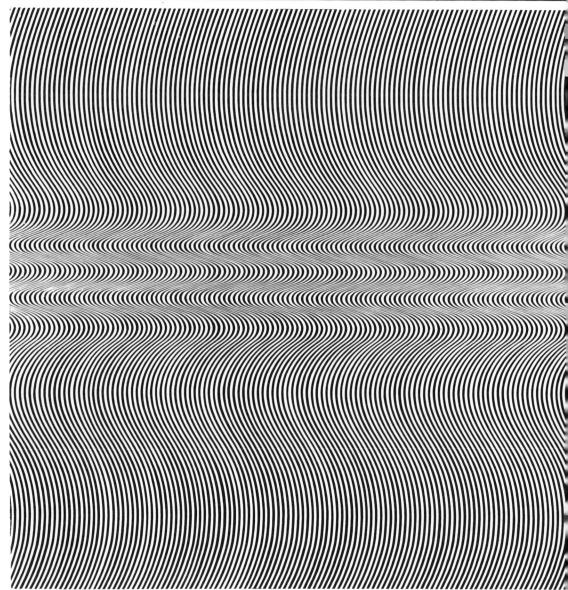

Bridget Riley, *Curr*

THE EYE THAT LOOKS...

Look at the painting on the opposite page. Examine it from all sides, from the top of the page, and from the bottom.

You will see that the lines in the painting seem to move, to wave and wiggle across the page. Why? Because you are experiencing an **optical illusion**.

You are seeing something that is not real. Your eye tells you that the lines are moving, but your head tells you that they can't possibly be moving across the page.

Which do you believe, your eyes or your head? Can you always trust what you see? Is seeing really believing? Are you ever fooled by the messages your eyes give you? Does your brain always give you the right messages?

This chapter will help you find answers to questions such as these. Read on and explore the world of **visual literacy**.

THE BASICS OF VISUAL LITERACY

More and more you live in a world in which pictures, or images, are important. Television, ads, billboards, posters — most likely you have had some contact with at least one of these media today. You should have the skills to understand and use these media. In other words, you need to become **visually literate**.

Activity 11A   Information Schedule

This activity asks you to think about how you receive information and to consider how much of this information is visual.

1. Complete this chart to describe your sources of information.
   a. Choose a three-hour block of time, preferably a stretch of time that includes both in-school and at-home activity.
   b. List all the information you receive during this time block.
   c. State the source of this information.
   d. Classify your sources of information: print, non-print (ear), non-print (eye), other.

2. Discuss how much of this information you receive visually. That is, how much of it came to you as images or pictures?

Kind of information	Source of information	Classification of information
1. score in football game	radio	Non-print (ear)
2. ad for new car	billboard	Non-print (eye) and Print
3. definition of photosynthesis	textbook	Print

Most likely your survey indicated that you receive a good deal of information visually.

The basic elements of a visual image, or picture, are these: **shape, line, colour, texture,** and **space**. The next activity will help you review these basic elements to see how they communicate meaning.

Activity 11B   Shape, Line, and Colour

1. In your notebook, match the adjective in Row B with the colour in Row A.

   Row A
      1) red   2) blue   3) yellow   4) green   5) purple
      6) white   7) black

   Row B
      a. life and energy   b. royalty   c. danger   d. death
      e. purity   f. sadness   g. growth

2. Is this hat taller than it is wide along its brim? Measure to find out.

3. What do the *crosses* in each of these signs mean?

a. (R X R) b. 7 X 3 c. ➕

d. grammer

4. As a whole class, share your answers.
   a. Try to find out *why* you and your classmates answered as you did.
   b. Are you still bothered by your answer to 2? Does your brain agree with what you saw on the ruler?

No doubt you reacted to the colours in 1 in much the same way as many of your classmates. Each of you attached the same meaning to the colours. The interesting question is *why*?

Like the optical illusion at the beginning of this chapter, the lines in the drawing of the hat confused your understanding of this picture. Yet you probably had little difficulty understanding the meanings of the X shape in 3.

In very simple ways, you arrived at understanding or meaning in these questions through your knowledge of **colour** and **line**.

Texture and **shape** are also part of the language of visual communication. The contrast in the **texture**, or surface appearance, in this illustration, for example, makes the star stand out. The larger space has a rough texture; the texture of the star is smooth and solid.

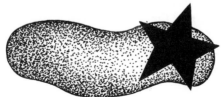

You also have definite reactions to the use of **space** in visual images. Some arrangements will be pleasing to you, and others will not be.

Activity 11C Texture and Space

1. Bring to class several examples of the use of contrast in texture in ads. (Be sure that you get permission before cutting out the ads.) Be prepared to explain to your class how contrasts in texture are used to highlight the central focus of the ad.

2. Which of these illustrations do you like better? How does the use of space affect your reaction to these illustrations? Why?

a. 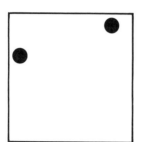 b.

OPTICAL ILLUSIONS

This section challenges you to figure out some more optical illusions.

Activity 11D Challenging Lines

1. Where do the three prongs in this illusion come from?

2. Can you draw this diagram?

3. Are these lines parallel? Lift up your book and look along the long lines from the point marked at the corner of the diagram.

   What happens to these lines now?

look along here ⟶

Activity 11E Figures that Change Shape

1. Stare at this bent card for several seconds. What happens? Is it facing towards you or away from you?
   Can you make it flip back and forth as you continue to stare at it?

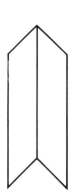

2. These are reversing cubes. Stare at each cube. What happens to the dark lines? Are they on the inside or the outside of the box?

3. Are these stairs upside down? Continue to stare at them to see what happens.

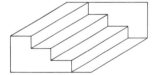

4. Are there six or seven stacked boxes in this diagram? Be careful! Look at it again.

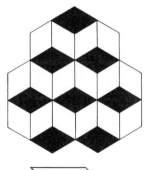

5. Does this box open toward you or away from you?

Activity 11F   The Questions Change the Shape

1. After you read each question, look at the optical illusion below to find your answers.
   a. Can you put a bouquet of flowers in this vase?
   b. What are the people in the picture saying to each other?

2. Look at the drawing above to find answers to these questions.
   a. Is the old woman looking at you?
   b. Is the beautiful woman wearing a necklace?

These optical illusions show you that you can't always trust your eyes when you look at something. Your eyes can be fooled into seeing things in certain ways. As you go further in this chapter, keep this fact in mind. The interesting question is, how is this fact used in **visual communication**?

LOOKING AT PICTURES

Photographers are able to determine the way you look at a picture. One way they do this is by controlling the angle from which you look at a photograph.

Activity 11G   Angle of the Shot

1. Describe the angles from which the photographer shot these photographs.

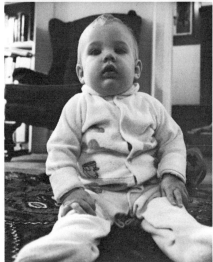

2. Why did the photographer shoot his photographs from these angles?

3. Talk as a class about your responses to these photographs. How could the photographers change their angles on these two pictures? What would be the result of such a change?

The next activities help you look at some photographs shot by a professional photographer. Your task is to look at them to find out exactly how they work. In other words, you will be practising your ability to see the elements of visual language in these photographs.

Activity 11H By Bedford Road

1. Look at "By Bedford Road" to find out how the lines work in this photograph.

By Bedford Road

    a. What is the focal point, or centre of interest, of the photograph?
    b. How do the lines in this photograph help to point out the focal point? Where are these lines repeated?

2. How do light and darkness, or contrast in colour, work in the photograph?

Activity 11I   City Castle

1. How do the lines work in "City Castle"?

   a. What is the focal point?
   b. How do the lines in this photograph emphasize the focal point? What lines repeat this emphasis?

2. How does texture add to the quality of the photograph?

Castle

Activity 11J   Sidewalk

1. After looking at "Sidewalk," list the visual elements in that photograph in your notebook.
   a. What different textures can you see?

    b. How does the photograph make use of the idea of shape and line?

    c. How does it make sure of light and shadow?

Sidewalk

Activity 11K *Which Photograph is Best?*

1. In your notebook, record your overall reaction to each of the photographs studied. Write four or five sentences for each photograph.

2. Which photograph do you like best? Why?

3. Use your knowledge of the elements of visual language to decide which is the *best* photograph. Why?

4. Is your overall response to 2 the same as your *analytical* response to 3?

Activity 11L   Your Family Album

1. Look in your family photo album, or at your family slides.

2. Choose six pictures.

3. Analyze these pictures, using your knowledge of the elements of visual language. Write notes to yourself in your notebook.

   It will be more interesting for you if you pick some pictures that aren't too successful. You should be able to find some pictures in which the elements of visual language are not used very well.

4. In a small group, talk about your six pictures. Explain how the elements of visual language are effective, or not.

   Remember: Even though your pictures may have some flaws, they are still valuable as a family record.

Activity 11M   A Dark Side

The photographs reproduced in this text are *nice* photographs. They show pictures of sunny days — where everyone lives happily and no one ever yells at anyone else. Life is not necessarily like this.

1. Look in magazines to find pictures in which the photographer has shown a harsher scene.

2. How are the elements of visual language used in these photographs?

3. Do these photographers use visual elements differently than the photographer who shot "By Bedford Road," "City Castle," and "Sidewalk"?

4. Be prepared to show your examples in class and discuss your photographs explaining what each photographer has done to make his or her photograph communicate a message. In other words, how does the technique of the photographer reinforce the message of the picture?

OUTDOOR SIGNS

City streets are full of signs. Many of the signs advertise a place of business — eat here, get your bike there, buy gas here. Have you ever stopped to think about the way these signs work to capture your attention? This section outlines some of the ways the elements of visual language work in signs.

The colour and shape of a sign give *psychological* meaning to the viewer. That is, the meaning is personal, dependent upon the viewer's cultural background and experiences.

The manufacturers of outdoor signs know a lot about how colour and shape affect people. If they use a colour or a shape that no one likes, their sign will not do a good job of selling its product.

A few years ago, a research firm did a study of the signs outside gasoline stations. The next activity helps you discover what they found out.

Activity 11N Gasoline Signs: Which One?

1. Look carefully at each shape.

2. Copy into your notebooks this rating scale, which shows your liking for each shape. Make a separate rating scale of each shape, from a to f.

Rating Scale	1	2	3	4	5	6
	I don't like this shape very much.			I like this shape and feel very comfortable with it.		

3. Then, show how much you like each shape by placing an X along the line.

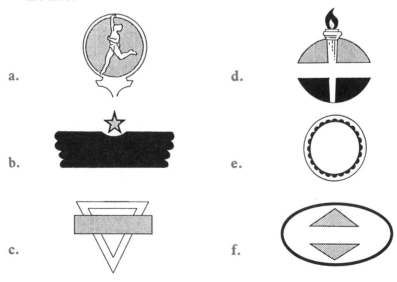

a.

b.

c.

d.

e.

f.

Now that you have stated your reaction, compare your results with those of the people reported in the research survey.

The researchers found that most people preferred the *oval shape*. They associated this shape with friendliness and cleanliness. The *circle* did not get much reaction from the people in the survey. The *angular signs* received a negative response. People associated them with dishonesty.

Were your results similar? Did you tend to like the oval shapes but not the angular shapes?

This same survey also showed that most people have an emotional reaction to colours used in signs. Here is a summary of the most common reactions.

red	danger
blue	coolness
green	growth
yellow	warmth/life
black	death
white	sickness

You might want to look back to Activity 11B to see your emotional or psychological reaction to colour.

Companies have learned a great deal from this research. They have designed signs with the shapes and colours that make people feel good about the products they are advertising.

Activity 11O Look at This Sign

Here are some outdoor signs commonly found in Canada.

1. Study the signs to see how they make use of the concept of shape to advertise their message.

2. As a class, discuss how the signs have, or have not, used a basic knowledge of people's reactions to shape.

a.    b.

c.

d.

e.

Activity 11P   Signs in Your Community

1. Use this research information to look at the signs in your community.

2. Look especially at the shape and colour of these signs.

3. Determine how shape and colour send out a message which is the same as, or different from, the words that appear on the sign.

4. Choose three signs that interest you and prepare a short talk for your class to report your information.

Activity 11Q   A Design Problem

Here is a problem for you to solve. A manager wants to set up an ice cream shop that will attract teens. The best place that the manager can find for this shop is a building which faces north and which is always in the shadow of a highrise apartment building.
The manager hires you to design the front of the shop.

1. What kind of sign would you use for the front? Why?

2. What colour would you paint the front of the shop? Why?

3. What colour would you paint the door? Why?

4. Share your responses as a whole class.

CREATING STORIES WITH PICTURES

Activities in this section provide you with practice in telling visual stories through pictures. This skill is basic to film and television.

Obtain permission to use old magazines and pictures for these activities.

Activity 11R   A Visual Story

1. Choose one of these themes: school, war, pride, youth, achievement, music, sport.

2. Select one element from the language of visual communication: shape, line, colour, texture, space.

3. Find five images or pictures that represent your theme, using the visual element you have chosen.

4. On a blank page, arrange your five images in an order so that they tell a visual story.

5. In small groups, ask members to describe and discuss the story you show them.

6. Tell the group the story you intended to communicate with this collage.

7. Talk about how different audiences would react to your visual stories.

Activity 11S   A People Story

1. Choose three people who are well known to your classmates. These people may be political figures, sports figures, local personalities, or any person whom most students in your class would know something about.

2. Choose one word for each person to tell what you think about him or her, and write these words in your notebook without telling anyone what they are.

3. Decide on the colour and shape that will communicate your ideas about each person.

4. Construct a collage from any material available to you. In your collage, surround each of the three people with the shapes and colours and images that communicate visually your thoughts about them.

5. Ask your small group to look at your collage to guess your one word for each person.

6. As a small group, discuss the overall effect of each collage.

An Illustrated Talk

In this chapter you have considered the visual language of communication. In the real world, these visual elements rarely occur on their own. Rather, they are combined with words to communicate meaning. These words can be either spoken or written. Together, the words and the images work to communicate a message. The image part of the message often operates to capture the attention of the audience, and the message is given in the words. Of course, the image also carries a subtle message.

This final activity asks you to present a message that uses both words and visuals.

Activity 11T A Visual Topic

a. Choose a topic you want to present to your class.
   Examples: You could choose a theme such as those you worked with in Activity 11R. Or you could communicate something more personal, like a family trip, or the story of your life.
b. In your notebook, make a tentative list of the information you want to communicate and the visual that could help you communicate the message.

Examples:

Topic: "The Story of Me"

Information	Visual
My first birthday	photograph or slide of my family

Information	Visual
Some animals have become extinct	drawing of dodo on an overhead transparency

c. Share your list of information and visual with your writing group. Ask for advice and additional ideas.

Activity 11U Planning

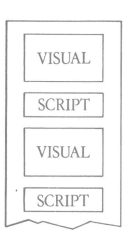

a. Use a story board format to plan your presentation. Make enough copies of this diagram so that you have one copy for each visual that you intend to use in your presentation. (You should make each sample the size of one of the pages in your notebook.)
b. In the rectangle at the top of the page, sketch the visual you intend to use.
c. In the rectangle at the bottom of the page, write out the script that goes with the visual.
d. Work with a writing partner. Show your partner your plans for your presentation, both your visual and word script.
e. Do the same thing for your writing partner. Use this chance to give some good advice. Comment on things which you feel are not very clear. If possible, help your partner think of some new information or new visuals for the presentation. Help your partner, too, with the written script.

Note: You may be surprised that a visual presentation involves so much writing. But, did you ever consider that almost everything that appears on your television screen was planned in written form first?

Activity 11V   Writing and Preparing

a. Now that your planning is finished, go ahead and prepare your visuals for your presentation.
b. Then, focus on your script. Write the commentary that goes with each one of your visuals.
c. Be certain that you use a system in which you can keep your written script and visual script in order.

Activity 11W   Presentation

a. Present your *illustrated talk* to your class.
b. Be sure to organize your talk so that students can see your visuals clearly. You may have to get someone to change your visuals for you as you talk.
c. Before you deliver your talk, do one last-minute check to make certain that your visual script and information script are in order.

In this chapter, you have explored the **language of visual communication**. In the final section, you combined visual, written, and spoken means of communication. Many speeches use this combination of types of communication.

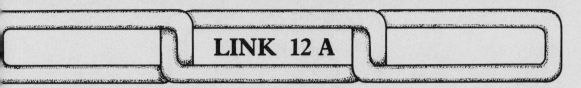

LINK 12 A

This link section is about **Readers Theatre**.

1. Place two chairs or stools at the front of your classroom.

2. Two volunteers will read this play, to explain what a *readers theatre* is all about.

Reader One:	A lone reader sits in a satin pool of light.
Reader Two:	He looks into the imagination of his audience.
Both Readers:	He believes,
Reader Two:	And velvet images touch the silent air of the theatre.
Reader One:	A second reader appears,
Reader Two:	Then a third,
Reader One:	And a fourth.
Both Readers:	All together they create
Reader One:	the setting,
Reader Two:	touch life to sleeping characters,
Reader One:	And the words on the page before them
Both Readers:	live again
Reader One:	as when the author had first sought to create.
Reader Two:	Readers theatre,
Reader One:	Readers theatre —
Reader Two:	a group activity in which the best of literature is communicated from the manuscript to an audience
Both Readers:	through the oral interpretation approach of vocal and physical suggestion —
Reader Two:	says one.
Reader One:	But more
Reader Two:	more
Reader One:	much more
Both Readers:	is readers theatre!
Reader Two:	For the audience,
Reader One:	For the reader,
Both Readers:	It is a shared experience.

Tim Bryson, *Creative Communication: Projects in Acting, Speaking, Oral Reading*.

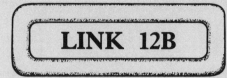

LINK 12B

This passage tells about the problems that a young girl has with osteomyelitis, a crippling disease of the bone.

1. Prepare this passage for the readers theatre session.

2. Remember, in readers theatre, you focus on the reading of the passage. There is no action in readers theatre, other than hand gestures or an occasional movement.

Reader One:	On New Year's Eve when I was thirteen, we were living in St. John's. Christmas had been happy, in an accustomed prosperity, but on this night . . .
Reader Two:	. . . the joyously intended clamor of church bells, car horns, ship's whistles, and signal guns . . .
Reader One:	. . . drove me to my room in sudden, unaccountable dread. Within the month, I was admitted to hospital with osteomyelitis in the left leg.
Reader Two:	The premonition of doom was being fulfilled, though not recognized in the fulfilling, for there was always the fear of worse to come.
Reader Three:	Before penicillin, osteomyelitis (inflammation of the bone and marrow) was a messy, dragged-out debilitating disease.
Reader One:	By the time I was able to have penicillin injections it was well established in my legs, arms, hip, neck, and shoulder . . .
Reader Two:	. . . and it was to be seven years before its course would be finally halted by amputation of the limb first affected.
	. . . .
Reader One:	The circumstances of my life since the ambulance took me to the hospital at the age of thirteen have not changed the personality that I had to begin with. I have only had to draw on my resources. I have learned that the premonition is always worse

than the event, and I have continued to believe in prayer as well as action.

If I were to choose my own epitaph, I think it would be . . .

Reader Two: "I was confident, even when I said I am greatly afflicted."

Reader Three: It is often said that there is no ecstasy without agony. What price is too high for having a husband and children who need me; for writing a poem that brings a smile; for hearing a violin concerto on the

Readers Two   car radio to the swish of windshield wipers in the
and Three: pouring rain?

Geraldine Rubia,
"A Space for me to Solve (1978)"

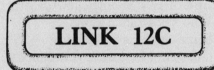

LINK 12C

Here is another poem that you can use for a Readers Theatre passage.

Reader One: INSTRUCTOR
Reader Two: the quickest draw in moose jaw
               is fred bsc engg
Reader One: he on his hip like a pistol wears
               his calculator
               electronic gunslinger/Reader Two: he swaggers
               down the hall
               his hewlett-packard swings easy
               in its padded vinyl holster
Reader One: Fred watches the eyes
               as he faces his pupils down
Reader Two: it's the eyes/ Reader One: lighting
               up like a switched-on
               texas instrument/ Reader Two: that
               give them away/ Reader One and Two: he guns
               them down with a flick
               of digits

E. F. Dyck

LINK 12D

Here is another poem that you can use for a Readers Theatre passage.

Readers One and Two:	Grade Five Geography Lesson
Reader One:	Children never get to the point, They surround it.
Reader Two:	The importance of the point Is the landscape of it.
Reader One:	You begin by discussing "The Rainfall of Vancouver Island" And somebody has an uncle who lives there.
Reader Two:	And there is an uncle in Alberta Who has a zillion cows, Some chickens and a horse
Reader Three:	(We get to feed the chickens And ride the horse),
Reader One:	Which brings us to an uncle In Saskatchewan, who has a house where Deer pass the kitchen window Every morning Reader Three: (He takes us out And shows us where they go).
Readers One, Two, and Three:	If there were no uncles on Vancouver Island It would never rain there.

Barry Stevens

LINK 12E

1. Form groups of three or four students, depending upon how many you need.

2. Select some passage to turn into a readers theatre presentation.

3. As a group, decide how you will read it, and then practise reading it.

4. Present your work to your class as an example of readers theatre.

Making a Readers Theatre Selection

Here are some suggestions:

1. The scripts for plays are the easiest material to work with because they are set up to read in parts, and the playwright has already designated the characters.

2. You can turn any piece of writing into readers theatre, however: letters, short stories, chapters from novels, histories, journals, poetry.

3. You may have to cut and edit some of the longer pieces of writing.

4. Try a composite program, in which you present several selections, all connected in some way. To do this, select works with a common theme, or by the same author, or of the same genre or type.

12

1-3-6 — ALL + *ACTION*

Everyone has to make a decision at some time. Which bike shall I buy? Shall I save money for a new sweater or spend it going to a movie?

There are also decisions made beyond the individual ones. Who is the best candidate for your local school board? Should the community put fluoride in its water supply? And on it goes.

This chapter is about decisions. It will give you a method you can use as a guide in making decisions.

Activity 12A   Tiger, Tiger

This activity gets you to look at the *Tiger* cartoon on the opposite page.

1. With what problem are these children wrestling?

2. How do they go about solving the problem?

3. What other solutions can you think of for this problem?

4. How might you have solved a similar problem when you were a young child?

Not all problems are easily solved, as is clear from the following story.

Jules and Andrea are very upset. They have just come out of a terrible class meeting. Everyone argued. No one listened. Yet the problem was one that concerned the whole class.

It all started several months ago. The grade eights held several fund-raising projects and collected five hundred dollars. This meeting was called to discuss ways to spend the money. The result was chaos.

Every time a person made a suggestion, another person argued against it. The class formed cliques, and one group wouldn't listen to another.

Nothing was accomplished. Jules and Andrea were decidedly upset. As they strode out of the room, Jules asked Andrea, "How in the world do we get our class to work together?"

PROBLEM SOLVING

This chapter will outline for you a process that will help answer questions like Jules's.

To understand the process, you will first have to study a problem-solving model. This model has two stages:

Stage One: The 1 — 3 — 6 — All Procedure
Stage Two: The Plan of Action

Stage One: 1 — 3 — 6 — All

Stage One has four separate steps. At Step One, you work on your own. At Step Two, you work in a group of three. At the third step, you work in a group of six, and at the fourth step, you work as a whole class. All of this thinking prepares you to set a plan of action.

Let's suppose you have a problem to solve. Here is how you might go through Stage One.

Step One: Working on Your Own

- On file cards, or some other small pieces of paper, write out your goal, idea, need, or concern — whatever it is you are trying to make a decision about.
  - This step is like brainstorming by yourself. Each goal, idea, need, or concern is written on a separate file card. Therefore, the number of file cards is the number of ideas you develop on your own.

- After you have written your ideas on the file cards, arrange them in order, from the best liked to the least liked.

Step Two: Working with Groups of Three

- Each person brings to the group the file cards that he or she developed individually and shares them.

- During the group discussion, each person clarifies and explains his or her ideas. If two ideas are the same, they are combined and put on one file card.

- After the group has shared, discussed, clarified, and explained all ideas on the file cards, the group arranges all of the file cards in order from best liked to least liked. The group must reach agreement on the order of the file cards, at least the top three or four ideas.

At the end of this step, your group of three will have developed one set of file cards. This set will contain at least three ideas that the group agrees with. They are arranged in order of preference.

Step Three: Working in Groups of Six

- Two groups of three now form one group of six students. The procedures for Step Two are repeated. Ideas are shared, clarified, and explained within the group. Similar ideas are combined and placed on one file card.

- Through agreement of all six group members, you arrange your file cards so that you have one set, arranged in order from best liked to least liked. This set should contain at least three ideas that the group agrees with.

Step Four: Working as a Class

- When your group has finished the 1—3—6 procedure, the next step is to list the ideas from all of the groups of six on the blackboard and have a class discussion.

- The result will be a list of ideas in order from the best liked to the least liked. This gives you a solution that everyone agrees with — without chaos and confusion.

At the end of Stage One you will have found an answer to your original question. Indeed, you will have a list of several possible answers, noted in order of group preference. The next step in the decision-making process is to move on to Stage Two: the plan of action.

Stage Two: A Plan of Action

At Stage Two you make these decisions:

1. **What** do you want to do with your idea?
2. **How** do you want to carry out your solution or idea?
3. **When** do you want to carry out your solution or idea?
4. **Who** is going to carry out your solution or idea?

When you have a personal problem that appears to have no satisfactory solution, you can share the problem with others. You can work together to develop solutions—*a plan of action*. Group problem-solving is a helpful process.

Activity 12B   Keeping Track of Problems in Journals

For the next month, write up a journal entry each time you find yourself in one of these situations:

1. Someone helps you solve a problem. The help may have come from a friend, a teacher, a counsellor, a member of your family, or from some other person.

- Describe in your journal the problem, your attempted solution(s), and how someone else helped you with the solution.

2. You help someone else solve a problem.
   - Describe the problem, how the person you helped was trying to solve the problem, and how you helped him or her solve the problem.

3. A group of you work together to solve a problem.
   - Describe the problem, who contributed each of the possible solutions, what the solution was, and how the solution was arrived at.

Journals are private writing. You should share them only with someone you choose to share them with. Your teacher may want to see your journal entries to find out how you are handling the problem-solving process.

Remember Jules and Andrea? They were left in a predicament. They had to find a way to get a class decision: how to spend money raised by their class. How can they use the problem-solving model to reach a solution?

Don't forget that Jules and Andrea must help their class reach *agreement* on how to spend the money. There has to be a plan of action that will work. They must reach this conclusion, with class cooperation, acceptance, and understanding. Will the group problem-solving model help them out? Let's apply the model.

THE MODEL IN ACTION

Stage One: 1-3-6 — All

Step One: Working Alone

Jules listed on file cards three separate ideas that he had to solve the problem. He next set them in order of preference.

Have a class party with a banquet and dance.

Buy a painting from a local artist for the school.

Buy football equipment for the interschool team.

Andrea also listed her three preferences on file cards and set them out in order of her preference.

All of the members of the class did the same thing: everyone set out at least three possible solutions and ordered them according to his or her preference. Here is Sylvia's list of possible solutions — she did a lot of thinking and came up with four solutions.

Step Two: Working in Groups of Three

When Sylvia, Jules, and Andrea got together, they discussed the ideas on their file cards. They found that they could agree to combine their ideas in the following way:

Although they felt their other ideas were good, these were the three they could all agree were the best ideas. They listed them in their order of preference.

Step Three: Working in Groups of Six

Two groups of three joined to form a group of six. This group had several ideas on their filing cards. Each group presented its ideas. They were discussed and examined. When all was finished, the group favoured two ideas:

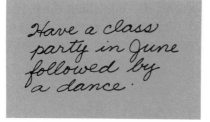

Step Four: Working as a Class

Following the 1 — 3 — 6 process, the class met as one group. The students agreed on the two best solutions: have a class party or adopt a child. But the class was divided on the best plan of action. Everyone wanted a class party, but many felt that spending five hundred dollars on themselves was selfish.

As they discussed and worked together, they arrived at a final solution:

1. **They would spend two hundred dollars on a class party.**

2. **They would spend three hundred dollars to adopt a child in a developing country.**

With this agreement, the class next needed a plan of action.

Stage Two: A Plan of Action

In completing the 1—3—6—All process, the class reached a decision— the first step of the plan of action.

1. **What** do you want to do with your idea or problem? The class already decided to have a party *and* adopt a child from a developing country.

2. **How** do you want to carry out your solution or idea?

3. **When** do you want to carry out your solution or idea?

4. **Who** is going to carry out your solution or idea?

There are two ways in which the class could complete Stage Two. First, the class could appoint committees of three or four students to study the questions and report back to the whole class. They could then discuss the committee's recommendations and vote upon decisions.

Or, the class could go through the 1—3—6—All procedures for each of the questions in the plan of action. In fact, they would have to go through this procedure twice, once to reach a decision about the party and once to decide how to adopt a child. This procedure takes longer, but it does involve all students in the class more actively in the process of making decisions.

Plainsville School: Using the Model

Plainsville School has been having serious behaviour and discipline problems in the school building, the classrooms, and on the playground. Kim Dogood, the principal, approached the Student Council for help. The principal suggested that the Student Council establish five rules for school behaviour. They should be rules that all students can accept and they should serve to improve the conduct among students in the school.

In addition, Kim Dogood asked the students to design posters to explain the rules. These posters or banners would be displayed throughout the school so that everyone would be aware of the rules. Kim Dogood and the Student Council are genuinely concerned to make Plainsville School a more pleasant place.

Activity 12C Plainsville School

1. Your class should use the 1—3—6—All procedure to arrive at the five rules for Plainsville School.

2. Remember that there must be common agreement among the class about the rules. And there can be only five rules.

3. After deciding upon the five rules, develop a plan of action. Posters and banners must be designed for display around the school. This activity itself will require more planning, more decision-making, and more problem solving.
   - For example, do you present all five rules on one poster? Or do you make five posters, one for each rule? Should the posters contain a visual image? Should they be written in prose or poetry? Do you need different posters for different grade levels?

Solve Your Own Problems

Chapter 12 has discussed one way in which people can work together to solve problems. Perhaps your class has some problems of its own to solve. Try using the **1—3—6—All + action plan** model to solve one of your problems.

LINK 13 A

The Phantom Hunter was painted by Blair Bruce from Hamilton, Ontario. This painting tells the story of the Walker of the Snow — a ghost who pursued trappers through the snow.

Use this painting to think about the questions on the next page.

The Phantom Hunter Blair Bruce

1. In your notebook, write a list of five *adjectives* that could describe the hunter, the phantom, and the landscape. Use this chart to organize your answer:

hunter	phantom	landscape
weary	mysterious	barren
1. _____	_____	_____
2. _____	_____	_____
3. _____	_____	_____
4. _____	_____	_____
5. _____	_____	_____

2. In your notebook, write a list of five *adverbs* to describe the actions of the hunter and of the phantom. Again, use this chart:

hunter	phantom
faintly	slowly
1. _____	_____
2. _____	_____
3. _____	_____
4. _____	_____
5. _____	_____

3. In your notebook, complete these two sentences:
   The hunter, who _____ , crouched in the snow.
   The phantom, who _____ , stalks the frozen land.
   Then, using these sentences as a model, write two more sentences about the hunter and two more about the phantom.

4. Write a paragraph to tell what is *not* in the landscape in this painting. Use as many of these words in your description as possible:
   not any, hardly any, little, no,
   few, not much, hardly, scarcely

5. In your notebook, use *The Phantom Hunter* to help you write sentences of at least ten words for each of these adverbial sentence starters:
   a. Last week, _____
   b. Yesterday, _____
   c. Right now, _____
   d. In a moment, _____
   e. Next week, _____

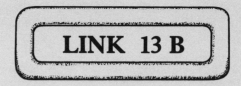

1. Use these discussion starters to look once again at *The Phantom Hunter*.
   a. What does *The Phantom Hunter* say about what nature is like?
   b. How does this concept of nature compare with that of the other paintings in this textbook?

2. This poem was written by Emily Dickinson, an American poet, who wrote about the same time that Bruce painted *The Phantom Hunter*.
   a. Read the poem to decide what Dickinson is saying about nature.

> **Apparently with no surprise**
> **To any happy flower,**
> **The frost beheads it at its play**
> **In accidental power.**
>
> **The blond assassin passes on,**
> **The sun proceeds unmoved**
> **To measure off another day**
> **For an approving God.**

   b. In your notebook, write three or four sentences to tell what the poem says about nature.
   c. Next, compare your answer to the answer you arrived at in 1.
      • Are the poet and the painter giving the same message?
      • Do you agree with what each or both are saying?

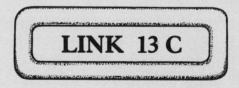

1. In your notebook, make a list of fifteen synonyms for the word *cute*.

2. List in your notebook ten different ways to say this sentence: "It's a *nice* day!"

3. Read at least three pieces of writing you have done this year. Find, if you can, any common *cute-and-nice* words you used and list them in your notebook. Beside each, write a synonym you could have used.

LINK 13 D

Idioms are colourful expressions used to communicate ideas. They usually create pictures. For example, *to break the ice* means *to begin something, but with some difficulty*. It creates the picture of someone starting something, but having a hard time getting going. This expression goes back many years. It originated from sailors having to break through ice before their boats could move.

Here are clues to the origin of some well-known English idioms. Write the answers in your notebooks.

1. The ancient Greek poet Homer talked of warriors killed on the battlefield as *lying in dust, biting the ground.*
   Someone who has died has _____ _____ _____ .

2. Horses fed on beans are full of energy.
   A person who is energetic is _____ _____ _____ .

3. Berserker was a mythical Norse warrior who could be very violent on the battlefield.
   Someone who becomes violent and wild has _____ _____ .

4. A common way to examine a horse before buying it is to check its teeth. We're told that when you receive a gift, however, you shouldn't be too critical of it, but accept it gladly.
   In other words, you shouldn't look a _____ _____ _____ _____ _____ .

At the Crease Line, Ken Danby

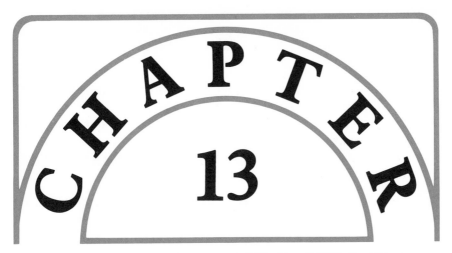

13

HERE IS HOW I SEE IT

Ken Danby's painting opposite is titled *At The Crease Line*. It celebrates the Team Canada/Soviet hockey series of 1972.

It was a great series. With a three-three record, and one game tied, Canada travelled to Moscow to end the series. The final game saw a five-five tie: with thirty-four seconds to the end of the game, Paul Henderson scored the winning goal.

Many Canadians still remember that moment.

Hockey has changed since 1972. Is Canada still a dominant force in international play? Can hockey truly be called Canada's national sport?

These questions call for statements of opinion. Opinions can't really be right or wrong. They are believable only if they have strong facts to back them up.

This chapter is all about what opinions are and how to write them.

WHAT IS AN OPINION?

Activity 13A   Talking about Hockey

Let's see what your opinion of hockey is.

1. In your notebook, write steadily for four minutes. Use this phrase to start your writing: *I think that hockey . . .*

2. Keep your pen working for the entire four minutes. If you can't think of anything to write, keep on writing *hockey* over and over. Some new ideas will soon come.

   Note: If you like, take a positive approach to this writing task, and explain what you like and admire about hockey.

   Or you can take a critical approach, pointing out what you dislike about the game of hockey.

   Or you can mix your ideas, writing about both the good and the bad points of the game.

3. Keep your writing handy in your notebook. You'll have to look at it again in a later exercise.

What Did You Write?

You may want to have a look at your writing to analyze your opinion about hockey. Before you can do this, you will have to learn to distinguish between **fact** and **opinion**.

A fact is something that can be measured by someone. For example, *The beaver are cutting down the trees* is a statement of fact. Anyone can count the number of trees that have been felled by the beaver.

An opinion, on the other hand, is a statement of personal belief. It may not be proven by measurement. *Team Canada is a lousy hockey team* is a statement of opinion. Someone else might have the opposite opinion: *Team Canada is the best hockey team ever.*

Activity 13B   Fact or Opinion

This activity will give you some practice in distinguishing between statements of fact and statements of opinion.

1. Read each of these statements. If you believe the statement is a fact, write *fact* in your notebook. If you believe it is an opinion, write *opinion* in your notebook.

2. For each statement that you note as fact, indicate in your notebook how it might be measured.

   a. It is 54 km from Vancouver to Abbotsford.
   b. Most of the Rocky Mountains have never been climbed.
   c. The age for getting a driver's licence should be raised to 20.
   d. The electronic game "Gorp Eater" costs $46.95 at the Bay.
   e. If there were no poverty, there'd be no crime.
   f. All societies must have a kind of government.

g. Convicted murderers should be executed humanely.

h. Heart disease is the biggest killer in Canada.

i. Television violence makes children more violent.

j. Education is the largest single item in Alberta's budget.

Activity 13C   Looking at Myself

1. Reread the statements you wrote in Activity 13A.

2. Classify each statement as a fact or an opinion.

3. Count your responses. How many were fact statements? How many were opinion statements?

4. Share your answers as a whole class.
   a. Did you class write more opinion or fact statements?
   b. Talk about the results of your survey.

That's an Unsupportable Argument

People usually make opinion statements, to convince someone else of something — in most cases, to accept their point of view. One way to convince others of your opinion is to give the supporting facts to back it up.

This next activity gives you practice in determining a writer's opinion and looking for the facts that support, or don't support, that opinion.

Activity 13D   The Opinions of Writers

1. Read each of the following paragraphs to discover the statement of opinion in each paragraph and the supporting facts.

2. Answer these questions in your notebook for each paragraph:
   a. What is the author's opinion?
   b. What facts does the author use to support this opinion?
   c. How are these facts measurable?

Paragraph 1

I think there were three reasons why *Pacman* was the most played computer game of the 1980s. First of all, it is a game played by both sexes. A Gallup poll indicates that both men and women like it for the skill involved. Secondly, *Pacman* received the most news coverage in magazines such as *Maclean's* and *Saturday Night*.

Because of that coverage, many occasional players tended to want to try *Pacman*. Finally, it is a game with many levels of difficulty. The amateur can feel happy making it through one round; the experienced player enjoys the new challenges of later rounds. Perhaps never again will a single computer game like *Pacman* capture so much public attention.

Paragraph 2

Pacman was the most popular game of the 1980s because it's the best game. *Pacman* is never boring. Sometimes the driving games can get boring if you've played them a while. *Defender* is never boring, but then it's hard to understand at first and you can lose a lot of money just figuring out how to move your ship and what the attackers can do. You can tell right away what to do in *Pacman*. Lots of other games are just imitations of *Defender*, but there is no other game like *Pacman*. That's why *Pacman* is the most popular game.

3. Select which of the following opinion statements you believe is true and write it in your notebook. Then, support your opinion with facts and examples taken from the paragraphs.
   a. The second *Pacman* paragraph is a poor opinion because it doesn't try to prove *Pacman* is the best game. It merely says that a few others aren't as good.
   b. The second *Pacman* paragraph was written by somebody a lot younger than the person who wrote the first *Pacman* paragraph.

4. Why is the first paragraph more believable than the second paragraph?

So far, you should have seen that a convincing opinion must:

- state the opinion
- present facts to support the opinion, and
- present evidence that the person holding the opinion is somewhat trustworthy.

The following section adds another dimension to the task of writing opinion.

The Effect of Strong Words

Sometimes writers of opinion get carried away with the words they use. These writers are so intent upon convincing you that they make sweeping statements, statements that include everything. These statements are called **broad generalizations.**

Activity 13E   Put the Blame on Parents

1. Read the following paragraph and answer these questions in your notebook.
   a. What is the author's opinion?
   b. What facts are presented to support this opinion? How can these facts be measured?
   c. What do the *italicized* words have in common?
   d. What effect do these kinds of words have on you as a reader?

> Parents have become *completely* dictatorial in the last few years as conservatism takes a *total* grip on the country. *Everywhere* in North America the average age of the population is getting older. *All* old people are conservative, don't like noise, don't like change, resent any hint of a lack of respect, and care more about money and security than idealism and improvement. As a result, I see a future *full* of quiet, downtrodden children, studying hard, respectful and money conscious, but also *totally* boring and *without any* of the bright, idealistic hopes which a young generation should have.

The kinds of statements that don't allow for exceptions are too harshly stated. They tend to turn the reader away, rather than persuade him or her to agree. Here is a list that will help you to identify statements that are too extreme:

1. Find words such as *none, all, always, never, every.*
2. Find superlatives such as *best, most, powerful, smallest, greatest, slowest.*
3. Find words that exclude other possibilities, such as *absolutely, completely, totally, entirely.*
4. Find particularly harsh words such as *dictatorial, money-grubbing, vicious,* or *contemptuous.*

Activity 13F   Parents Again

1. Rewrite the paragraph about the growth of conservatism among parents, in Activity 13E.

2. Make it more convincing and appealing as a statement of opinion by adding more facts and softening the overly harsh statements.

HOW DO YOU GATHER FACTS TO SUPPORT OPINIONS?

When you have lived a long time and have experience, it will be easy to support your opinions with facts and examples from memory. But when you have only been on Earth some twelve to fourteen years, it is often necessary to gather information to support your opinion. This section will show you two ways to do this: **interviews** and **discussions.**

Tell Me about It: Interviews

You can interview other people to assemble their opinions and the reasons for them. As a writer, you can then use this information to prepare an opinion paragraph. This task has been done when you read or hear about such facts as

- Seventy percent of Canadians are concerned about the effects of acid rain.
- Sixty-five percent of Prince George parents favour a two-month spring break for their children.
- Sixty percent of Canadians say they would vote for the Rhinoceros Party if an election were held today.

At least two types of errors can occur when you use interviews as your method of gathering facts to support your opinions: **personal knowledge** and **interview bias.**

Ask What They Know: Personal Knowledge

Public opinions can be simply a collection of ignorance. Public opinion polls work best with simple questions about which you can expect the public to be informed. For example, there's no point in expecting a sensible public opinion on whether the 747 or the 727 is a better plane for fuel efficiency per passenger kilometre. It's better to ask an engineer.

Don't Bias the Response

Interview questions can bias the response by the way they are worded. For example, it is difficult to get an unambiguous (or clear) response to the following question: Have you stopped biting your fingernails yet? If the man you ask answers yes, you can conclude that he used to bite his fingernails. If he answers no, you can conclude that he still bites his fingernails.

A less obvious example of an interview question that can bias the response is: Do you favour the punishment of students who are late for school by expelling them from school? From this question you could not come to any conclusion about how many people favour expulsion for being late for school for the following reasons:

1. Some people might prefer a different punishment for students who are late.
2. Some people might want it clearly specified that only students who are late without a good reason should be expelled.
3. Some people may not favour punishing students at all who are late for school.

Where the Action Is: A Questionnaire

It's time now for you to try constructing a questionnaire that you can use to support your opinion. To get the least biased questionnaire, you should ask a mixture of closed-ended and open-ended questions.

	Closed-Ended Questions	Open-Ended Questions
1.	Single answer, usually *yes* or *no*.	Respondent is allowed to give reasons for the answer.
2.	Can be tabulated as percentages.	Can't be tabulated.
3.	Easy to report, but can be misleading.	Hard to report, but allows a greater understanding.

In preparing your opinion statements, you will want to be able to give some specific details, in the form of percentages, for example. You will also want to offer some of the reasons behind those opinions.

Therefore, a combination of closed and open-ended questions is most valuable.

Look at the *Sample Opinion Questionnaire*. Responses to this questionnaire will give you information on the TV viewing habits of the people you use in your sample.

Activity 13G   TV Watching Habits

1. Answer these questions about the sample opinion questionnaire:
    a. Which questions are open-ended?
    b. Which questions are closed-ended?
    c. What is the best way of combining the results of questions 1 to 6?

SAMPLE OPINION QUESTIONNAIRE: TV WATCHING HABITS

1. I watch TV an average of:

0	hours per week
5–10	hours per week
11–20	hours per week
21–50	hours per week
over 50	hours per week

2. My three favourite shows are: _____

_____

_____

3. On the average, I watch TV:

by myself	___ hours per week
with friends	___ hours per week
with my brothers and sisters	___ hours per week
with my parents	___ hours per week
with my whole family	___ hours per week

4. When I watch TV with other people, the shows are usually picked by:

myself	___
my friends	___
my brothers and sisters	___
my parents	___
my whole family	___

5. During the rest of my spare time,
   when I'm not watching TV, I:
   (List at least three activities and ____ ____ hours per week
   how many hours per week you ____ ____ hours per week
   spend on each.) ____ ____ hours per week
   ____ ____ hours per week
   ____ ____ hours per week

6. My mathematics mark on the last
   report card was _____

7. I am ____ 13 or under ____ over 13

    d. How could you report the results of questions 1, 3, and 5?

    e. What would you find by putting together the results of questions 3 and 4?

    f. How could you report the results of question 2?

    g. Why was question 6 included?

    h. Can you assume that the people in your class would know enough about this topic to give informed opinions on this questionnaire?

Activity 13H   Your Own Questionnaire

1. Design a questionnaire with six to ten questions about this topic: *Students and the Future.*

2. In small groups, select the six best questions from the questionnaires on students and the future. Put them on the chalkboard or on a large piece of newsprint.

3. As a whole class, look at the group questions and then compile a set of the best six to ten questions for a class questionnaire.

Activity 13I   A Questionnaire in Action

1. Divide the class in half. One-half of the class will conduct the questionnaire on TV watching. The other half will conduct the questionnaire on students and the future.

2. Form groups of eight—four with one questionnaire and four with the other.

3. Survey each other.
   a. The students with the TV questionnaire survey those with the future questionnaire. Then, exchange roles.
   b. Students with the TV questionnaire move on to another group, and repeat the surveying process.
   c. Repeat this procedure one more time, with the students with the TV questionnaire moving on to yet another group.

   Each of you will now have answers from at least twelve students. This should give you a good sample of the opinions of the students in your class.

4. Compile your results and then analyze them. *For example:* Are the answers of people who are 13 and under 13 years of age different from those who are over 13?

Activity 13J An Opinion Statement

1. Write an opinion paragraph on either Students' TV Watching Habits or Students and the Future.

2. Use this guide to help you construct this opinion paragraph:
   a. State your opinion.
   b. Present at least three facts or examples from your questionnaire to support your opinion.
   c. Draw a conclusion without repeating your opening opinion statement.

Talk About It: Discussion

A discussion can also provide you with the facts you need to support your opinion. Both open and guided discussions are valuable, but only if the topic under discussion is one about which your class can be considered to be informed.

Activity 13K A Discussion

1. Form small groups of three to five students and discuss this topic: *The Value of Pets*.

2. Take some notes from this discussion to collect as many facts and opinions as you can.

3. Use these questions to guide your discussion, but don't let them limit your flow of ideas:
   a. Who keeps pets?

b. What are the advantages of owning a pet?

c. Are these advantages the same for all people?

d. What are the disadvantages of owning a pet?

e. What facts can back up your opinions?

4. One member of each group should report a summary of the group's discussion to the whole class. Be sure to take down more notes from this whole class discussion.

Activity 13L   Writing About the Value of Pets

1. Write an opinion paragraph about the value of pets, based upon the information you collected from your discussions.

2. Use this outline as a guide for constructing your opinion paragraph:

a. State your opinion about the value of pets.

b. Present at least three facts or examples, which you have in your discussion notes, to support your opinion.

c. Write a final sentence that summarizes and reinforces your statement of opinion.

WHAT IS YOUR OPINION ABOUT HOCKEY?

This final section asks you to put together an opinion paragraph about hockey.

Activity 13M   Prewriting About Hockey

1. Look back at the paragraph you wrote for Activity 13A. From this paragraph, choose the opinion statement about hockey that you feel most strongly about and write it in your notebook.

2. Find support — facts and examples — for this opinion:

a. What facts do you know that support your opinion?

b. What facts will you have to get from others or from a book?

3. Find at least three support statements for your opinion and write them in your notebook following your original opinion statement.

4. Exchange work with a writing partner:

a. Read your partner's paragraph.

b. In your partner's book, list at least two facts or examples or opinions that are contrary to what your partner has written. That is, think of facts and examples that support some other opinion about hockey.

5. Get your work back from your partner and read the new facts or examples that do not support your opinion. If you can think of any additional facts that do not support your first opinion, add them to your partner's list.

6. Write a paragraph that refutes the facts and examples that appear in your partner's list. That is, find examples and facts that support your opinion and show these new facts to be wrong, or at least weak.

7. Finally, write a two- or three-sentence paragraph that restates your original opinion from 2 and 3.

Activity 13N Audience and Form

In this writing task, the audience and form have been determined for you.

Audience: Your audience is a knowledgeable adult reader, someone who is interested in hockey and will have his or her own opinions.

Form: The form for this writing task is a short essay. Write an essay of at least three paragraphs to convince the reader about your opinion.

1. In your writing groups, discuss these questions:
   a. What is a knowledgeable adult reader like?
   b. Should you use standard or non-standard usage, or a mixture of both? Why?
   c. What kind of sentence structure is appropriate to use for a knowledgeable adult reader?
   d. What can you do to convince this kind of reader to support your opinion?

2. How will a knowledgeable adult reader look at your use of the short essay form?
   a. What might be this reader's reaction to spelling errors?
   b. What kind of margins and other spacing will this reader expect?

Activity 13O Writing About Hockey

You now have the prewriting done for a three-paragraph statement of opinion.

1. Put the three paragraphs (or more) that you wrote in the prewriting stage into an essay. Write legibly, with adequate margins on all sides of your page.

2. Think of a title and place it at the top of your essay.

Activity 13P Revising Your Paper

1. Exchange work with a writing partner.

2. Help your partner examine his or her work, using these points as a guide:
   a. Underline the opinion that is the main point or forms the backbone of this essay.
   b. Number each of the supporting facts for this opinion.
   c. Use letters to indicate the facts or examples that refute, or go against, the main opinion statement. (You should find these in the second paragraph.)
   d. Do the facts and examples given in the first paragraph support the main opinion statement?
   e. Are there enough facts and examples in the first paragraph to convince you?
   f. Does the second paragraph do a good job of refuting any contrary facts or examples?
   g. Are there any too harshly worded statements that need softening?
   h. Does the author sound as if he or she is somebody whose opinion you would trust on this matter?
   i. Is there a final conclusion? If the essay simply ends, suggest a conclusion.

Activity 13Q Editing and Proofreading Your Paper

Meet as a writing group to go over the mechanics of your paper:

1. The first student reads your paper to look for errors in spelling.

2. The second student looks for errors in punctuation.

3. The third student looks for errors in capitalization.

4. The fourth student checks to make certain that each sentence is a complete sentence.

Activity 13R   Publishing and Sharing Your Paper

1. After your writing team has edited your work, write your final copy, which is ready for sharing with others.

2. Send your opinion statement about hockey to an adult reader and ask that person to write back to you, commenting on how well you convinced him or her that your opinion was right.

3. Or, you might try one of these ideas to share your work:
   a. Give it to the editor of your school newspaper for publication.
   b. Send it to your local paper to see if they will publish it.
   c. Send your letter to the coach of your favourite NHL team to see if he (or she) will respond to your ideas.
   d. Send your work to a high school classroom to get those students' reactions to your ideas.

You'll Continue to Have Opinions!

In this chapter, you have looked at the process involved in writing an opinion paragraph. Keep these ideas in mind. The opinion statement is one type of writing you will almost certainly have to do in future years.

ENDINGS

1. Study these cartoons. What is each one about? What is the theme or main idea for each cartoon? How are these cartoons different? How are they alike?

2. Put your ideas together and write a paragraph or two in your notebook about these cartoons. What do they say about living? What do they say about your life? Have you ever had similar experiences?

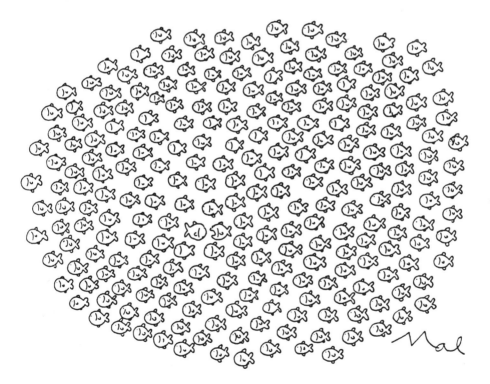

"Damn it, Mortimer, can't you do anything right?"

3. Think about your ideas and then write a letter to yourself in which you talk about your response to the cartoons. Also talk about the way you think you should live the next five years of your life.

4. Seal your letter in an envelope. Address the letter to yourself. On the envelope, write this special notice:
   To be opened on my eighteenth birthday.

RESOURCE CHAPTER — GRAMMAR

GRAMMAR CONCEPTS

All writers need to know the building blocks of language. In other words, they need to know **grammar**.

What is grammar, you ask? You can look at it one way, as a kind of giant puzzle, with millions of pieces to put together. The surprising thing is that you only rarely make mistakes in putting together the grammar puzzle.

As soon as you started to speak, you began to learn grammar. Many of you learned English grammar because English is your first language. Others learned the grammar of some other language, such as French or Ukrainian or Cree, and then you learned the grammar of English as your second language.

Grammar is a system that describes how words fit together to communicate ideas and thoughts.

This chapter is about the puzzle of grammar. At least, it's about part of the puzzle of grammar. It will introduce you to the eight parts of speech, and it will show you how to use this knowledge of the parts of speech to build sentences.

PARTS OF SPEECH

There are eight different kinds of words that are called parts of speech: **noun**, **verb**, **adjective**, **adverb**, **preposition**, **conjunction**, **interjection**,

Resource Chapter

pronoun. But, before reviewing the parts of speech it is important to understand the structure of the **sentence**.

The Sentence

Parts of speech make sense only as they fit into sentences. They don't stand by themselves very often. Sentences have two main parts: a subject and a predicate.

The *airplane* / *flew*.
subject   predicate

The huge *engine* / *roared*.
subject   predicate

Activity 14A   Subjects and Predicates

Write these sentences in your notebook and draw a line between the subject and the predicate.

1. The red light flashed.
2. The pilot blinked.
3. The propeller turned.
4. The fog appeared.
5. The runway disappeared.
6. The radio died.
7. The emergency light flashed.
8. Disaster loomed ahead.

Very few sentences are written this simply. Writers expand them so that they contain more words than just a subject and a predicate. So, you need to learn a new label: *complete subject* and *complete predicate*.

A complete subject is the simple subject and all of the words that go with it, like this:

The huge *engine* in the centre of the transport plane / *roared*.

             simple subject   simple
                                                       predicate
                       complete subject

A complete predicate is the simple predicate and all of the words that go with it, like this:

The *pilot*   /   *turned* the transport plane to the right without hesitating.
     simple   simple
     subject   predicate
                           complete predicate

Activity 14B   The Complete Subject

Here is a group of basic sentences. Divide them into two parts—the simple subject and the simple predicate. Then add your own words to the simple subject to expand it. Write your answers in your notebook.

Try to see how much information you can add to each basic sentence and still write a good sentence.

1. The car stops.
2. The driver looks.
3. The dog runs.
4. The bird sings.
5. The road continues.
6. The traffic stops.
7. The police officer whistles.
8. The ambulance comes.

Activity 14C   The Complete Predicate

This exercise is the reverse of Activity 14B. Add words to expand the simple predicate in each of these basic sentences.

1. The train whistles.
2. The tracks hum.
3. A crowd collects.
4. The train stops.
5. The passengers appear.
6. The conductor waves.
7. The engineer nods.
8. The train starts.

The complete predicate has some odd characteristics. You will have to look inside the complete predicate to understand it more fully.

The *racehorse* in its stall / *ate* the yellow oats.

simple subject	simple predicate
complete subject	complete predicate

The complete predicate sometimes contains a noun. This noun follows the verb. It completes the thought or action suggested by the verb. It tells *what* or *who* receives the action suggested by the verb. The noun that follows the verb is called a *noun object of the verb*.

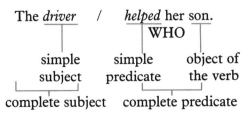

The *driver*   /   *helped* her son.

	WHO	
simple subject	simple predicate	object of the verb
complete subject	complete predicate	

Activity 14D   Noun Object of a Verb

Write these sentences in your notebook.

Draw a line between the complete subject and the complete predicate.

Show the *noun object of the verb* by using an arrow:

Puzzle: **One of these sentences does not have a noun that is the object of a verb. Can you find it?**

1. **The artist dropped her brushes on the floor.**
2. **The paint spattered the canvas and ruined the painting.***
3. **The artist called her helper.**
4. **The helper washed the floor with cold water.**
5. **The sun lit the room.**
6. **The artist walked out of the room.**
7. **She closed the door quietly.**
8. **She scolded herself in anger.**

*Watch this one. It's a little harder than the others.

There is one more fact about nouns that you need to know before you can find your way around a sentence. This fact requires a knowledge of prepositions.

Prepositions are words that connect nouns with nouns or nouns with verbs. A preposition and the noun it goes with are called a *prepositional phrase*. Notice the prepositions and prepositional phrases in these sentences:

The little girl *in the green jacket* walked *to the edge of the pond*. The geese swam quickly *to her*. They squawked as they swam *over the waves*. They had seen the breadcrust *in her hand*. She ran *around the edge of the pond* and started *for the car*. The geese followed *in hot pursuit*.

Prepositions are joining words, like these: *in, over, into, for, at, around, beside, to, by, under, beside, of, with, from, among*. They connect nouns with nouns. These nouns can be either part of the complete subject or the complete predicate. They also connect nouns with verbs. Follow the arrows in the example above to check out this rule.

Activity 14E   Nouns and Verbs with Prepositions

Write each sentence in your notebook. Circle each prepositional phrase and draw an arrow to the noun or verb to which it is connected.

Note: There are ten prepositional phrases in these sentences.

Example: The magician walked to the centre of the stage.
1. He winked to the leader of the band.
2. The music started with a huge drum roll.
3. The magician reached into his black hat.
4. The hat with its black velvet band fell to the floor.
5. A dove flew from the hat and sat among the ceiling lights.
6. The magician, with tears in his eyes, left the stage in disgust.

Nouns and Verbs

Nouns are words that name things. They name people, places, and objects, as well as ideas.

Verbs are words that tell what the action of a sentence is. Some verbs, like *is, am, was, were,* or *are,* are words that do not describe an action, but express the existence of something.

The following examples show that some words can be both a noun and a verb. They change their part of speech, depending upon how they are used within a sentence.

As Nouns	As Verbs
The *house* stood silently on the corner.	The museum *housed* the priceless treasures.
The catcher hit a home *run*.	The motor in this used car *runs* smoothly.
The dog's *bark* echoed across the yard.	The dog *barked* at the foot of the tree for two hours.

Activity 14F   Nouns and Verbs

Study this jumble of words and decide which are nouns and which are verbs. Use the definitions to help you decide.

In your notebook, create two columns and title them *Nouns* and *Verbs* and write each word in its proper column.

eel   prairie   precede   satisfy   mayor   conquest   ocean   oppose   elope   confuse

How to Identify Nouns

The definitions for noun and verb cannot always help you decide which is which. Other clues can help you out. The features that go with nouns and verbs also help to identify them. The following example outlines these features:

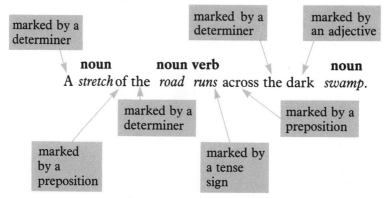

Here are some of the markers that help you identify nouns:

1. Nouns occur in specific positions, or places, within a sentence:

   a. as subjects   The cat likes the dog.

   b. as objects   The cat does not like her food.

   c. with prepositions   The cat with the black foot caught its tail in the door.

2. Nouns can be preceded by *determiners*, or words like:

   a. articles: *an, a, the*

   b. possessives: *my* hat   *our* hats   *your* hat
                 his hat   *her* hat   *its* hat   *their* hats

   c. numbers: such as *one, five, eight, twelve*

3. Nouns are sometimes modified or described by adjectives:

   The *big black* bug bit the *beautiful bobbing* bird.

Activity 14G   Identifying Nouns

1. **Add as many feature markers as you can to the nouns in these sentences and write your answers in your notebook.**

   Example: Birds eat worms.

   determiner adjective   prepositional phrase   determiner

   The little birds *in my yard* eat *six* worms each day.

a. Dogs chase cats.
b. Birds sing songs.
c. Horses eat grass.
d. Goats eat everything.

e. Canaries eat seeds.
f. Seagulls eat garbage.
g. Mosquitoes annoy people.
h. Spiders spin webs.

2. Fill in each blank with a noun.
   a. One day a little _____ went walking in the _____ .
   b. She met a big, bad _____ who asked her a _____ .
   c. The little _____ replied, ''I'm going to visit my
      _____ .
   d. The big, bad _____ sneaked through the _____ .
   e. He reached the _____ first and hid, waiting for the little
      _____ .
   f. The poor little _____ was in real _____ .

How to Identify Verbs

1. Verbs are marked by the endings they may have. These endings are called tense markers. They show the time at which something happens: the present, the past, or the future.

to talk	the infinitive form
I talk	present tense
he talk*s*	present tense
I talk*ed*	past tense
he talk*ed*	past tense
he *has* talked	past tense

The verb *to talk* is a **regular verb**. It simply adds tense markers to the main verb: talk + s; talk + ed.

Other verbs are **irregular**. The main verb itself changes when the time or tense changes.

I teach and he teaches   teach + es
I taught and he taught.

2. Some verbs can be identified by an **auxiliary verb**. Here is an example of an auxiliary verb with a main verb:

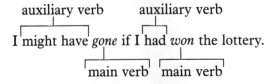

auxiliary verb   auxiliary verb

I might have *gone* if I had *won* the lottery.

main verb   main verb

Here is a list of possible auxiliary verbs:

be, am, is, are, was, were, been   will, would
can, could   may, might
have, has, had   must
do, does, did   shall, should

Activity 14H   Identifying Verbs

1. Copy and complete this chart of irregular verbs in your notebook.

Present Tense Form		Past Tense Form	
I swim	he swims	I swam	she has swum
I begin	he _____	I _____	she _____
I break	_____	_____	_____
I bring	_____	_____	_____
I choose	_____	_____	_____
I come	_____	_____	_____
I do	_____	_____	_____
I drink	_____	_____	_____
I drive	_____	_____	_____
I fall	_____	_____	_____
I freeze	_____	_____	_____
I give	_____	_____	_____
I go	_____	_____	_____
I run	_____	_____	_____
I see	_____	_____	_____
I speak	_____	_____	_____
I throw	_____	_____	_____
I write	_____	_____	_____

2. Decide which auxiliary verb could go in each blank:
   a. I _____ do my homework with you.
   b. She _____ finished her report before me.
   c. The quiz master _____ not know the correct answer.
   d. You _____ keep any of the prizes which you win.
   e. I _____ show you how to find a short cut to answer that question.
   f. We _____ sing in the festival about noon.
   g. I _____ given him the answer before.

Adjectives and Adverbs

Adjectives are words that tell more about nouns. They describe or modify nouns, like this:

The *large*, *happy* crowd cheered as the *Olympic gold* medalist skated to the podium.

How to Identify Adjectives

1. Adjectives are usually, but not always, placed before the nouns that they modify:

   The green, powerful ocean swept over the sandy beach.

   But:
   The ocean, green and powerful, swept over the sandy beach.

2. Suffixes mark the degrees of comparison of adjectives.

Degrees of Comparison		
The dog is small.	positive	(Only one dog is referred to.)
This dog is small*er*.	comparative	(Two dogs are compared.)
This dog is small*est*.	superlative	(Three or more dogs are compared.)

With long adjectives, the words *more* and *most* are used to form the degrees of comparison:

This painting is beautiful	(Only one painting is referred to.)
This painting is *more* beautiful.	(Two paintings are compared.)
This painting is *most* beautiful.	(Three or more paintings are compared.)

3. Some adjectives have suffixes that mark them as adjectives:

able/ible	irritable/defensible
ar	solar, lunar
ful	beautiful
less	hopeless
ous	gracious
y	windy
ate	fortunate

4. Adjectives sometimes follow words called qualifiers:

A *very* windy day . . .   A *rather* hopeless situation . . .
A *quite* beautiful pose . . .   An *almost* happy loser . . .

Activity 14I Adjectives

In your notebook, list the fifteen adjectives in the following story. Then list the two qualifiers in the story.

Nothing
The young singer climbed onto the high platform. The huge audience, quite happy by this time, sat with eager expectation. The big room became quieter as the singer stepped to the metallic microphone. The quietest person of all was the unfortunate singer. He could not remember a word, not a single note. His mind, open and empty, refused to work. It was his most hopeless moment.

How to Identify Adverbs

1. *Adverbs* answer some definite questions:

   a. They tell *when* something happened or will happen.

      We will fly to the moon *tomorrow.*

   b. They tell *where* something happened.

      We went *there.*

   c. They tell *how* something happened.

      We made our decision *quickly.*

2. Adverbs often end with the suffix -ly.
   Note: This is the form you can add to most adjectives to turn them into adverbs.

adjective form	adverb form
happy	happily
sad	sadly
hopeless	hopelessly
silent	silently

3. Adverbs can usually be compared in the same way as adjectives. Most adverbs use the words *more* and *most* in their comparison:

He went happily.   (One person is referred to.)
Serge went *more* happily.   (Two persons are compared.)

Katerina went most *happily* of (Three or more persons are
all.   compared.)

A few shorter adverbs use the suffixes *-er* and *-est* in their comparative form:

far   farth*er*   farth*est*
near   near*er*   near*est*
late   lat*er*   lat*est*

4. Adverbs sometimes follow qualifiers, just as adjectives may. Some qualifiers are *very*, *too*, *quite*, and *somewhat*.

He walked *very* quietly.   He sang *very* loudly.
She ran *slowly*.   She talked *somewhat* boldly.

5. Adverbs can often be placed at several spots in a sentence.

The announcer *quietly* spoke the bad news.
Quietly the announcer spoke the bad news.
The announcer spoke the bad news *quietly*.

Activity 14J Adverbs

1. In your notebook, write three adverbs that could modify or tell more about each of these verbs:

   a. sing   e. talk
   b. shout   f. shoot
   c. write   g. read
   d. run   h. play

2. Complete each of these sentences by writing your answers in your notebook. Be sure to include the adverb in parenthesis in your sentence.

   Example:
   Suzanne walked . . . . (quietly)
   Suzanne quietly walked through the hospital ward.

   a. Ralph waited until . . . . (nearly)
   b. Mike will apply . . . . (soon)
   c. Jessie looked . . . . (rather anxiously)
   d. He worked . . . . (patiently)
   e. She stopped and . . . . (cautiously)
   f. As he . . . he would . . . . (often)

3. Here is a game with adverbs.
   a. Choose two students to go out of the room.
   b. Choose two more students to act at the front of the room.
   c. Select an action that the actors can perform: clean the board, write a letter, open a window.
   d. The actors select an adverb to describe how they perform the action: angrily, happily, slowly, quickly.
   e. The actors perform their action for the students who were out of the room.
   f. The students who were out of the room guess the action and the adverb.
   g. Your class should repeat this activity several times, just to see how many different adverbs members of the class can perform. You can make the game harder by not allowing anyone to choose the same adverb twice.

Prepositions and Conjunctions

You have already studied prepositions and prepositional phrases in Activity 14E, and you will study conjunctions and clauses in the next chapter. This section is a quick review of these concepts so that you will remember prepositions and conjunctions as two of the eight parts of speech.

How to Identify Prepositions

Prepositions are often little words, which join a noun with a noun or a verb with a verb. One of the easiest ways to learn about prepositions is to become familiar with a list of the most common ones.

Here is a list of common prepositions:

above	before	during	over
across	behind	for	to
along	below	from	through
among	beneath	in	under
around	beside	into	up
at	between	of	with
	by	on	

Activity 14K Prepositions

In your notebook, write complete sentences that contain the prepositions and prepositional phrases included in parentheses.

Example: _____ (out the gate) (over the hill).
The goat galloped out the gate and raced over the hill.

a. _____ (into the forest)   (beside a lake)
b. _____ (around the curve)   (to the stop sign)
c. _____ (above the clouds)   (among the eagles)
d. _____ (under the roof)   (beside the castle)
e. _____ (between periods)   (around the microphone)

How to Identify Conjunctions

Conjunctions: are joining words that link together both large and small units. You should become familiar with some of the most common conjunctions.

---

and, but, or
after, although, because, before, if, since, that, unless, until
when, while

Activity 14L   Conjunctions

1. In your notebook, explain what the difference in conjunctions makes in each set of sentences:
   a. To find the clue, you should walk up *and* down the street.
      To find the clue, you should walk up *or* down the street.
   b. Father said I cannot play basketball *unless* I have a C average.
      Father said I cannot play basketball *because* I have a C average.

2. These sentences contain incorrect conjunctions. Rewrite each sentence in your notebook. Choose one of the conjunctions from the list above to correct each sentence.
   a. I sang well *but* the audience applauded my performance.
   b. I read my history text *unless* it contained the answers I needed.
   c. Science is my best subject *unless* I like it.
   d. We painted portraits of our friends *although* we had art class last week.
   e. Our gym class was cancelled *until* the floor was painted.
   f. You should not walk on the gym floor *after* you are wearing street shoes.
   g. We had a spare during first period *or* we had a surprise quiz in period two.

3. Here is a game that encourages you to use conjunctions and some other parts of speech.
   a. Your class should divide into teams of about eight or ten players per team.
   b. Player 1 for each team writes a word on the blackboard.
   c. Player 2 goes to the board and adds a word to this first word, either before or after it.
   d. The other players, in order, keep adding words to make a sentence.

   Caution:
   Team members are not allowed to discuss their work with each other while the game is in progress.

   e. The winning team is the one that has the longest and most logical sentence at the end of six minutes.
   f. Play this game several times, until you get skillful at using prepositions and conjunctions to add words to your sentences.

Interjections

A part of speech that isn't used very often is the **interjection**. Interjections are words that express anger, surprise, joy, or almost any emotion. As a rule, interjections are followed by exclamation points:

Example:
Wow! You fanned him with that pitch.
Gee whiz! I couldn't have done it without you.
Oh! You make me so mad.
Well! What do you think you're doing?

Activity 14M   Interjections

1. Make a list of all of the interjections you can think of.

2. Look through a magazine. After getting permission, cut out examples of interjections. You will find these most often in advertisements and headings. Make a poster of *Interjections in Action.*

Pronouns

Pronouns are the eighth part of speech.
   Look carefully at this sentence:

> Marion dove into the pool so that Marion could test the tempera-
> ture of the water in the pool which Mukhtar, Hans, and Ricardo
> said would be too cold for Mukhtar, Hans, and Ricardo.

Would you write a sentence like this one? Probably not! You would
probably say something like this:

> Marion dove into the pool so that *she* could test *its* water
> temperature, which Mukhtar, Hans, and Ricardo said would be
> too cold for *them*.

The italicized words in the second version of the sentence are called
personal pronouns.

You use personal pronouns in your writing to stand for people and
things you have already mentioned. The words the pronouns stand for
are called **antecedents**.

Pronoun	Antecedent
she	Marion
it	pool
them	Mukhtar, Hans, Ricardo

Activity 14N Personal Pronouns

1. Replace each noun or noun group in the first sentence with a
   suitable pronoun in the second sentence. Write your answers in
   your notebook.
   a. The twelve skiers warmed up in the lodge. _____ enjoyed
      resting _____ in front of the fire.
   b. John's skis rested against the wall. _____ said, " _____
      skis can't take the kind of punishment _____ am giving
      _____ ."
   c. The other skiers all laughed. " _____ told _____ to
      stay on the paths, John. _____ are made for _____
      comfort and safety."

2. To answer this first question, you had to use your knowledge
   about personal pronouns. You probably know quite a lot about
   them. On the next page is a chart that will help to organize all that
   you know about personal pronouns. Write it in your notebook,
   filling in the blanks.

Resource Chapter

Subject Form	Object Form	Possessive Form
First person (singular) I (plural) _____	_____ _____	_____ , min‹ our,
Second person (singular) _____ (plural) _____	you _____	your, _____ _____, your
Third person (singular) he _____ it (plural) they	_____ her _____ _____	her, _____ their,

Activity 14O   Third Person and First Person

Here is a paragraph written in the *third person*. That is, it uses personal pronouns such as he, she, and they.

Change this *third person point of view* to *first person point of view* by substituting the first person pronouns I and we for the third person pronouns.

As you write this new version in your notebook, think of yourself in the situation described by the author, Margaret Laurence. You are forced to survive in the wilderness and your food is running out.

The leaves of the poplar were turning a clear yellow, and I knew it was autumn. She looked with sudden terror at the tins of food on the shelves and saw they were almost gone. She picked berries and cooked them on the wood stove, wondering how long they would keep. She had fished only to provide her daily needs, but now she caught as many fish as she could. She slit and cleaned them and laid them out in the sun to dry. One afternoon she found a black bear from the forest, feeding on the outspread fish. She had no gun. At that moment she was not afraid of the animal. She could think only of the sun-dried fish, hers, the food she had caught. She seized a stick and flew at the bear. The creature, taken by surprise, looked at her with shaggy menace. Then it lumbered off into the green ferns and the underbrush.

Margaret Laurence, *A Queen in Thebes*

Now that you are becoming skilled at working with personal pronouns and point of view, you have a job to do.

Activity 14P   The Newspaper and Pronouns

Someone has written this news story in your school newspaper, but this person is a visitor from a foreign country whose language does not use pronouns.

Revise this story, using personal pronouns where you think they would improve the article. Make this story ready for publication.

> Yesterday, Central School's basketball team defeated Central School's basketball team's arch rival, Forest Grove. The final score of this exciting game was 85–83.
>
> Central School's team was cheered on by Central School's excellent cheerleaders and coached to victory by Central School's basketball coach, Mr. Evans. Mr. Evans said after the game that Mr. Evans was sure Mr. Evan's well-prepared team would win the team's game against the team's greatest rival. "Mr. Evans knew the team would win from the end of the first quarter," Mr. Evans said after the game.
>
> The team members were enthusiastic about the team member's victory. "The team members deserve all the glory the team members can get at this time," the team members said.
>
> Central School's basketball team's next game will be Central School's Basketball team's last regular game of the season. The team will play Eastide on Tuesday. The game should be a great game for coaches, teams, cheerleaders, and spectators.

Activity 14Q   The Correct Pronoun

Rewrite each sentence in your notebook, choosing the right personal pronouns from those in parentheses:

Hint: Do you need the subject, object, or possessive form of each pronoun?

1. John called loudly to Jason and *(I, me)*.

2. *Last week (she, her)* and Len visited Banff.

3. Mr Prasad showed Marcel and *(he, him, his)* the otters in the creek.

4. Neither Lech nor *(he, him)* saw the comet.

5. Call Chantal or *(I, me, mine)*.

6. Sarah found out that both Joseph and *(I, me, mine)* had seen her.

7. Devin said he would help you and *(I, me)* with our homework.

8. Mario helped *(she, her)* and *(I, me)* make the cake.

9. Mr. Knudsen chose *(she, her)* and Helga to go to visit the Legislature.

10. Marcia and *(I, me)* have joined the orchestra.

REVIEW OF PARTS OF SPEECH

In this chapter we have studied eight parts of speech. They are listed in the chart below.

NOUN VERB ADJECTIVE ADVERB

PREPOSITION CONJUNCTION INTERJECTION PRONOUN

The next section contains some puzzles dealing with the parts of speech.

Activity 14R   A Parts of Speech Crossword Puzzle

Do you know the names of the parts of speech? Let's see how you do with this crossword puzzle.

Write your answers to this puzzle in your notebook.

ACROSS

1. A word that serves as a noun marker: *a, an, the*

3. A word that names things: people, places, ideas

4. Oh! Help! No!

5. A word that can take the place of 3 Across
7. A joining word like *and* or *but*
8. A word that suggests action or being

DOWN

2. Words that begin phrases, like *in*, *over*, *under*, or *on*
6. A word that describes 3 Across
9. A word that describes 8 Across

Activity 14S   Following a Pattern

Here are some sentence patterns from which you can make non-sense sentences. Copy these sentences into your notebook and fill in the blanks with the appropriate parts of speech. Your results can be as crazy as you like.

Example:

The _____ climbed _____ and _____
    noun   **prepositional phrase**   **verb**

_____ .
prepositional phrase

The *elephant* climbed *up the CN Tower* and danced *on the top*.

1. A(n) _____ _____ shouted _____ and _____
     adjective   **noun/subject**   **prepositional phrase**   **verb**

   a(n) _____ .
     noun/object

2. Why did _____ sing _____ when the moon rose?
      proper noun   **prepositional phrase**

3. _____ _____ burn _____ _____ .
  adjective   **noun/plural**   **adverb**   **prepositional phrase**

4. _____ _____ _____ _____ and then stumbles
 prepositional phrase **proper noun**   **verb**   **noun/object**

  _____ _____ .
    adverb   **prepositional phrase**

5. _____ eat _____ _____ so that _____ can drive
    noun/plural   adjective   noun/object   noun

_____ _____ .
    noun/object   prepositional phrase

Activity 14T Parts of Speech

Here's another chance to write some odd sentences. All you have to do is to fill in the blanks. Write your answers in your notebook.

_____ *is* _____

that _____ .

1. Place a *noun* in the first blank as subject of the sentence.

2. Place an *adjective* in the second blank.

3. Write a humorous or ridiculous consequence in the third blank to complete the *predicate* of the sentence.

Example:

My *bedroom* is so *small* that *flies must file a flight plan*.
   noun   adjective   words to complete the predicate.

My *friend* is so *cheap* that *going out to eat means sharing a sandwich*
   noun   adjective   words to complete

in his backyard.
the predicate

You might wish to share your exaggerations in small groups, or make a display on your classroom bulletin board.

PARTS OF SPEECH AND WRITING

In the last section you looked at the parts of speech. The next section shows you how these parts of speech work in sentences and gives you practice using them as you write sentences.

Most sentences follow a basic pattern with a *noun* and a *verb*, like this:

noun verb prepositional phrase

The sun set beyond the hill.

noun verb noun/object adverb

The car crossed the intersection cautiously.

This basic pattern can be changed. You can end up with a different sentence structure if you start moving things around. The next set of activities looks at ways to change this basic structure.

Activity 14U An Adverb Opener

Adverbs can quite easily move to the beginning of a sentence. Look at these examples:

> *Thoughtfully*, the teacher set down his book.
> *Sadly*, he walked through the dark streets.
> *Quickly*, the answer came to her.

1. Rewrite these sentences in your notebook and place the adverb at the front of the sentence:

   a. The space ship drifted *aimlessly* in its new orbit.
   b. The ship's captain called *repeatedly* for help.
   c. Her super lasar beams drifted off *suddenly* into space.

2. Create a sentence of your own, using each of these adverbs as an *adverb sentence opener*.

   a. Frankly, _____
   b. Quickly, _____
   c. Fearfully, _____
   d. Bravely, _____

Activity 14V Prepositional Phrase Opener

You can also move prepositional phrases around to act as openers for your sentences. Here are some examples:

> *In the morning*, I feel sleepy and tired.
> *On my way to school*, I begin to see things clearly.
> *At noon*, I have conquered the day.
> *In the evening*, I really come alive.

1. Write sentences of your own, using these prepositional phrases as sentence openers:
   a. Through the telescope, _____
   b. Over the blueline, _____
   c. Across the ocean, _____

Activity 14W   Predicate and the Subject

Another way to vary sentence structure is to exchange the subject and the predicate. In this way, you use the predicate as the sentence opener. Here are some examples:

In the field grazed two old cows.
complete predicate   complete subject.

In the shade lay two young calves.
complete predicate   complete subject.

Over the hill crept the prowling coyote.
complete predicate   complete subject.

1. Write your own sentences in which you exchange the subject and the predicate. Start your sentences with these phrases as part of the complete predicate:
   a. In the distance _____
   b. Out of his desk _____
   c. Throughout the year _____

Activity 14X   Adjective Openers

You can also use adjectives as sentence openers, but they are a little tougher to move around than adverbs. Look at this example:

> *Independent*, he stood with his arms crossed.
> *Insistent*, she argued her case.
> *Happy*, they walked away together.

1. Write sentences of your own that begin with these adjectives:
   a. Sad, _____
   b. Silent, _____
   c. Free, _____
   d. Resolute, _____

Activity 14Y   Direct Object Openers

You can also change some sentences around so that the noun, direct object of the verb, is the sentence opener. These examples show how this can be done:

> *Two correct answers* **John wrote on his paper.**
> *Her future* **Jacqueline chose to ignore.**
> *Her concern* **Marika placed before the committee.**
> *Her answer* **Natasha gave easily.**

1. Try writing your own sentences with these direct objects of verbs as openers.
   a. The exam _____
   b. The ball _____
   c. The concert _____
   d. The holiday _____

In this section, you tried out several different ways to begin sentences. These ways are listed in this chart.

Sentence Openers
1. Adverb opener
2. Prepositional Phrase opener
3. Predicate/Subject exchange
4. Adjective openers
5. Direct Object openers

Activity 14Z   Working with Sentence Openers

1. Choose a paragraph that you wrote some time ago — perhaps this year, or even in an earlier grade. It should be a paragraph of about eight to ten sentences in length.
   a. Rewrite this paragraph in your notebook.
   b. Where possible, change the order of each sentence so that it begins with a different opener. Use your work in this section to give you ideas.

    c. Underline each new opener and write above it the kind of opener that it is.

2. Find a paragraph in a story that you are reading in literature class. Choose a paragraph of about six sentences.
    a. Rewrite this paragraph in your notebook.
    b. Underline each opener for each sentence, including the regular noun as subject opener.
    c. Above each opener, write the kind that it is.

At the End of Things

This chapter has introduced you to a grammar system. In it, you learned about the *eight parts of speech*, and some of the characteristics of these parts of speech.

You also practised using your knowledge of the parts of speech to look at sentences. You most likely pushed the order of words in some sentences around so that they looked, and sounded, pretty odd. And other sentences probably sounded all right.

You now have the skill to experiment with the order you use when you put words together. This skill will help you out when you are *revising* your writing. You won't want to change every sentence that you write into some odd order, but you can change the occasional sentence. These changes will give variety to your writing, and better hold the attention of your reader.

This information you should keep in mind. Probably it will help you out someday. Skillfully you will write unusual sentences. Awe-struck, your readers will admire your skill. Happily you will keep on writing.

CHAPTER
15

RESOURCE CHAPTER: SENTENCE COMBINING

WORKING WITH SYNTAX

-]20 PRINT "LEFT 2"
-]21 PRINT "FORWARD 11"
-]22 PRINT "LEFT 7"
-]23 PRINT "RIGHT 29"
-]24 PRINT "BACKWARDS 5"
-]SYNTAX ERROR

If you've worked with a computer, you have probably seen messages like this one. When you make a mistake in giving it directions, the computer will let you know. The message **syntax error** means that the order of your directions just doesn't make sense.

The word **syntax** refers to the order in which things go together. Here is an example of a **syntax error** in written language:

Scary a went to Monique movie.

You can't get any meaning from this sentence because its syntax is wrong — the words are not in the right order.

This chapter is about **syntax** — but it is not about errors. Rather, it's about improving your ability to handle syntax. In other words, it will help you write better, stronger sentences.

THE BASIC SENTENCE

The main unit of English syntax is the **sentence**. You, as a speaker of English, have developed a feeling for a sentence. It is a unit of words that communicates a thought to you in a special form. Most sentences have a **subject** and **predicate**. If communication in English does not follow this form of subject and predicate, it is not a sentence.

Activity 15A   The Basic Sentence

1. Some of these units of words are complete sentences, with subjects and predicates. Others are not.

   In your notebook, tell whether each unit of words is a *sentence* or a *non-sentence*.

   For those that you classify as non-sentences, rewrite them in your notebook to make them complete. You may add, subtract, or substitute words to create your complete sentences.

   a. Newfoundland is Canada's newest province.
   b. Beside the cold Atlantic Ocean.
   c. The highest tides in the world occur in the Bay of Fundy.
   d. Nova Scotia is the home of the Bluenose Schooner.
   e. Famous for fiddleheads, which grow in the St. John Valley.
   f. Maine, which is New Brunswick's American neighbour.
   g. Canada's smallest province, with miles and miles of sandy beaches.
   h. Nova Scotia, famous for fishing, attracts many tourists each year.
   i. A ferry service connects Nova Scotia with Prince Edward Island.
   j. The Cabot Trail up the west side of Cape Breton Island.

2. The following units of words look like complete sentences. But they are not sentences, for they don't make sense.

   Rewrite each unit of words. Add a logical predicate to each subject, and add a logical subject to each predicate.

Example:

   complete subject   complete predicate
   _____   _____
          | |
The St. Lawrence River / waves to the cheering crowd.

Rewrite:

<u>complete subject</u>   <u>complete predicate</u>

The St. Lawrence River / *flows into the Atlantic Ocean.*

<u>complete subject</u>   <u>complete predicate</u>

The captain on the deck of the ship / waves to the cheering crowd.

   a. The Ottawa River / munched peanuts on the quiet deck.
   b. The Niagara Falls / lay on the deck in a lounge chair.
   c. Hudson Bay / sent a telegraph to the keeper of the lighthouse.
   d. Labrador, which is part of Newfoundland, / quietly sipped a refreshing drink.
   e. The CN Tower, the highest free-standing structure in the world, / listened to her new stereo.

JOINING WORDS TO LINK TWO BASIC SENTENCES

When you write, you often join two or more basic sentences. There are several words that allow you to do this. These words are called **conjunctions**.

One set of joining words is the **coordinating conjunctions**, *and* and *but*.

> Ontario is Canada's largest province, *and* it has an interesting history.
> French is the main language of Quebec, *but* English is readily understood in the large urban centres.

The second group of joining words is called **subordinating conjunctions**. Some subordinating conjunctions are these: *when, because, after, while, as, before.*

> Montreal gained national prominence *when* the World Fair, Expo '67, was held there.

> Quebec City attracts many tourists *because* they enjoy the French flavour of the city.

> *Because* Canada has two official languages, English and French, we hold a unique position among the nations of the world.

The following activities will give you some practice with **sentence combining** — joining two basic sentences to make one large sentence. To do these activities you need to understand a signal system that tells you how to join the basic sentences. Here's an example:

1. The lighthouse stood on a rocky coast. ◄── | Sentence 1 is called the base sentence |

2. It saved many a ship from disaster.   (combine . . . and)

| base sentence |

1. The government spent a lot of money to maintain the lighthouse.

2. The government knew that the lighthouse saved many human lives.   (combine . . . because)

The directions tell you to combine each set of sentences. In the first set, you must add Sentence 2 to the base sentence by using the joining word *and*. Here is a rewrite of the first set of sentences:

The lighthouse stood on a rocky coast *and* it saved many a ship from disaster.

In the second set, you have to join Sentence 2 to the base sentence by using the joining word *because*, like this:

The government spent a lot of money to maintain the lighthouse *because* the government knew that the lighthouse saved many human lives.

Sometimes the directions tell you to leave some words out when you are joining them. The signal to delete or leave out a word is this: X. The first set of sentences could also have been written like this:

1. The lighthouse stood on a rocky coast.

2. X̶ saved many a ship from disaster.   (combine . . . and)

Rewrite: The lighthouse stood on a rocky coast and saved many a ship from disaster.

Activity 15B Joining Words

1. Following the joining signals, write each sentence in your notebook.

    a. Newfoundland was first settled in the seventeenth century.
       It is Canada's newest province.   (combine . . . but)

    b. I remember my trip to Fredericton.
       I saw the wide St. John River.   (combine . . . where)

    c. The seagulls looked like little peas in a pod.
       They sat on the roof of the fishing shed.   (combine . . . as)

    d. The old fishermen from Lunenburg met the tourists.
       He showed them how to make lobster traps.   (combine . . . and)

    e. The Bay of Fundy will be a future source of energy.
       Someone can find a way to use the swift tides to generate hydro-
       electricity.   (combine . . . if)

    f. Peggy's Cove was a quiet fishing village in Nova Scotia.
       It became a major tourist attraction.   (combine . . . before)

    g. The north shore of Prince Edward Island can be cold in winter.
       It is open to the winds off the Gulf of St. Lawrence.
                                                  (combine . . . because)

    h. I knew that we were approaching Cape Breton Island.
       We reached the Canso Causeway, a bridge linking the main-
       land and the island.   (combine . . . when)

    i. I stood on Citadel Hill in Halifax, looking at the harbour.
       The old town clock rang the hour.   (combine . . . as)

    j. You will never truly experience the marvels of Atlantic Canada.
       You get to know the small fishing villages.   (combine . . . unless)

2. Combine each set of sentences by choosing one joining word
   from the box. Place this joining word before the first sentence,
   like this:

   **As I watched the boat sail away from the wharf, a seagull stole
   my sandwich.**

a. ∧ We went to Toronto for our vacation.
We made a list of places to visit.

b. ∧ The tour guide drove along Spadina Crescent.
She hummed a verse of *O Canada*.

c. ∧ The bus drove up to Ontario Place.
The tourists poured out to take pictures.

d. ∧ The wind was blowing off Lake Ontario.
We returned to the tour bus to find our sweaters.

e. ∧ The tour guide took our order.
She went to the hamburger stand.

f. ∧ You want to watch the Argonauts practise football.
Let's go to the CN Tower.

g. ∧ You want to see people of many ethnic heritages.
You should take a ride on Toronto's street cars.

h. ∧ We visited the Toronto Art Gallery
We caught the subway to our hotel.

i. ∧ You go to the top of the CN Tower.
You haven't really seen Toronto.

j. ∧ The tour of Toronto came to an end.
I have been very lonely.

unless
after
when
since
if
because
before
as
while

3. Combine each group of basic sentences into one sentence and write your answers in your notebook.

   Your sentence should contain at least one of the join words (or conjunctions) listed in the box. You may place the join words before any basic sentences You may also change any of the basic sentences you choose. When you finish this exercise, you should have used each join word at least once.

when	because	before
although	since	as

Gabriel Dumont

a. Gabriel Dumont was young.
He lived on the Prairies.

b. One day his family camped for the night.
It was 1848.
They had travelled all day.
They had travelled with a caravan of Métis people.

Gabriel Dumont

c. Gabriel watched.
   His father hobbled the horses.
   His uncle hobbled the horses.
   His uncle was Alexis.

d. Gabriel was sent to make a smudge fire.
   Isadore was sent to make a smudge fire.
   The flies were very bad.
   The mosquitoes were very bad.

e. Gabriel loved Uncle Alexis.
   Uncle Alexis did not tease him.
   Gabriel's body was stocky.
   Gabriel's legs were short.

f. Gabriel put his ear to the ground.
   He heard a rumbling noise.

g. He ran to his father.
   He thought the Sioux were attacking.

h. He asked for a gun to help fight.
   His father had little time to think.

i. The noise sounded like horses' hooves.
   It was a herd of buffalo.
   The buffalo were stampeding.

j. Uncle Alexis admired Gabriel's bravery.
Uncle Alexis gave his gun to Gabriel.

k. Gabriel named his gun *Le Petit*.
Le Petit means ''small one.''
The gun was small like him.

l. Gabriel grew to be a man.
He was brave.
He fought with Louis Riel.
Louis Riel and Gabriel fought in the Métis War of 1885.

m. Gabriel Dumont was a leader.
He lead the Métis people.
He was called *Prince of the Plains*.

In Activity 15 A you practised sentence combining using *and* and *but*
as joining words, or coordinators. Another word, like *and* and *but* is the
word *or*. It, too, can be used to join basic sentences.

The next activity requires you to use your knowledge of these joining
words with your understanding of pronouns.

Activity 15C *Joining Words and Pronouns*

1. Combine the following sentences as directed by the signals.
The Signal *P* indicates that you should substitute a pronoun for a
noun.

Example:
Motorcycle enthusiasts in the Vancouver region are 25 000 strong.

Motorcycle enthusiasts' numbers are growing daily.
           P   (combine . . . and)

Rewrite:
Motorcycle enthusiasts in the Vancouver region are 25 000 strong

and **their** numbers are growing daily.
     P

Example:
Motorcyclists used to have a bad reputation.

Motorcyclists do not deserve **a bad reputation** today.
    P   P   (combine . . . but)

Rewrite:
Motorcyclists used to have a bad reputation, but they do not

deserve **it** today.
      P

a. There are many who drive large motorcycles.
    The majority of motorcycles are small, off-road vehicles.
                                    (combine . . . but)

b. Abandoned gravel pits are traditional motorbike terrain.
    Unused dirt trails are used as well.   (combine . . . and)

c. Motorbike drivers drive just for fun.

    Motorbike drivers become involved in serious competition.
            P   (combine . . . or)

d. Serious road races involve extremely high speed.

    ~~Serious road races involve~~ hairpin turns.   (combine . . . ,)
    ~~Serious road races involve~~ a dirt or gravel track.
                                     (combine . . . , and)

e. Cross-country racing also involves very high speed.

    Cross-country racing can involve as many as five hundred bikes.
        P   (combined . . . and)

f. Time trials are the most challenging of the motorcycle events.

    Time trials test the bike as well as the rider's skill.
        P   (combine . . . and)

g. Speeds seldom exceed eighty kilometres per hour.
    The rider must show skill by not touching the ground with his
    or her feet.

                                      (combine . . . but)

h. Riders can join a motorcycle club.

    ~~Riders can~~ ride alone   (combine . . . , or)
    ~~Riders can~~ ride with friends.   (combine . . . , or)

i. Vancouver had one motorcycle club in the 1920s.
    There are many motorcycle clubs now.   (combine . . . but)

j. Some motorcycle clubs are highly organized.

    Some motorcycle clubs work for the improvement of motor-
    cycling.   P   (combine . . . and)

    k. **Motorcyclist** can choose to become serious competitors.

                                                      (combine . . . or)

    ~~Motorcyclists~~ ~~can~~ ~~choose~~ ~~to~~ ~~become~~ serious club members.

                                                        (combine . . . and)

2. In the previous exercise, you practised sentence combining using *and, but,* and *or* as your join words. This exercise will give you practice with three more join words: nor, either-or, neither-nor.

Example:

Snakes are dangerous.

~~Snakes~~ ~~are~~ harmless.   (combine . . . either-or)

Rewrite:

Snakes are either dangerous or harmless.

    Use these new join words to combine the following groups of sentences. When you finish this exercise, you will have constructed a paragraph about *Snakes in Canada*.

    a. People have a great fear of snakes.

        People have no fear of **snakes.**   (combine . . . either-or)

    b. Rattlesnakes are the only dangerous Canadian snakes.

        Rattlesnakes are found in the southern parts of British Columbia,

        Alberta, and Saskatchewan.   (combine . . . and)

    c. The garter snake is native to most parts of Canada.
       There are no snakes native to Newfoundland.   (combine . . . but)

    d. The common garter snake has stripes which are white or yellow.

       ~~The~~ ~~common~~ ~~garter~~ ~~snake~~ ~~has~~ ~~stripes~~ ~~which~~ are orange or green.

                                        (combine . . . either-or)

    e. When disturbed, these snakes may bite in self-defence.

       ~~When~~ ~~disturbed,~~ **these snakes** may emit a foul-smelling fluid.
                                       (combine . . . and)

    f. The bite is not harmful.
       The fluid is not dangerous.   (combine . . . and)

NOUN CLAUSES

Sometimes you will find sentences in which the object is one word:

The *storm* / *hit* the unsuspecting *coastline*.

subject   verb   object

It is possible to have a whole group of words act as an object in a basic sentence, like this:

He knew *something*.
The path ahead would be covered with nettles and thorns.

(combine . . . that)

He knew *that the path ahead would be covered with nettles and thorns*.

subject verb   object

She could not decide *something*.
Winnipeg or Thunder Bay would be the better location.

(combine . . . whether)

She could not decide

subject   verb

whether Winnipeg or Thunder Bay would be the better location.

object

The combining signal *something* indicates this word-group kind of object, called **noun clauses**.

Activity 15D   Noun Clauses

1. **Combine these sentences about Louis Riel, a Canadian Métis hero.**
   Use the new signal —*something*,— to create noun clauses in your rewrite sentences.

   a. Riel thought *something*.

   Riel must have all the Métis people on his side.
   P
   (combine . . . that)

b. He had to decide *something*.

He should do som̶e̶thing about the government's threat to the Métis way of life. (combine . . . what)

c. He finally realized *something*.
He must make his move quickly. (combine . . . that)

H̶e̶ m̶u̶st let the government in Ottawa know *something*. (combine . . . and)
He believed in the rights of the Métis people. (combine . . . that)

d. Riel discovered *something*.

P **Riel** had a faithful ally in Gabriel Dumont. (combine . . . that)

e. He decided *something*.
Dumont would be his close advisor. (combine . . . that)

f. The Canadian government soon concluded *something*.
Riel had to be stopped. (combine . . . that)
He could cause dangerous unrest. (combine . . . because)

2. Combine these sentences, using the new signal *something*.

a. Alain could not decide *something*.

Al̶ain co̶u̶ld take Marsha to the movies. (combine . . . whether to)
Al̶ain co̶uld t̶ake Ma̶rsha to the carnival. (combine . . . or)

b. He knew *something*.
The message had gotten through. (combine . . . that)

Th̶e̶ mes̶s̶age h̶a̶d go̶t̶ten to the other side. (combine . . . 0)

c. Tell me *something*.
I should buy that old car now. (combine . . . if)

X̶ sho̶uld wait for a better deal. (combine . . . or)

d. Sonja decided *something*.
She would stay home. (combine . . . that)

S̶h̶e sho̶uld study for the English test. (combine . . . and)

e. Davinder did not know *something*.
He should go down the steepest waterslide alone. (combine . . . whether)
He should wait for Pat to join him. (combine . . . or whether)

PREPOSITIONS AND PREPOSITIONAL PHRASES

Prepositions are the words that begin phrases. **Phrases** are groups of words that tell more about nouns or verbs.

Here is a list of the prepositions you meet often:

> **after, against, along, among, around, at**
> **before, behind, below, beneath, beside, besides, between,**
> **beyond, by**
> **despite, down, during**
> **except, for, from**
> **in, inside, into, like, near**
> **of, off, on, onto, out, outside, over**
> **round, through, throughout, to, toward**
> **under, underneath, until, up, upon**
> **with, within, without**

Prepositional phrases are combinations of prepositions with nouns or pronouns. Here are some examples of prepositional phrases — preposition + noun/pronoun.

prep + noun	prep + noun
over the rainbow	into the sky
prep + pronoun	prep + noun
through him	in school
prep + pronoun	prep + adj./noun
to her	beside the still waters

Activity 15E   Prepositional Phrases

1. Combine these simple sentences. You're on your own with them: no signals have been provided. Most sentences can be combined by collapsing some of the basic sentences into prepositional phrases.

   a. The trip takes over twelve hours.
      The trip is to Edmonton.

    The trip is by train.
    The trip is from Vancouver.

b. My father hunts ducks.
   My fathers hunts in the fall.
   My fathers hunts in Saskatchewan.
   My father hunts with his friends.
   My father's friends are from work.

c. The car travelled.
   The car travelled at a very high speed.
   The car travelled through Saskatchewan.
   The car travelled toward the Manitoba border.

d. The young woman drove.
   She drove in a Toyota.
   She drove from Halifax.
   She drove to Vancouver.
   She drove the trip in nine days.

e. Dalginder got up.
   She got up in the morning.
   She washed her hair.
   She washed in the sink.
   She washed in the usual way.
   She discovered grease.
   The grease was in her hair.
   The grease came from the bottle.
   The bottle was for shampoo.

f. Shane wandered into the forest.
   He wandered early.
   He wandered in the morning.
   He wandered to find the path.
   The path was old.
   The path was to the mine.
   The mine was deserted.

2. This exercise is more difficult than the first one. Combine these sentences and you will build a paragraph about the famous Ogopogo of Okanagan Lake in British Columbia.

a. The pioneers soon learned *something*.
   The pioneers lived around Okanagan Lake.
   They learned about the Lake Demon.
   The Lake Demon was Ogopogo.
   Pioneers learned from the Indians.

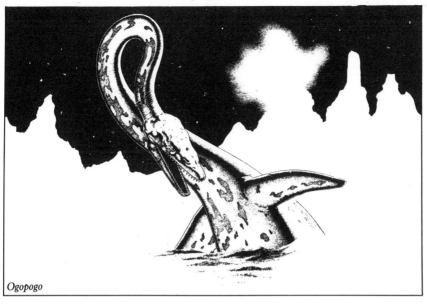

Ogopogo

b. One observer said *something*.
Ogopogo shone like diamonds.
The diamonds were in the sunshine.
Ogopogo swam through the water.
The swimming was like a snake.

c. The monster is said to rise.
He rises from the depths.
The depths are of the lake.
He rises in weather.
The weather is warm.
The weather is still.
He rises to the fear.
The fear is great.
The fear is of the fish.
The fear is of the birds.

d. Ogopogo can swim.
He swims at various speeds.
The speeds are incredibly fast.
The speeds are leisurely.

e. Ogopogo is not afraid of people.
People have sighted Ogopogo.
He was at the edge of the gardens.
The gardens were beside the lake.
People have seen Ogopogo near the downtown areas.

The areas are of the three cities.
The cities are on Lake Okanagan.
The cities are Penticton, Kelowna, and Vernon.

f. Ogopogo remains a mystery.
Ogopogo might be a large sea serpent.
Ogopogo might be a giant reptile.
The reptile might be left over from prehistoric times.

g. Scientists might decide *something*.
The scientists are Canadian.
They should have a closer look.
They should look at Lake Okanagan.
They should look in the future.
They should find out about the Ogopogo.
They should look once and for all.

Adapted from *Ogopogo*, by Mary Moon.

ADJECTIVE CLAUSES

Look at how these basic sentences are combined:

Alexander Graham Bell is a famous inventor.
Alexander Graham Bell lived at Baddeck, Nova Scotia.
(combine . . . who)

Alexander Graham Bell is a famous inventor who lived at Baddeck, Nova Scotia.

These basic sentences have been joined by (1) deleting the subject in the second sentence and (2) joining them with the join word *who*.

The group of words, *who lived at Baddeck, Nova Scotia*, is called an **adjective clause**.

You will need more skill to join sentences using adjective clauses than you did with the other joining words such as *and, because,* or *when*.

Here are some more examples of adjective clauses.

• Bell is a man.
Bell is a Canadian.   (combine . . . who)
Bell is a man *who is a Canadian*.
Note: Who takes the place of the subject of the clause.

- Bell invented the telephone.
  The telephone is a modern miracle.　　　(combine . . ., which)
  Bell invented the telephone, *which is a modern miracle*.
  Note: Which takes the place of the subject telephone.

- The telephone is an invention.
  Many people would not give up this invention.　(combine . . . that)
  The telephone is an invention *that many people would not give up*.
  Note: That takes the place of the object, *the invention*.

- Bell is a Canadian.
  Many Canadians admire Alexander Graham Bell.
  　　　　　　　　　　　　　　　　　　(combine . . . whom)
  Bell is a Canadian whom many Canadians admire.
  Note: Whom takes the place of the object, *Alexander Graham Bell*.

- Bell is a man.
  All Canadians are proud of Alexander Graham Bell.
  　　　　　　　　　　　　　　　　　　(combine . . . whom)
  Bell is a man *of whom all Canadians are proud*.
  Note: Whom takes the place of the noun or pronoun in a prepositional phrase.

Here is a chart to show how all of these join words are used.

join word	used to replace	takes the place of
• who	people	nouns (or pronouns) in the subject
• that	people or things	nouns in the subject or the object
• which	things	nouns in the subject or the object
• whom	people	nouns in a prepositional phrase

The units of words that are introduced by these join words are called **adjective clauses**. The join words are called **relative pronouns**. They act both as conjunctions and as pronouns.

Activity 15F   *Adjective Clauses*

1. In your notebook, combine these basic sentences by following the directions of the sentence-combining signals.

   a. Bell was interested in helping deaf people.
      ∧
      　This caret tells you to place the adjective clause here.

      Bell had a deaf mother.　　　　　　(combine . . ., who,)

b. Bell's father invented *visible speech*.

   Vis~~i~~ble spe~~e~~ch is a method of teaching deaf people to speak.

   (combine . . ., which)

c. Visible speech is a set of pictures.
   T~~he set of~~ pic~~t~~ures shows deaf people the action of the vocal organs.

   (combine . . . that)

This caret tells you to place the adjective clause here.

d. The work ∧ led to the invention of the telephone.

   Bell did ~~the~~ w~~o~~rk with the deaf.   (combine . . . ∧that)

e. Bell also worked with some experiments.

   T~~he~~ expe~~r~~iments formed the basis of the first airplane flights.

   (combine . . . that)

f. One memorial to Bell is a house near Brantford, Ontario.

   P **Bell** once lived in t~~hi~~s ho~~u~~se.   (combine . . . that)

g. There is a sign.

   T~~he~~ s~~ig~~n stands in the front yard of the Brantford house.

   (combine . . . that)

   T~~he~~ s~~ig~~n says "Here the telephone was invented."

   (combine . . . that)

h. Bell finally moved to Baddeck, Nova Scotia.

   P **Bell's** assistant ∧ helped him with his telephone work.

   (combine . . . and)

   T~~he~~ assi~~s~~tant was Thomas Watson.

   (combine . . ., who,) ∧

i. One of Bell's good friends was J. A. D. McCurdy.

   Mc~~Cu~~rdy made the first public plane flight in the British Empire

   at Baddeck in 1907.   (combine . . ., who)

j. Baddeck is privileged to host the Bell Museum.

T~~he~~ citizens ~~of~~ Bad~~d~~eck are proud of Bell.

(combine . . .ᴧwhose)

T~~he~~ B~~ell~~ Mus~~e~~um contains many of Bell's experiments and possessions.

(combine . . ., which)

2. Combine each of these sets of basic sentences into one sentence that contains an adjective clause.

Sport in Canada's Past

a. Lacrosse is Canada's national game.
Few Canadians have played lacrosse.

b. The Canadian-bred thoroughbred, Northern Dancer, won the Kentucky Derby in 1964.
All Canadians were proud of Northern Dancer.

c. Harry Jerome was a famous Vancouver sprinter.
Harry Jerome was co-holder of the world record for one hundred metres.

d. Maurice Richard was a colourful and controversial figure.
Maurice Richard played forward for the Montréal Canadiens.

e. In 1954, Marilyn Bell swam across Lake Ontario.
Marilyn was sixteen years old.

f. Ernestine Russell was an outstanding Canadian gymnast in the 1950s.
Ernestine Russell won the Canadian championship seven times running.

g. In 1950, sports writers voted Lionel Conacher the greatest athlete in Canada's first half century.
Lionel Conacher was a professional hockey player.

h. An athlete has to perform in the white heat of the spotlight.
An athlete is like an actor.

i. The elements are found among athletes of all nations.
The elements produce the great athlete.

j. Our pioneers had little time to become involved in sport.
The pioneers settled the cold, open spaces of our country.

THE APPOSITIVE PHRASE

You can now do interesting things with adjective clauses. This section will show you how to shorten adjective clauses by changing them into **appositive phrases**.

These examples explain what appositive phrases are. Have a look at this series of sentence combinations:

> The giant panda bears lives in China.
>
> ~~The giant panda bear~~ is a very shy animal.
>
> (combine . . . which)
>
> The giant panda bear, which is a very shy animal, lives in China.
>
> *New signal*   (combine . . . APP)
>
> The giant panda bear, *a very shy animal*, lives in China.

Notice what the signal APP prompts you to do:

> The giant panda bear, ~~which is~~ a very shy animal, lives in China.

The signal gets you to delete the join word *which* and the verb *is*. The group of words that remains is called an appositive phrase.

The word itself gives you a signal about what it means. It comes from a Latin source. Appositive means placed beside; hence, a word that is an appositive is placed beside a noun and means the same things as the noun: *giant panda bear = a very shy animal*. In the example, the group of words, *a very shy animal*, was placed directly beside the subject, *the giant panda*. This new method of combining basic sentences does not use any join words at all. This fact makes the appositive phrase different from all the other sentence combinations you have learned about. Here are some more examples, using the new signal, APP:

> The Chinese people love the giant panda.
>
> ~~The giant panda is~~ their national treasure.
>
> (combine . . ., which + APP,)
>
> *Rewrite:*
>
> The Chinese people love the giant panda, *their national treasure*.

In the next examples, one step is omitted: the signal to convert the second basic sentence to an adjective clause. The signal APP is used, but you must delete some words and place the appositive phrase in the right place in the base sentence.

> Panda bears live in Central China.
> Central China is their natural habitat.
>
> (combine . . ., APP,)

Rewrite:
Panda bears live in Central China, *their natural habitat.*

Pandas live on bamboo plants.
Pandas are fussy eaters.   (combine . . ., APP,)
Rewrite:
Pandas, *fussy eaters*, live on bamboo plants.

Activity 15G   Appositive Phrases

1. Combine these sentences so that the base sentence contains an appositive phrase:
   a. This signal indicates water.
      The signal is H_2O.
   b. H_2O is a chemical formula.
      H_2O represents two atoms of hydrogen and one of oxygen.
   c. Water is abundant on earth.
      Water is rare in the solar system.
   d. The world faces a crucial question.
      The crucial question is the growth in population.
   e. The sea may be our source of survival.
      Our source of survival is food, energy, and minerals.
   f. The ocean is the source of our only renewable resource.
      The renewable resource is solar energy.
   g. Space exploration has shown humans the interdependence of the world.
      Space exploration is the study of the universe.
   h. Space exploration has given humans a strange gift.
      That strange gift is a global consciousness.
   i. The sea will help out humankind.
      The sea is the great unifier.
   j. An old phrase describes the human situation.
      The old phrase is "We are all in the same boat."

SOME SENTENCE MODELS

This section gives you some handy models to follow when you are giving information. You may find that you can use this kind of sentence in social studies or science reports.

Here is a basic model:

I like doing homework *for two reasons. One is* that I learn something. *The second is* that I like to get it finished.

Note that the first, or topic sentence, signals that some information will be given in the following sentences. It also tells exactly how much detail will be provided. The second sentence provides the first piece of information; the third, the second bit of information.

Let's see how well you handle this model for writing sentences that give information.

Activity 15H   Sentence Models

1. Ice cream tastes better than potatoes for two reasons. One is _____. The second is _____.

2. Canada has two important cities. One is _____. The second is _____.

3. I know two good summer vacation spots. One is _____, and the second is _____.

4. On Saturdays, I like to do two things. _____.

5. I like holidays for two reasons. _____.

6. I like two kinds of TV programs. _____.

You can expand this model by including details. So now the sequence looks like this:

Statement + one piece of information + some detail + second piece of information + some detail.

Here is what this model looks like.

I like *two kinds* of food. *One is* hamburger. I enjoy its juicy taste. *Another is* pizza. It has a spicy, tangy flavour.

Or:

Canada has *several* major river systems. *One is* the Saskatchewan river system. It stretches across the three Prairie provinces and flows into Hudson Bay. *Another* river system is the St. Lawrence. It flows from Ontario, through Quebec, and out into the Atlantic Ocean.

Activity 15I Mini-Paragraph Models

Try completing these mini-paragraphs, following the model of the example.

1. I know two people whom I admire a great deal. One is _____. (Now add a sentence giving at least one detail about this person.) Another is _____. (Add some detail about this second person.)

2. I have read two books that I enjoyed very much. (Follow the model to complete this mini-paragraph.)

3. I can think of two unusual uses for a piece of string.

4. I like winter for two very special reasons.

5. I can remember two things that happened to me a long time ago.

6. I have two special abilities.

7. In my own way, I have achieved success.

8. I like the colour red very much. (or substitute your own colour)

9. I have seen some strange sights in my day.

10. My friends have been kind to me.

11. Last month had its troubles.

12. Here are my wishes for the future.

Terminate the Program

It's been a long time since you started this program. Remember, you considered the word *syntax*. The computer tells you when you have made syntax errors. This chapter has helped you build sentences with more mature syntax. You have gained the skills to understand and use methods to change sentences around. You can shorten them or lengthen them. You can join them or pull them apart.

The computer is signaling again: it's time to terminate this program.

INDEX